Discovering the Roman Family

DISCOVERING THE ROMAN FAMILY
Studies in Roman Social History

Keith R. Bradley

New York   Oxford
OXFORD UNIVERSITY PRESS
1991

Oxford University Press

Oxford   New York   Toronto
Delhi   Bombay   Calcutta   Madras   Karachi
Petaling Jaya   Singapore   Hong Kong   Tokyo
Nairobi   Dar es Salaam   Cape Town
Melbourne   Auckland

and associated companies in
Berlin   Ibadan

Copyright © 1991 by Oxford University Press, Inc.

Published by Oxford University Press, Inc.,
198 Madison Avenue, New York, New York 10016-4314

Oxford is a registered trademark of Oxford University Press

Library of Congress Cataloging-in-Publication Data
Bradley, K. R.
Discovering the Roman family : studies in Roman social history /
Keith R. Bradley.
p.   cm.   Includes bibliographical references.
ISBN 0-19-505857-7—ISBN 0-19-505858-5 (pbk.)
1. Family—Rome—History. I. Title.
HQ511.B73 1991   306'.0945'632—dc20   90-34248

9 8 7 6 5 4 3 2

Printed in the United States of America
on acid-free paper

For
Marsh McCall

Preface

This book brings together a series of individual studies intended, as a collection, to make a positive contribution to the fast-developing field of Roman family history. Each study is a unit in itself and can be read independently of the others, but a continuity of theme will be evident throughout. I hope that historians of Roman society and social relations will find something of merit both in the parts and in the whole.

The studies were severally written over a period of five years. During that interval I received help of many kinds, and it is a pleasure at this juncture to be able to acknowledge it publicly. A succession of awards from the Research and Travel Fund at the University of Victoria and the Social Sciences and Humanities Research Council of Canada greatly facilitated basic research; I am grateful to both institutions. Three of the studies (Chapters 3, 5, and 6) were previously published in *Historical Reflections/Réflexions Historiques* [12 (1985): 485–523; 12 (1985): 311–30; 14 (1987): 33–62]; and although they have now been completely revised and, in some aspects, augmented, I must nonetheless thank Stanley K. Johannesen for permission to reuse material that first appeared in the journal he edits. Those earlier versions benefited from the critical attention of Samuel E. Scully, Peter L. Smith, and Susan M. Treggiari; to all three scholars I should like to renew my appreciation of their advice. Three of the studies (Chapters 2, 6, and 7) began life as conference papers. I am indebted therefore to Sarah B. Pomeroy for asking me to speak at the Seventh Berkshire Conference on the History of Women at Wellesley College in June 1987; to William V. Harris for suggesting that

I participate in a panel on the Roman family at the 118th Annual Meeting of the American Philological Association at San Antonio in December 1987; and to Beryl M. Rawson for inviting me to a marvelous conference on the Roman family at the Australian National University in Canberra in July 1988.

From conversations and correspondence with Beryl Rawson and Susan Treggiari in particular I have learned much, and I wish to express my special thanks to both for their interest in my work. I am also very grateful to my former pupil and now colleague, Patricia A. Clark, first for help in compiling some of the epigraphical material discussed in the book and secondly for encouraging me, in the late stages of composition, to bring it to completion. To William P. Sisler of Oxford University Press thanks are due for converting a notion into a reality. And to A. Nancy Nasser I am, once more, deeply thankful for her incomparable assistance as my typist.

My greatest debt, as in the past, is to my wife, Diane Bradley, without whose unfailing understanding and constant inspiration nothing would be possible, and without whom, indeed, nothing would even be worthwhile. My deepest gratitude must therefore, as always, be reserved for her alone.

Victoria, British Columbia   K. R. B.
April 1990

Contents

Abbreviations

In the interest of clarity, abbreviations are kept to a minimum. Ancient works are cited by English or Latin title, with intelligibility being the only guiding principle. Translations are those of standard Loeb or Penguin editions. For Cicero's correspondence, I use throughout the numbering system of Shackleton Bailey. For papyri, I follow the abbreviations of Turner (1968), 154–71, with the single exception below.

AE	*L'année épigraphique*
CIL	*Corpus Inscriptionum Latinarum*
ILS	*Inscriptiones Latinae Selectae*
MRR	T. R. S. Broughton, *The Magistrates of the Roman Republic*
NS	*Notizie degli scavi di antichità*
*ORF*³	H. Malcovati, *Oratorum Romanorum Fragmenta*, third edition
*PIR*²	*Prosopographia Imperii Romani*, second edition
P. Wisc.	P. J. Sijpesteijn, *The Wisconsin Papyri I*
RE	*Paulys Realencyclopädie der classischen Altertumswissenschaft*
TLL	*Thesaurus Linguae Latinae*

Discovering the Roman Family

1

Introduction

In contemporary North America, most people belong to a family and have no difficulty understanding what is meant when "the family" becomes an item of conversation or discussion. But the term baffles easy definition. Imagine, for a moment, that you and I were to meet somewhere for the first time, say on a plane or at a conference, somewhere where we were inescapably thrown together for a certain length of time. At some stage, you would probably ask if I had a family—the topic is standard—and as a middle-aged husband and father, I would assume that you were asking whether I were married and had any children. So I would tell you at once about my wife and my three sons—my immediate family, that is—before politely asking you about your family. If the conversation continued, and you learned that I am an immigrant to the country in which I live, you might go on to inquire, simply as a courtesy, whether I still had any family in my country of origin. I would assume that you were asking about parents and siblings, and so I would tell you about my mother and father, my brother and his wife, and perhaps, too, if you were really interested or there were absolutely no line of retreat at your disposal, a host of aunts and uncles and cousins—the people, that is, who populated my childhood world a generation ago. (The lives of my grandparents could only be spoken of as a memory in all of this.) If relief were still not in sight, you might conceivably next ask about my wife's family, my relatives by marriage, and so on, endlessly.

My point is that even at the level of ordinary discourse, *family* is an ambiguous, elusive term, whose meaning for any individual is shaped primarily by the variables of age and marital status, and if divorce and remarriage have anywhere entered the picture, the complications of understanding and defining are greater still. All this is elementary. But for the historian the simple fact that the family is a constantly changing entity, the nature of which depends on the individual's point of progress through the life course, functions as a warning of the dangers inherent in trying to characterize or to classify families in past societies too readily. Hence the rather informal way in which I have begun.

This book is about the Roman family. Or better, given what I have said so far, it is about some aspects of family life in Roman antiquity. By *Roman* I mean pertaining to Rome in the central period of its history, roughly from 200 B.C. to A.D. 200, so that the term has a generic meaning and refers not merely to the city of Rome and its inhabitants but to any place and people imbued with Roman culture in a broad sense. And by *aspects* I mean topics or issues of the sort covered in the following definition of family history given by a leading modern historian:

> the history of the family . . . embraces not only the demographic limits which constrain family life but also kinship ties, family and household structures, marriage arrangements and conventions and their economic and social causes and consequences, changing sex roles and their differentiation over time, changing attitudes toward and practice of sexual relations, and changes in the affective ties binding husband and wife, and parents and children.[1]

Implicit throughout, however, is the question of capturing what is meant when "the Roman family" is written or talked about by historians, and it is with elaborating that question that this introductory chapter is concerned.[2]

The Romans themselves knew, of course, what they meant when they used the word *familia*—the root of the English *family*—and the jurist Ulpian, who lived right at the end of the central period of Roman history, has even left a legal definition of the word, or rather a series of definitions, since, like *family, familia* changed its meaning according to context.[3] None of its senses, however, corresponds precisely to English *family* in the varied way I used the word in my opening paragraph. For that purpose Romans might draw on the alternative *domus* (literally "house" or "household") or simply choose to use possessive adjectives like *mei* or *tui* (literally "my people" or "your people"). Yet these terms, too, were elastic in meaning, and they could include, strangely to the modern mind, persons who were not related to each other by blood or marriage. Like the contemporary family, therefore, the Roman family is an ambiguous concept and defies easy definition.

Nevertheless, Roman family life has hardly been neglected by historians, and to anyone educated in the last generation, under the dominant regime of prosopographical history, the value attached to family connections for political and administrative history scarcely needs to be pointed out. But as practiced by historians involved with revealing shifts in the political landscape or with disclosing administrative trends, family history has for the most part consisted just of reconstructing marital ties and lines of descent—little more than genealogy, in other words. The result has been that no notion has emerged from the use of a mode of historical analysis that is essentially mechanistic and emotionless of what life within the Roman family may actually have been like, and prosopographical studies have, of course, centered only on a very small sector of the Roman population, the social and political elite.[4]

At the present time, however, under the impact of what is called the new social history, it is becoming more and more possible to gain some appreciation of the dynamics of Roman family life, at more than one social level indeed, and to understand the family as a social organism.[5] This book is intended as a contribution to that process. But it is a book that offers no more than a collection of self-contained studies on particular features of Roman family life, with no pretense to being a complete history. Its origin lies in fact not so much in a long-standing interest in the history of the Roman family as in the history of Roman slavery, and especially in the tantalizingly skeptical remarks of M. I. Finley on the difficulties of making any sense of what he called "the nursemaid-governess-*paedagogus* class among domestic servants."[6] Thus, in studying Roman nurses (*nutrices*) recorded on sepulchral inscriptions, most of whom were slaves or of servile stock, I found that it was impossible to pursue the study within the context of slavery alone. Equal attention had to be given to the children associated with the nurses, many of whom were not slaves.[7] Interest then began to focus more on the nature of the Roman family, its composition and shape, and quite fortuitously this happened to coincide with the emergence of family history, in the sense described in the quotation above, as virtually a new field of Roman historical scholarship. The contents of this book have therefore largely been written in counterpoint to the appearance of a body of highly creative and exciting new work.[8]

A notable element of this scholarship is the emphasis historians have placed on the predominance in Roman society of the nuclear family—even though there is no Latin equivalent for the modern phrase—to the point that it is now almost unorthodox to think of the Roman family in any other way.[9] To the extent that the Romans were monogamous and that they produced legitimate children in marriages whose fundamental purpose was procreation, this stress on nuclear organization is unobjectionable. But to my mind the phrase *nuclear family* is so overloaded with modern connotations that it is misleading to take the concept as the key to understanding Roman familial behavior, and this is part of the problem of defining the Roman family. In today's world, the phrase *nuclear family* conjures up an image of a domestic unit comprising two parents and their children who live together in a single-family residence and who share a deep affective intimacy with one another. The family unit is a whole, a totality. It will usually have started its life with the parents' union (marriage for most) and their establishment of a physical household before the birth of their children. In turn, the union will usually have followed the development of a romantic attachment between the couple and a period of courtship or preparation for living together, and, whether formalized in marriage or not, it will in principle usually be egalitarian in character. Under these conditions, the modern nuclear family is an institution that is characterized above all by privacy.[10]

Should, then, the Roman family be thought of in the same way? It is certainly true that Roman parents and children lived together. But it cannot be assumed that the affective bonds between them were for that reason alone identical to those generally understood to form the foundation of the modern family, with all its trappings of intimacy and privacy. Consider for a moment the fact that one of the cardinal characteristics of a good Roman marriage was *concordia,* a state of harmony between husband and wife that was hoped for when marriage began and that was celebrated, once attained, by outsiders or commemorated at the time of spousal death by a surviving partner. So, for example, Cicero once noted the *concordia* of his friend Atticus's marriage to Pilia; an anonymous husband who set up an elaborate epitaph to his wife in the late first century B.C. testified to the *concordia* that had marked their life together; and Tacitus, in the biography of his father-in-law, wrote of the "mira concordia," the exceptional concord, that Agricola and Domitia Deci-diana had shared.[11] No doubts should necessarily be entertained about the success in Roman terms of any of these marriages. But think how odd it would seem if you were to describe a successful marriage today by saying that it was full of concord or harmony between husband and wife. The virtue is rather passive in its associations, implying a state of tranquil and stable unanimity but suggesting little of the romance or intimacy typical of modern marriage. It is equally odd from a modern perspective to find that the relationship between husband and wife is openly acknowledged to be asymmetrical, analogous to that between father and child or tutor and ward, and that a husband's display of restraint (*moderatio*) toward his wife can be taken as a sign of his affection (*caritas*) for her.[12] A suspicion that the affective dimension of a Roman marriage might have differed significantly from its modern counterpart thus becomes legitimate. After all, why should Roman husbands and wives not have been concordant?

The question is not merely rhetorical. But to answer it, another context in which *concordia* figured must be considered: that of Roman public life. For throughout the central period of Roman history, the virtue term always maintained a high profile both as a political slogan and, personified, as a goddess. So at various times politicians reiterated the value of concord in the civic community, temples to the goddess were built in one generation after another, and representations of the divinity appeared on coins and in the form of statues.[13] Yet the tendency was for *concordia* to be given all this attention in moments of crisis, at times of actual discord, such as "during the Samnite and Punic wars, because fear of the enemy often drove the Romans to concord; and again at the time of the Gracchan revolt when internal order was threatened."[14] Similarly, "Caesar began his consulate of 59 with a speech about concord with his fellow consul Bibulus, thus following Cicero's example in 63, and there is no doubt that at first he tried to act in this spirit. [But] the consulate ended in discord."[15] Under the Principate, the legend "concordia exercituum" (concord among the armies) made periodic appearances on the Roman coinage, in response to episodes of military unrest or outright civil war.[16] Celebration of concord therefore frequently signified an absence of peace and harmony in the public sphere, and more often than not *concordia* was a term whose relationship to political reality was not descriptive but only prescriptive.

Perhaps it would be too cynical to maintain in consequence that it was all a sham when Romans lauded marital concord, and there is no reason to impugn the essential truthfulness, as he perceived it, of a verdict like that of Tacitus on Agricola's marriage: "they lived in rare accord, maintained by mutual affection and unselfishness.''[17] But what can be inferred is that because marriage at Rome was generally a matter of outside arrangement, not of personal choice on the part of the marrying couple (among the prosperous, at least), there could never at the outset be any assurance of harmony between husband and wife, and in the likely absence of any strong affective tie characteristic of modern marriage, the potential for discord was always as great as that for concord. Affective expectations in Roman marriage had to be low, and it is for this reason that spousal commemorations of deceased partners often draw on phraseology of a highly dispassionate tone, even as the ''success'' of the union is being signaled. Thus, it is common to find statements of the sort that for a certain number of years the surviving partner had lived with the spouse ''without any complaint,'' ''without any quarrel,'' or ''without any discord.''[18] The emotional point of departure in Roman marriage was not highly charged, and for men like Agricola and his peers it was the public image of a union that was most important, not its inner life, since in the Roman system of values a good match was chiefly a source of ''social distinction and aid to ambition for advancement.''[19] This being so, there is no obvious reason to believe that the life of the Roman family followed a pattern comparable to that of the modern affective or companionate nuclear family just because the members of the reproductive triad shared the same living space. In my view the pattern was altogether different, and the modern terminology should be applied to the Roman past only in a very qualified manner. On a minimal estimate, attention to the ramifications of *concordia* in Roman marriage suggests the need for a cautious approach to the subject.

The same point emerges from comparing modern and ancient attitudes toward the family's living space. For the modern family the domicile is primarily a place of retreat or refuge, in which family members seclude themselves from the world of work and education that lies outside the home; for most people the home is not a place in which parents earn a living or children are schooled but a place characterized by and valued for the familial privacy that a strict physical distinction between work and home allows. Roman houses also catered to the need for privacy, and the notion that the physical dwelling afforded refuge (at least in the sense of protection, if not comfort) was certainly known.[20] But the cleavage between public and private life that is so strong a feature of contemporary society was unknown in Roman antiquity. The value Romans put on personal or familial privacy was in fact very low, and for them the house was multifunctional, a place of constant social, economic, and some-times political intercourse, not simply a place of habitation. It was a place in which the owner could make his way in the world by receiving and working with a daily stream of visitors whose influence or services impinged on his public standing and his prospects for advancement in society, a place in which status was both displayed and acquired, given that worldly aspirations were inextricably bound up with domestic conventions.[21] Thus, the relationship of the residents of a Roman house to their domestic space was vastly different from the modern archetype, which means that their concepts and forms of family life are likely to have been equally distinctive.

For one thing, it is a patent fact that Roman houses occupied by the socially and materially successful were not at all single-family residences in the modern sense; rather, they gathered under one roof whole commu-nities of people in which a cluster of reproductive, nuclear groupings might coexist. The community centered on the owner, his wife, and his children. But it embraced, too, a highly visible and constantly circulating domestic staff, slaves for the most part, whose relationships with the members of the core unit intersected those of the core unit's members themselves, and among whom independent nuclear attachments could and did develop.[22] Hence the cluster. But it is noteworthy that the sleeping quarters of the domestics were not segregated from those of the core unit by being set, for example, in structures apart from the main house, as happened in the slave society of the American South; instead, they comprised part of the house itself. This meant that despite differen-tials of status, the communal aspect of life in the house could never be utterly interrupted; and, in fact, slaves might sleep in the same rooms as their owners, husband and wife might not always share the same room, and the owner's children might sleep with their servile chaperons.[23]

The privacy of the nuclear family might also be affected in ways that have nothing to do with the presence in the household of domestic servants. In the modern family it sometimes happens at one stage of the life course that coresident parents and children are joined in their domicile by other people related to them—an older parent (the children's grandparent) or the spouse of a marrying child (and then perhaps a grandchild). The nuclear family becomes a multigenerational family. Of Roman society it is often said that the multigenerational family was a rarity, and with considerable justification, since only a few instances of the phenomenon appear in the sources.[24] Yet there still may be a danger in insisting on the typicality of any one family configuration, apart from the complications raised by coresident servants. What is to be made of statements such as those in legal sources that a woman to whom the right of use of a house has been left may live in the house not only with her husband but also with her father-in-law;—not just with her husband, children, and freedmen but with her parents, too?[25] Does that evidence imply, in fact, a high incidence of multigenerational families in Roman society, despite the paucity of attested specific cases? Once more the need for caution is clear, especially if the additional factor is noted that the Roman household often also contained foundlings (*alumni, alumnae*), children biologically related to no one in the community but part of it nonetheless.[26]

What results from examining the composition of the Roman house is a pattern of social organization in the family that is unique to Rome. It becomes evident that the male head of the family was severally bound by various ties of authority to his children, his wife, and his servants, and that any number of independent relationships existed alongside—between children and mother, wife and servants, children and servants, and among the servants themselves. Given this power structure, and the heterogeneous population of the house on which it depended, it was impossible for a social milieu to be created that was in any way comparable to that represented by the modern nuclear family. Roman parents were not linked in egalitarian marriage, and their offspring did not rely exclusively on them for all their household and material needs. The concept of the family as an integrated whole that is ideally associated with the companionate family of today could not therefore be a Roman concept.

By this point, you will have noticed, the Roman *family* has become almost synonymous with the Roman *household*. The two are obviously connected: to clarify the nature of the household is to clarify the nature of the family. But the two are not identical, if only for the reason that the life of the family is not confined to what occurs within the domicile but extends beyond it, too. So this again forms part of the question I have had uppermost in mind: how the Roman family should be defined. To suggest an answer, the chapters that follow pursue and develop the themes that have been adumbrated here: the nature of Roman marriage, parent-child relationships within and without the household, the place of servants in the structure of the Roman family, and the communal aspects of Roman family life. An attempt is made to dispel some of the ambiguities that surround the Roman family and, above all, to understand the Roman family on its own terms. It must be remembered, however, that the topics dealt with are piecemeal in character and limited in scope; much of the history of the Roman family still remains to be discovered.

Notes

1. Stone (1987), 25.
2. See as essential introductions to modern study of the Roman family B. Rawson (1986a) and Garnsey and Saller (1987), 126–47.
3. *Digest* 50.16.195.1–5 (cf. 21.1.25.2). With *familia* represented by English *household*, the meanings may be summarized thus:

(i) the physical household;
(ii) the persons who comprise a household (e.g., patron and freedman);
(iii) a body of persons "covered by a legal status peculiar to its members or common to an entire related group" (e.g., *paterfamilias, materfamilias, filiafamilias, nepotes, neptes*, etc.);
(iv) "all the agnates under a single legal rule";
(v) a body of slaves;
(vi) "people who descend by blood from the same original founder"; for example, "the Julian household."

For discussion, see Saller (1984); cf. Corbier (1987), 1267–68.
4. See Bradley (1984) and Bradley (1989a).
5. On the character of the new history, see Stone (1987), 3–44; and, from an antagonistic point of view, Himmelfarb (1987).
6. Finley (1980), 105.
7. Bradley (1986).
8. Apart from the bibliography of this book, see for access to the new material Binkowski and Rawson (1986) and Golden (1988a).
9. Saller (1984), 355; Saller and Shaw (1984), 137, 145; cf. B. Rawson (1986a), 7; Dixon (1988), 13–21. Cf. the passing generalization in P. Brown (1988), 16: "It appears that the nuclear family, and with it a tendency to lay stress on the affective bonds between husband and wife and parents and children, was already [i.e., by the second century A.D.] a well-established feature of Roman society, at least in the West."
10. See the discussion of Mitterauer and Sieder (1982), 48–70; and cf. Goldthorpe (1987), 56–62.
11. Cicero, *Letters to Atticus* 154.5; *ILS* 8393.45 (the so-called Laudatio Turiae); Tacitus, *Agricola* 6.1. See *TLL* s.v. "concordia." The notion of marital concord is complemented by the phrase "consortium omnis vitae," used by the jurist Modestinus at *Digest* 23.2.1 in defining marriage as a joining of male and female, a partnership in every respect of life. The Republican ideal of marital *concordia* is overlooked by P. Brown (1988), 16.
12. Quintilian, *Institute of Oratory* 6.2.14.

13. See Weinstock (1971), 260–66; Levick (1978).

14. Weinstock (1971), 260–61.

15. Weinstock (1971), 263.

16. Levick (1978), 228.

17. Tacitus, *Agricola* 6.1: "vixeruntque mira concordia, per mutuam caritatem et in vicem se anteponendo."

18. Lattimore (1962), 279, provides a convenient catalogue of examples. It should be noted, of course, that "records of devotion between husband and wife are enormously frequent in Latin inscriptions, both prose and verse." Lattimore (1962), 277. But this does not affect my point about expectations at the outset of marriage; cf. the almost clinically detached evaluation of his new wife, Calpurnia, given by Pliny, *Letters* 4.19; cf. Bradley (1985), 91–92; and Aulus Gellius, *Attic Nights* 1.17.4–5, for the notion that a husband should eradicate his wife's faults (from a book, *On the Duty of a Husband*, by Varro). Precisely how this was to be done is not made clear, but verbal and physical abuse of wives by husbands was occasionally recognized as a matter for the attention of the courts: Quintilian, *Institute of Oratory* 7.3.2, 7.4.10, 7.4.24, 7.8.2.

19. Tacitus, *Agricola* 6.1: "idque matrimonium ad maiora nitenti decus ac robur fuit." Rousselle (1988), 2, makes the valid point of how difficult it is to speak of love in antiquity given the absence of evidence from women.

20. *Digest* 2.4.18.

21. See Wallace-Hadrill (1988), a brilliant study. Observe Cicero's image of the Roman noble advising visitors to his house on matters of the law, arranging a betrothal, buying an estate, leasing land, on every kind of *officium* and *negotium*: *De Oratore* 3.133.

22. For the impact of slavery on Roman family life, see Saller (1987a); and on family life among slaves, Bradley (1987), 47–80.

23. See *Digest* 29.5.14, 29.5.1.28; Tacitus, *Dialogus* 28.4; Pliny, *Letters* 9.36.1–2 (where is Calpurnia? cf. 9.36.4), 7.5.1 ("quibus horis te visere solebam").

24. B. Rawson (1986a), 14; Dixon (1988), 14.

25. *Digest* 7.8.4–6.

26. On *alumni,* see most successfully B. Rawson (1986b); cf. also Nielsen (1987) and Boswell (1988), 116–21 (the last, however, is flawed in some respects).

2

The Social Role of the Nurse in the Roman World

*W*hen Apuleius's Lucius, the hero of the *Metamorphoses,* encounters Byrrhaena in the city of Hypata in Thessaly, it comes as a surprise to learn that he is meeting a relative. But as the truth is revealed, Lucius discovers that Byrrhaena and his mother had been brought up together, that as infants they had shared the same nurse, and that they were in fact maternal cousins: "nam et familia Plutarchi ambae prognatae sumus et eandem nutricem simul bibimus et in nexu germanitatis una coaluimus."[1]

The detail on the nurse is just one of many in literary sources that provides unambiguous evidence that the primary meaning of the word *nutrix* in Latin was "wet nurse," and indeed the *nutrix* was a very common figure at Rome in the central period of its history, employed by women of means to breast-feed their children and at times by slave owners to nurse the offspring of their slaves.[2] The convention of using a wet nurse, it was believed, went all the way back to the beginning of the city's history, for Romans of the historical age could still name the women who had nursed Romulus and Remus, and Aeneas, too.[3] It is hardly surprising, therefore, that stories were handed down from generation to generation on how the nurse might best maintain a plentiful supply of milk.[4]

The story of Byrrhaena suggests, however, that the wet nurse was also to be found in many other regions of the Roman world than at Rome itself, a commonsense inference supported, for example, by the legal knowledge that it fell within the provincial governor's jurisdiction to hear claims for *nutricia,* the costs of child maintenance owed to nursing women.[5] Accordingly, the concern of this chapter is twofold: first, to present an analytical description of nurses identified in Latin inscriptions from Italian and provincial towns and cities, and, second, to assess the significance of this material in the context of the history of the Roman family. The evidence, it must be made plain at once, is often difficult to evaluate because the inscriptions—of the sepulchral sort for the most part and at times either fragmentary or elliptical or both—are often susceptible of more than one interpretation. Nevertheless, the inscriptions have a certain advantage over literary sources, where the nurse, when mentioned, is usually an anonymous figure, in that they allow specific individuals to emerge into the historical record. Moreover, the implications of the material for a fuller appreciation of child-rearing practices in the Roman world are important and worth pursuing.

II

Tables 2.1 and 2.2 provide lists of *nutrices* from Italy and the provinces, the nurslings associated with them, and the locations of the inscriptions identifying them. The geographical range of the evidence is substantial, but the total number of texts is not great, rather less than the number available for the city of Rome alone. Their significance therefore is not to be exaggerated. However, there is no reason to assume that the inscriptions, when set alongside casual literary information, are not representative of widespread social behavior and practices. Even in late antiquity, for example, Augustine, when writing of his own infancy, took wet-nursing for granted in his native North Africa.[6]

Of the nurses listed in Table 2.1, four must be regarded as somewhat exceptional, since the women concerned were all related to their charges, and so were not wet nurses proper. Postumia Paulina (no. 2) is described in her inscription as the grandmother and nurse of Cavarasia Faustina, and Cantria Paulla (no. 7), Halicia Severa (no. 13), and Ragonia Eutychia (no. 23) are all described as the mothers and nurses of their charges. The father of Cavarasia Faustina, it may be imagined, was one of Postumia Paulina's two recorded sons, M. Cavarasius Maximianus and M. Cavarasius Aurelianus. But if so, it would seem implausible that a grandmother breast-fed her own son's child, and her function as nurse is thus more likely to have been custodial: she simply raised, or helped to

Table 2.1. Italian *Nutrices*

No.*	Nurse	Nursling	Location
1	Paperia		Nemi
2	Postumia Paulina	Cavarasia Faustina	Verona
3	Clodia Verna		Arusnates
4	Cassia Prisca	Cassius Karicus	Segusio
5	Aste	Silvanus	Uria
6	Clodia Jucunda	Mucia Maxima	Canusium
7	Cantria Paulla	Cn. Ennius Dexter	Aeclanum
8	Adv[e]nta	Lucceius	Aeclanum
9	ignota	ignotus	Anxanum
10	Lucceia Donata	Hyalissus, Vic[. . .], Hyacint(h)us?	Teate Marrucinorum
11	Vibpsania Capriola	Vibpsania Severa	Teate Marrucinorum
12	Pompulla Nemaesis	L. Laberius Lupus	Marsi Marruvium
13	Halicia Severa		Trebula Mutuesca
14	Multasia Felicitas		Salvia
15	Ediste	domini sui	Locri
16	Caecilia Eupraesia	Sabina	Puteoli
17	Lucceia Herophil		Puteoli
18	Servea Marcellina	Victoria	Puteoli
19	Rasinia Pietas	filiae L. Burbulei Optati Ligariani	Minturnae
20	Musa	Praesens	Ostia
21	Egr[ilia		Ostia
22	ignota		Ostia
23	Ragonia Eutychia	. . .]us Firmus	Ostia
24	Calpurnia Lupula	Val. Vic(t)orinu(s)	Aricia
25	Casp(eria) Zotice	L. Casperius Latinus	Ager Albanus
26	Ammia		Tusculum
27	Tyche		Tusculum
28	Sperata	L. Sentius Pietas	Cesi
29	Livia Benigna		Parma
30	Cominia Secunda	L. Nutrius Gallus	Brixia
31	Birria Cognit[a	P. Birrius Gallus	Brindisium

*For various details of information pertinent to the case histories and the inscriptions providing them, consult the appropriately numbered Table Notes at the end of this chapter.

raise, her granddaughter. In the other cases, however, there is no cause to doubt that the three mothers nursed their own children in preference to using a nurse. One may compare Varro's remarks on female pastoral slaves: "As to feeding their young, I merely remark that in most cases they suckle them as well as bear them," where the Latin uses the phrase

Table 2.2. Provincial *Nutrices*

No.*	Nurse	Nursling	Location
32	Clovatia Irene		Emerita
33	Pont]iena [N]ovel[l]a	Domitius	Valeria
34	Valeria et Amabilis	filii Proculini	Guarda
35	Fabia Tertulla		Barcino
36	ignota		Corduba
37	Justina Virginia	Julius Vaentinus	Salonae
38	C. Epic(h)aris	filius Romullae	Salonae
39	Desidiena Primitiva	C. Desidienus Proculus	Salonae
40	Iri[. . .		Salonae
41	Fl(avia) Tatta	Fl(avia) Prisca	Pozega
42	Dianadre	Caius Julius Certus	Raetinium
43	Par]thenope	T. Dindius [. . .	Scupi
44	Jul(ia) Donata	Ti. Jul(ius) Princeps	Scarbantia
45	Aurelia Sura	M. Aur(elius) Maximianus	Gorsium
46	Julia Pistrix	Julius Bassus	Lambaesis
47	Julia Almyrde	C. Julius Quintinus	Lambaesis
48	Ateria Januaria	Cerdon[iu]s	Theveste
49	. . .]illia En[. . .		Carthago
50	. . .]dore	. . .] Amabilis	Catina
51	ignota		Forum Julii
52	Rubria Acte	Aquilina	Arelate
53	Titia Epictesis	L. Sennius Hermogenes	Nemausus
54	Fabia Rustica	M. Fab[ius] Stabilio	Narbo
55	Leda	ignotus	Mediomatrici
56	Marciana	Cl(audius) Rufinus	Lugdunum
57	Flavia Cal]lityche	Flavia Parthenope	Scupi
58	Julia Musa	Classicus et Lucius	

*For various details of information pertinent to the case histories and the inscriptions providing them, consult the appropriately numbered Table Notes at the end of this chapter.

"et nutrices et matres."[7] But use of the phrase "mother and nurse" in inscriptions must signify that in some social circles maternal breast-feeding could be considered unusual and hence worthy of later comment. Cantria Paulla (no. 7) was a freeborn woman who became a priest of the imperial cult; she should thus perhaps be regarded as a woman of some means. Like their counterparts in Rome, women of relatively prosperous status in Italy may well have favored the use of wet nurses over maternal feeding.[8]

What can be learned of the remaining women in the Italian inscriptions and the children associated with them? The following remarks focus principally on matters of social status, for both nurses and nurslings. The girls cared for by Rasinia Pietas (no. 19), one of whom was named Procula, belonged to a socially prominent family. Their father, L. Burbuleius Optatus Ligarianus, held the consulship around A.D. 135. Although Burbuleius's family origins perhaps lay in Africa, this case is thus comparable to many from the city of Rome where the senatorial status of families using wet nurses, often drawn from their domestic *familiae,* is well attested. However, Rasinia Pietas is known from an Italian rather than a Roman inscription because Burbuleius became patron of the colony of Minturnae. If it is correct to believe that he had a residence there, it may well have been at Minturnae that the nurse attended his daughters. It is noteworthy that Rasinia Pietas herself set up a text recording the details of Burbuleius's career, her knowledge of which, combined with the fact that she had responsibility for more than one child, suggests a long-standing association with his family. Indeed, a certain pride is detectable in Rasinia's description of herself as the nurse of Burbuleius's daughters, comparable perhaps to that observable in an illustration of a nineteenth-century Brazilian nurse that appeared in Jean Baptiste Debret's *Voyage pittoresque et historique au Brésil* (1834–1889). The nurse was shown sumptuously dressed and bejeweled, being carried in a litter with her nursling to the infant's baptism. In the slave society of Brazil, such women could be "living evidence of their owners' wealth and high social status," and something of the same *éclat* may have surrounded Rasinia Pietas, as though the celebrity of the consular patron of Minturnae in part reflected upon the woman who had charge of his children.[9]

With the case of Cominia Secunda (no. 30), a far different social level for the nursling's family becomes apparent. The nurse was commemorated by the freeborn L. Nutrius Gallus on an inscription set up under the terms of the latter's will. Since the inscription also commemorates two of Nutrius's freedmen and two of his slaves, it can be inferred that Gallus was a man of moderate estate, of the resources available to a legionary soldier in the Roman army such as his apparent brother, C. Nutrius Gallus.[10] The use of a *nutrix* at an intermediate level of society is thus indicated, as perhaps also with the freeborn charges of Pompulla Nemaesis (no. 12) and Musa (no. 20).

At a lower remove again was the family of the nursling associated with Casperia Zotice (no. 25). Here a father and mother, L. Casperius Abascantus and Casperia Aeliane, share a common *nomen,* which is often a strong sign that a couple had once been slaves in the same household. However, that may not be strictly true in this instance, for Aeliane's father was himself free at the time of his death, and so Aeliane may have been freeborn. Nevertheless, since a Casperius Aelianus is on record as praetorian prefect under Domitian and Nerva, the Casperii are probably best understood as members of his dependent *familia* or close descendants of such. At most, they were people not far removed from slavery. Several individuals are commemorated in their inscription: first, the parents made a dedication to their freeborn son, L. Casperius Faunus; then Abascantus alone commemorated his father-in-law, his wife, a second freeborn son, L. Casperius Latinus, the freed nurse, and the *verna* Prosdecte. Zotice the nurse had obviously once been a slave in the same *familia* as that from which the core family of Abascantus derived, but it cannot be determined whether her former owner was Abascantus or the praetorian prefect. Nor is it clear whether Zotice had nursed one or both of Abascantus's sons; the abbreviated phrase "nutrici fil." could be taken either way. However, the use of a nurse by parents of servile extraction is certainly in evidence, and if Zotice had indeed nursed both Latinus and Faunus, then she nursed at least one child while the nursling's mother was still living. Further, it should be noted that Abascantus chose to remember Zotice in her role as nurse long after Latinus reached maturity, for the son was aged eighteen when he died. That fact implies that the association between nurse and nursling (or nurslings) had been maintained well beyond the child's (or children's) infancy.

A similar social background obtains for the nursling of Sperata (no. 28). L. Sentius Pietas was a freeborn child, but his father, L. Sentius Lucrio, was a freedman. The father made a dedication to three people: the freeborn Pontia Procula, his wife; his son, dead at the age of seventeen; and the freedwoman Sperata. Again, nursing of a child of servile extraction is evident, as is the implicit maintenance across time of a bond between child and nurse, given the nursling's age at death.

Nursing of actual slave children is attested in the case of Lucceia Donata (no. 10), who apparently made a dedication to three of her charges, slaves owned by a certain Flavia Procula. Elsewhere, on the assumption that the use of a single name alone in an inscription is a sign of servile status, three further nurslings should also be considered slaves: Silvanus, the charge of Aste (no. 5); Sabina, the charge of Caecilia Eupraesia (no. 16); and Victoria, the charge of Servea Marcellina (no. 18).

Despite the difficulties of interpretation the inscriptions raise, then, it is unquestionable that the use of *nutrices* in Italian towns was not confined to any single social stratum but covered a range of familial situations. Parents of substantial means would obviously have had little difficulty in finding nurses for their children, whether hired or drawn from their slave personnel; but families of lesser estate also found it possible to gain access to nurses when they were needed, as did slave owners who were sufficiently interested in the survival of slave nurslings in their possession to guarantee them adequate care.[11]

The status of the nurses should not be expected to show a great deal of variation from one case to another, and predictably upper-class women do not enter the picture at all. In some instances status is recorded precisely. Thus, Aste (no. 5) and Musa (no. 20) were imperial slaves. They died at the respective ages of fifty-five and twenty-two. Women with single names—Ammia (no. 26) and Tyche (no. 27)—may also have been slaves. Ediste (no. 15) must once have been a slave, because she is described in her inscription as the "nurse of her owners"; but since she had a free husband, she may possibly have been set free by the time of her death at the age of thirty-five. Other women had definitely been released from slavery: Lucceia Herophil (no. 17), Casperia Zotice (no. 25), Sperata (no. 28), and the unnamed nurse from Anxanum (no. 9) were all *libertae,* and the same may be imagined for Adventa (no. 8), given the fact that she set up a dedication to a man she called her patron. Those for whom *nomina* and *cognomina* are given in their inscriptions were free women, but whether freeborn or freed it is usually difficult to say. Three nurses—Cassia Prisca (no. 4), Vibpsania Capriola (no. 11), and Birria Cognita (no. 31)—shared their *nomina* with their nurslings; like Casperia Zotice (no. 25), they are likely to have been *libertae,* or close descendants, from the same households or families as their charges. Multasia Felicitas (no. 14) could perhaps be included in this category as well, because although her nursling's name is missing from her inscription, the child was commemorated not just by the nurse but by another person who shared her *nomen,* P. Multasius Felix. Women whose *nomina* differed from those of their nurslings—for instance, Pompulla Nemaesis (no. 12) and Calpurnia Lupula (no. 24)—could have been either freedwomen associated with their nurslings' *familiae* or free mercenary nurses. However, the only certain freeborn woman in the Italian inscriptions is Cantria Paulla (no. 7), and, as already seen, she was not a *nutrix* proper. All in all, therefore, the nurses on record were woman of no more than humble circumstances—slaves, former slaves, and women close to slavery.

Since, strictly speaking, the *nutrix* was a wet nurse, it might be assumed that the care she afforded her charge extended only through the child's infancy, approximately until the age of weaning. But in the evidence so far described, several indications have emerged—in the particular cases of Rasinia Pietas (no. 19), Casperia Zotice (no. 25), and Sperata (no. 28)—that the association between nurse and nursling persisted over a long period of time. The point can be illustrated further: thus, Pompulla Nemaesis (no. 12) and Multasia Felicitas (no. 14) commemorated charges who were respectively thirty and fifteen years old when they died, and Aste (no. 5) and Birria Cognita (no. 31) were respectively fifty-five and sixty when they were commemorated by their nurslings. Moreover, although the nursling who set up a dedication to Musa (no. 20) cannot have been a mature adult when Musa died at the age of twenty-two, evidently he was no infant; and even in the single example where a child of very young age was commemorated—the five-year-old charge of Servea Marcellina (no. 18)—it is likely that the boy was beyond the age of weaning. The reason for celebrating, after many years, a connection between a nurse and her young charge was doubtless in part simple sentiment. In their inscriptions the nurses are sometimes honored with the label "well-deserving," and Musa (no. 20), very specially, is called by her nursling a "nutrix sanctissima."[12] However, nurslings who had reached adulthood are not likely to have remembered their nurses or to have been remembered by them if their association had been utterly terminated in infancy. It is plausible to believe, therefore, that wet nurses regularly continued to function as nannies to children they had previously nursed, as alternates to or companions of other child minders such as male *nutritores* and *paedagogi,* once breast-feeding was no longer required.[13] In other words, the inscriptional evidence implies that the job of the *nutrix* might well continue until her nurslings reached maturity, a point to which I shall return below.

III

Generally speaking, the provincial inscriptions that identify *nutrices* are even more intractable than those from Italy. But the information they convey essentially complements the Italian evidence.

Firm indications of the status of the provincial nurslings are sparse. One of the Dalmatian inscriptions reveals at the top of the social hierarchy a nursling whose family became successful enough to acquire senatorial standing: Flavia Prisca, *c(larissima) f(emina)*, the charge of Flavia Tatta (no. 41). A second Dalmatian nursling, C. Desidienus Proculus, the charge of Desidiena Primitiva (no. 39), can be presumed to have belonged to a relatively prosperous family, since he became a decurion at Salonae. Three nurslings appear as legionary soldiers in their inscriptions—T. Dindius, the charge of Parthenope (no. 43); Julius Bassus, the charge of Julia Pistrix (no. 46); and C. Julius Quintinus, the charge of Julia Almyrde (no. 47)—so the convention of wet-nursing at the intermediate social level is again indicated. The nursling of C. Epicharis (no. 38) was almost certainly a slave: the child, who was five years old at his death, was commemorated by his nurse, the freedman L. Saloninus, and his mother, Romulla, whose single name suggests servile status for her and hence for her son. It looks as if a pair of child minders had in fact been found for the boy, perhaps to allow Romulla to continue with her normal work as a slave woman.[14] The inscription of Julia Musa (no. 58) was set up by the decurions of an unknown city and the *familia* of a certain Theopompus; the reference to a *familia,* together with the single names, points to servile status for her nurslings Classicus and Lucius. Similarly, Amabilis, the nursling of the Sicilian nurse (no. 50), and Aquilina, the nursling of Rubria Acte (no. 52), might also be considered slaves.

Of the nurses themselves, five were certainly *libertae:* Clovatia Irene (no. 32), Flavia Tatta (no. 41), Julia Donata (no. 44), Aurelia Sura (no. 45), and Flavia Callityche (no. 57). Four of them shared their *nomen* with their nurslings and have to be regarded as former slaves from the households of their nurslings' families. Other freedwomen can be sought in similar cases of shared *nomen* (nos. 39, 46, 47, 54), though the possibility has to remain that these women were freeborn. Given that her inscription labels her as nurse and maidservant, Justina Virginia (no. 37) must also have been a freedwoman. None of the provincial nurses is specifically designated a slave, but servile status is highly probable for Leda (no. 55), who made a dedication to her fifteen-month-old nursling, together with the nursling's foster brother: all three individuals have only single names. Likewise, Marciana (no. 56) and other women with single names may have been slaves. Several cases must remain problematical because of the fragmentary nature of the evidence. However, there is no positive evidence that any of the nurses was freeborn, and the probability that the majority were either slaves, former slaves, or women close to slavery is again high.

A greater number of the provincial inscriptions record ages at death for either the nurses or the nurslings. The details are summarized in Table 2.3. As with the Italian evidence, this information strongly implies that contacts between nurslings and nurses were often maintained for many years. Nurses were at times fondly remembered when they died. Aurelia Sura (no. 45), for example, was described by her nursling as "nutrix pientissima," and Julia Pistrix (no. 46) as "nutrix optima."[15] But whatever the bonds of sentiment, it again seems sensible to believe that contacts over time were in some cases attributable to the fact that the nurse continued to function as a child minder for her nursling beyond the age of weaning.

One provincial nurse, finally, must be dismissed from consideration as a *nutrix* proper. Dianadre (no. 42) was called by C. Julius Certus his "amita dignissima et nutrix." Two alternatives are possible: the aunt nursed the child either because his mother died in childbirth or because, for some indeterminate personal reason, the mother simply opted not to breast-feed her son herself. It can be noted, however, that the aunt was aged sixty-one when she died and Certus commemorated her.

Table 2.3. Ages at Death

No.	Name	Y.	M.	D.
	Age at Death of Provincial Nurses			
41	Flavia Tatta	50	—	—
44	Julia Donata	25	—	—
45	Aurelia Sura	35	10	—
46	Julia Pistrix	100+	—	—
47	Julia Almyrde	63	—	—
50	. . .]dore	60	—	—
57	Flavia Cal]lityche	60	—	—
	Age at Death of Provincial Nurslings			
37	Julius Vaentinus	21	—	—
38	filius Romullae	5	3	—
52	Aquilina	1	6	—
53	L. Sennius Hermogenes	22	7	—
55	ignotus	1	5	22

IV

Of course, wet-nursing as a social phenomenon has a history that extends far beyond Roman antiquity. In eighteenth- and nineteenth-century France, for example, the practice is especially well attested, not just in the upper reaches of society but at many lower social levels as well.[16] Yet despite its prevalence, commentators from antiquity on have always been quick to denounce its inadequacies. So, advising against the use of a bibulous nurse, the Greek physician Soranus observed that such a woman "leaves the newborn untended or even falls down upon it in a dangerous way," and he urged his preference for an affectionate nurse on the grounds that "some wet nurses are so lacking in sympathy towards the nursling that they not only pay no heed when it cries for a long time, but do not even arrange its position when it lies still; rather, they leave it in one position so that often because of the pressure the sinewy parts suffer and consequently become numb and bad."[17] Another Greek doctor of the imperial age, Galen, reports that when he once had to deal with an unusually cranky infant boy, he found that the child's dirty body and bedding were the causes of the baby's distress. To make him more comfortable, Galen had to give the child's nurse specific instructions to wash him and to change the bedclothes.[18] Comparably, in Brazil of the mid-nineteenth century, the use of wet nurses was regarded as a prime cause of infant mortality in Rio de Janeiro, while the eighteenth-century Englishman John Gabriel Stedman wrote as follows of his own childhood experience:

> Four different wet-nurses were alternately turn'd out of doors on my account, and to the care of whom I had been entrusted, my poor mother being too weak a condition to suckle me herself. The first of these bitches was turn'd off for having nearly suffocated me in bed; she having sleep'd upon me till I was smother'd, and with skill and difficulty restored to life. The second had let me fall from her arms on the stones till my head was almost fractured, & I lay several hours in convulsions. The third carried me under a moulder'd old brick wall, which fell in a heap of rubbish just the moment we had passed by it, while the fourth proved to be a thief, and deprived me even of my very baby clothes.[19]

Such flirtations with death form a common theme in the litany of complaints, remarkably consistent across time, directed against wet nurses: the women morally corrupt their charges, transmit diseases to them, fail to provide adequate care, and actually kill babies, accidentally or otherwise.[20] Thus, recourse to the nurse has been stigmatized as a "form of institutionalized abandonment."[21] True, this is an extreme view, and evidence of parental concern for the welfare of children entrusted to wet nurses can be found in the modern record, though without necessarily exonerating the women from the charge of neglect.[22] Indeed, the subject of parental interest in children's well-being in the early modern period and of the relationship between wet-nursing and parental indifference to infants is highly contentious. But whatever the truth, the modern evidence suggests, for a fuller understanding of the role of the nurse in the Roman world, that a distinction should be drawn between free mercenary nurses on the one hand and slave nurses on the other. French mercenary nurses, for example, tended to have control of their nurslings only until the age of weaning, whereas slave nurses in Brazil might continue to care for their nurslings much later. For Parisian infants put out to mercenary nurses in the rural district of Evreux in the early nineteenth century, the "normal pattern appears to have been for the child to be restored to his parents soon after his first birthday."[23] But in Brazil, where slave nurses were used for the offspring of the white elite, such abrupt separation of nurse and child was not so likely to occur. One critic, for instance, referred to the "effects of the bad personal behavior of slave nurses, and, *at a later age,* the same nurses inducing a precocious development among the children of those activities which normally begin at the age of puberty, thus exposing them at a tender age . . . to the evils of immoderacy."[24] In a slave-owning society, the capacity of the nurse to become a nanny as her nursling advanced in years was much greater than in a non-slave-owning society, where the services of the nurse were engaged only for a specified and relatively brief amount of time.

The mercenary pattern of wet-nursing was not unknown in the Roman world. It is best observed in contracts for wet-nursing services that have survived in papyri from Roman Egypt, where the stipulation is some-times found that the nurse is to care for the infant entrusted to her in her own home.[25] It is evident, too, in a legal text that discusses the validity of a grant of freedom to a slave named Thetis, a girl or young woman who was raised by a nurse named Seia Procula, a free woman presumably. Procula had occasion to sue the slave owner for Thetis's maintenance costs and must therefore have been hired by him.[26] However, the inscriptional evidence from Italy and the provinces has made clear the fact that nurses tended not to be freeborn women and that at times they maintained contacts with their nurslings well beyond the children's earliest years. Doubtless there were other free mercenary nurses like Procula, some of whom had never been slaves. But the dual function of wet nurse and nanny is likely in many more instances in view of the pure manipulability of the slave and ex-slave woman.

Indications that the servile wet nurse regularly became a nanny and chaperone for her growing nursling, especially when the nursling was female, can be found in Roman literary sources. Consider, for example, Livy's account of the young Verginia, who at an early date in Roman history was supposedly killed by her own father to save her from the lustful advances of a cruel magistrate. The latter, impelled by his mad desire to possess the girl, suborned a dependent to claim Verginia as a slave when she entered the forum one day to attend school. Despite the public outcry against the patent enormity of the action and the protests of both Verginia's betrothed and her father, Appius Claudius the magistrate confirmed his client's claim and judged Verginia his slave. It was at that point, however, that the father took his daughter aside and stabbed her to death before the magistrate's wicked design could be fully accomplished.[27]

The story has no historical foundation.[28] But two details in Livy's narrative are of implicit importance for present purposes. First, although her attendance at school is plainly anachronistic, it can be noticed that when Verginia appeared in the forum she was accompanied by a *nutrix* who, once the claim of slavery was made, was the first to cry out for help.[29] Second, immediately before Verginia's death, it is again the same nurse whom her father, Verginius, says he will question to determine his daughter's paternity.[30] And so, too, in one of the declamations attributed to Quintilian that concerns a question of paternity, it is likewise the nurse—on this occasion an old slave woman—who, naturally, holds the key to unlocking the truth.[31] For Livy and his audience, therefore, it can be assumed that the custodial role of the nurse, her attendance upon a girl old enough to be close to marriage, and her intimacy with her charge since the latter's infancy were all aspects of contemporary social custom familiar enough to require no explanation.

Other literary evidence could be invoked. In one of two Propertian examples, the married woman Arethusa, pining for her absent soldier-husband, is found attended by an anxious nurse, while in the other

Propertius himself is exhorted by Cynthia's ghost to take care of her former nurse in the nurse's declining years.[32] So, too, in a list of those able to exploit an ardent lover's wealth, the nurse, according to Ovid's *lena,* is placed alongside the woman's mother and sister.[33] Again, the old nurse of Charite in Apuleius's *Metamorphoses* assists her widowed mistress to accomplish the destruction of Thrasyllus, Charite's lover and her husband's killer, by admitting Thrasyllus to Charite's bedroom in the dead of night for what Thrasyllus mistakenly believes will be an ecstatic session of lovemaking.[34] Admittedly, the juxtaposition of mistress and nurse in Roman imaginative literature could simply be dismissed as a literary motif devoid of any realistic significance. But more substantially, the younger Pliny provided a farm worth one hundred thousand sesterces for his former nurse and was concerned that it remain a profitable enterprise, seeing that the nurse was to continue to benefit from his generosity; and in his portrait of Minicia Marcella, prematurely dead at thirteen, Pliny included among the entourage of her attendants the nurses for whom she had maintained an affection until the end of her young life.[35] According to Fronto, a foolish nurse was likely to resent the arrival of her nursling's adolescence, for it was then that she had to relinquish him to the training ground and forum.[36] In sum, the evidence of literature, deriving from authors of very diverse geographical origins, complements the evidence of the inscriptions, and it cannot be doubted that the *nutrix* was often an integral part of a child's life from birth to maturity.[37]

Various reasons why parents in the Roman world chose to use wet nurses for their infants can be posited. Many women must have died in childbirth, and at all levels of society. In this respect, the upper-class daughters of Helvidius Priscus, who died, it seems, almost simultaneously when each had given birth to a daughter, were no better off than the slave woman Augustus commemorated, who perished soon after bearing quintuplets.[38] Other women who survived may have been averse to breast-feeding or unable to perform: a new pregnancy, or sickness, may have intervened, circumstances under which Galen recommended the immediate use of a nurse.[39] Slave mothers may at times have been discouraged from nursing their own children by their owners. It could be expected, for instance, that a husband would find a nurse for children born to the slave women in his wife's dowry.[40] As a result, it was the *nutrix,* predominantly, who for about three years or so (in Galen's view, again) took responsibility for the chores associated with early infant care:

breast-feeding, powdering and swaddling, bathing and massaging, rocking and singing the child to sleep, weaning the child from milk to solid
food.[41] And although it should not be thought that every wet nurse
automatically later became a nanny and chaperone, the existence of slavery as a fundamental element of Roman society made that progression
possible, as parents continued to be able to control the labor of dependent
personnel at their disposal. So, in her developing role as a provider of
extended child care, the *nutrix* became the equivalent of the *educatrix* or
paedagoga, comparable to figures such as the *liberta* Caesia, a woman
commemorated on an inscription from Verona by a certain C. Romana as the *educatrix* of Romana's four sons; or the *paedagoga* Cornelia
Fortunata, known from an African inscription.[42] The *nutrix,* in fact, was
only one of a sequence of child-minding functionaries who influenced the
early lives of children.

The chief significance of this fact lies in its relevance to the issue of
how the Roman family, as a social unit, is to be conceptualized. The
nurse's social role can be defined from two points of view: at the
functional level, first, the nurse provided early infant care, including
breast-feeding, and for older children supervision of a custodial sort; but
at a more underlying level, secondly, the nurse also acted, with parents
and other child minders, as an instrument of socialization and became an
important element in the child's emotional framework of reference. This
is acknowledged, across time, in the way nurses were commonly associated with storytelling, in the commemorative expressions of the inscriptions, and perhaps also in the popular saying that the grief of a nurse
was second only to that of a mother.[43] The nurse consequently was in a
real sense part of the child's familial world, but as a nonkin member of the
family—a reality illustrated in the legal provision that one of the few
women permitted to bring an action for untrustworthiness against a tutor
on behalf of a ward was the *nutrix,* the others being the mother,
grandmother, or sister; or in the rule that a slave *nutrix,* like other slave
child minders and blood relatives, could be set free by a slave owner who
was below the normal statutory age for granting slaves their freedom.[44] A
view of the Roman family that will accommodate the relationship
between nurse and nursling is thus clearly desirable.

Of course, since the *nutrix* entered a child's familial world through
compulsion rather than choice, there could never be any guarantee of
a positive emotional bonding between nurse and child. The inscriptions reveal only one side of the coin, and what could happen on the

reverse is hinted at in a decree issued at Aquileia by Constantine in A.D. 326:

> Since the watchfulness of parents is often frustrated by the stories and wicked persuasions of nurses, punishment shall threaten first such nurses whose care is proved to have been detestable and their discourses bribed, and the penalty shall be that the mouth and throat of those who offered incitement to evil shall be closed by pouring in molten lead.[45]

Nurses were vulnerable. But the willingness of parents to rely on them is a firm indication that the Roman sense of family was much more diffuse than the narrow conception that dominates the modern Western tradition. The inscriptional evidence shows the presence of nurses in Roman domestic groups diverse in geographical location and social standing. Its limitations, again, must always be kept in mind. As a whole, however, it points to a communal character in the Roman family, a character that had the capacity for embracing extensive, nonkin relationships as well as connections of blood.

V

A final question remains. Was wet-nursing a symptom of widespread parental indifference to children in Roman society, connected in some way to the very common reality of premature child death?[46] So much is suggested by Soranus's generalization that Roman women of his day neglected the responsibilities of caring for children; and yet the detailed advice doctors gave on how to select nurses could just as well imply that parents were intent on providing their children the best care possible.[47]

The question is, in fact, too broad to allow for a single, simple answer. A variety of parental attitudes must be acknowledged, dependent on specific circumstances and analogous to the variety of attested responses to children's deaths in antiquity. In the case of the latter, one could take, on the one hand, Quintilian's chronicle in the *Institute of Oratory* of the loss of his two young sons (and of his wife, as it happens), which leaves no doubt of the intensity of Quintilian's grief; the account is profoundly disturbing.[48] Again, one could point to the letter Fronto wrote to Marcus Aurelius when his three-year-old grandson died, a fully convincing expression of personal loss made all the more poignant by the knowledge that Fronto had never actually seen the child. The grief he experienced, indeed, brought back to life sad recollections of the five children he had lost himself.[49] On the other hand, Cicero wrote that "if a small child dies, the loss must be borne calmly; if an infant in the cradle, there must not even be a lament."[50] In the face of demographic reality, the attitudes of Quintilian and Fronto may have been aberrant.[51]

It is unlikely therefore that attitudes to wet-nursing were universally identical. From case to case, the use of the nurse may well have signified both parental indifference to and parental regard for Roman children. It is better consequently to set the question aside as inappropriate and to concentrate instead on the practical effects of the convention. If, for instance, a child were taken at birth from the mother, handed over to a nurse, and sent, as happened, from the city to the healthier environment of the country, parents normally resident in the city will not have been able to maintain daily contact with the child.[52] If a child were kept in the city, to be attended by a nurse from within the parents' urban *familia,* the parents may well have directed the nurse's regimen and seen the child at intervals throughout the day, but continuous contact will not have been the norm. If parents in the city entrusted their child to a free nurse who maintained the child in her own place of residence, ease of association between parents and child will again have been affected. Variations of practice no doubt occurred. But in all cases nursing implies a general disruption of contact between parent and child, and it seems plausible that physical distancing was matched by emotional distancing. It might have happened as a result that when a nursling died prematurely, the loss experienced by parents was to some extent cushioned. More importantly, however, the physical and perhaps emotional distancing of parents and children does not fit comfortably with conceptions of the Roman family that focus exclusively on the core unit of father, mother, and children. To the degree that child-rearing practices illustrate familial behavior, it is again the communal aspect of the process that stands out in the Roman record. Byrrhaena, after all, was not only raised together with Lucius's mother—in turn, she also became one of Lucius's *educatores.*[53]

Notes

1. Apuleius, *Metamorphoses* 2.3. On Lucius's descent from Plutarch, see C. P. Jones (1971), 11; and on historical realism in Apuleius, see Millar (1981).

2. On wet nurses at Rome in general, see Bradley (1986) and Joshel (1986); cf. also

Treggiari (1976), 87–89; Kampen (1981), 109–10; Gourevitch (1984), 233–59; Gardner (1986), 241–45; Fildes (1986), 26–36; Fildes (1988), 4–25. Beard (1986) questions the "primary meaning" of *nutrix*, which may mean "either wet-nurse or nursemaid"—for the phraseology cf. Bradley (1986), 202—but without evidence or discussion. It is obvious that many occurrences of the word must be subject to a certain ambiguity, but note, for example, Vitruvius, *On Architecture* 2 Preface 3: "natus infans sine nutricis lacte non potest ali"; *Digest* 50.13.1.14: "quoad infantes uberibus aluntur"; Celsus, *On Medicine* 5.28.15D, 6.11.3–4 (where Celsus, referring to the sick child at the breast, simply assumes that the nursing woman is a *nutrix*); Pliny, *Natural History* 13.131, 22.89, 37.162. It would be foolish to ignore such evidence, or to imagine that a wet nurse could never have later become a nursemaid to the infant she had nursed. That the nurse was not merely associated with the care of upper-class children or children in an urban environment is implicit in Galen's remarks on bathing at *Hygiene (De Sanitate Tuenda)* 1.10.

  3. Pliny, *Natural History* 3.82, 18.6 (cf. 15.77); Scullard (1981), 210–11.

  4. According to Pliny, the gemstone galaxias assured nurses a good supply of milk (*Natural History* 37.162), as did a drink made from the stem of the sow thistle (22.89); the remedy for insufficiency was a drink made from the shrub cytisus, dried and boiled and mixed with wine (13.131).

  5. *Digest* 50.13.1.14. The papyrological evidence of wet-nursing contracts from Roman Egypt is also relevant, of course; see below, n. 25.

  6. The inscriptions used in the preparation of the tables have been collected from the various volumes of *CIL* and *AE*. The lists could doubtless be expanded from the contents of highly specialized epigraphical publications not easily accessible; note that Curchin (1982), 44, provides some additional evidence for Spain. For the inscription reference numbers, see the list accompanying the table notes. For Augustine's evidence, see *Confessions* 1.6.7, 1.7.11, with Shaw (1987a), 41–42.

  7. Varro, *On Agriculture* 2.10.8: "De nutricatu hoc dico, easdem fere et nutrices et matres."

  8. Obviously enough, individual preferences will not always have conformed to type. The implication of maternal breast-feeding at Apuleius, *Metamorphoses* 3.8, evidently of a lower-class but not necessarily impoverished provincial woman, should be noted, as should that of Augustine, *Confessions* 1.6.7, that the infant Augustine was nursed both by his mother and by wet nurses; cf. also Martial, *Epigrams* 11.78.7, "nutrix materque." Note that Livia Benigna (no. 29) must also be removed from consideration as a wet nurse. In her inscription she is called the wife and nurse of the *eques* C. Praeconius Ventidius Magnus, which must mean that she took care of her husband, in sickness or old age, in the selfless manner of the wife of the invalid Domitius Tullus known from Pliny, *Letters* 8.18.8–10; a certain L. Sentius September commemorated a woman named Barbara on an inscription from Comum (*CIL* 5.8902) as "nutricula senectutis suae."

  9. Quotation from Conrad (1983), 139. For the illustration, see Conrad (1983), 224. For the need nevertheless to keep in mind that nurses may not always have shared the attitudes of the elite, see Joshel (1986).

  10. On soldiers' economic circumstances, see in general Campbell (1984), 176–81.

  11. It might be expected, of course, that very poor women, with access neither to cash nor to slaves, were obliged to nurse their own children; observe Juvenal 6.592–593, with Courtney (1980), 340. What practices were like among lower-class women in rural districts

is difficult to say, but the rural nurse of fable literature (e.g., Avianus 1; Babrius 1.16) should be noted.

12. The epithet "well-deserving" is used of Cassia Prisca (no. 4), Aste (no. 5), Caecilia Eupraesia (no. 16), and Calpurnia Lupula (no. 24).

13. On *nutritores* and *paedagogi*, see Chapter 3.

14. For child-minding couples, see below, Chapter 3, n. 45.

15. For discussion of terms of endearment in some provincial inscriptions, see Curchin (1983) and Curchin (1984).

16. See, in general, Fildes (1988); on France in particular, see Sussman (1982).

17. Soranus, *Gynecology* 2.91.

18. Galen, *Hygiene* 1.8.

19. Quoted in Pollock (1983), 218. For Brazil, see Conrad (1983), 137–39.

20. See Bradley (1986), 214–15; DeMause (1974), 32–39; J. Brown (1986), 24–25; Fildes (1986), 186–204. Observe especially Edward Gibbon's remark, in *Memoirs of My Life:* "My poor aunt has often told me with tears in her eyes, how I was nearly starved by a nurse that had lost her milk."

21. DeMause (1974), 34.

22. See Pollock (1983), 212–22.

23. Sussman (1982), 147.

24. Conrad (1983), 138; my emphasis. Cf. Fildes (1988), 139–43, on the use of slave nurses for white children in the U.S. South.

25. See Manca Masciardi and Montevecchi (1984), 22. It has recently been argued that nursing contracts from the village of Tebtunis belonging to the mid-first century A.D. conceal fictitious loans secured by nursing women with their nurslings (their own children or slaves) as surety; see Montevecchi and Manca Masciardi (1982). The notion of a fictitious loan has also been used to explain a text from Oxyrhynchus, but see Whitehorne (1984). In any case, the point about mercenary wet-nursing is not affected.

26. *Digest* 41.7.8. The facts of the case were as follows: Procula sued Sempronius for the cost of maintaining his slave Thetis, a child born of a slave woman and a man named Lucius Titius. Sempronius responded that he could not pay and that Thetis should be handed over to Titius. Titius then paid Procula's expenses and set his daughter free, whereupon Sempronius contested the manumission. On the ground that Sempronius had apparently abandoned Thetis, the grant of freedom was upheld. This seems to be an authentic case history, but certainty, of course, is impossible. As for the availability of mercenary nurses, it can be supposed, on the analogy of the *columna lactaria* at Rome, that many communities had spots where women seeking work could customarily be found. For the practice generally, see Fildes (1988), 18. Boswell (1988), 110, seems to misunderstand Festus, *On the Significance of Words* s.v. "lactaria": the column was not a place where children were abandoned but a place where nurses could be hired.

27. Livy 3.44–48. The story of Verginia is told also by Dionysius of Halicarnassus, *Roman Antiquities* 11.28–29, who gives Verginia's age at the time of the episode as fifteen; her mother, who breast-fed her daughter, had been dead long since, but Verginia was now attended by several nurses (11.28.4, τὰς τροφοὺς). Cf. also Cicero, *De Republica* 2.63; *Digest* 1.2.2.24, but without any mention of chaperones.

28. See Ogilvie (1965), 476–88.

29. Livy 3.44.4.

30. Livy 3.44.7.

31. Ps.—Quintilian, *Declamations* 338. The facts are as follows. The parents of an adult son have divorced, and the father has remarried. Stepmother and stepson quarrel. A pauper claims the son as his own. To ascertain the truth, the son's nurse is tortured twice, first asserting that the father is the father, then the pauper. She dies from her torment. The father is prepared to abandon the son, when the mother claims him for herself.

32. Propertius 4.3.41, 4.7.73.

33. Ovid, *Amores* 1.8.91.

34. Apuleius, *Metamorphoses* 8.10–11.

35. Pliny, *Letters* 6.3, 5.16.3.

36. Fronto, *Epistles* 2.124, Loeb.

37. Note also Martial 11.78.7–8; Cassius Dio 77.8.1; and, on the custodial role, Pliny, *Natural History* 28.39. Pliny's story of Livia (*Natural History* 10.154) is good enough to quote: "Moreover eggs can be hatched even by a human being. Julia Augusta in her early womanhood was with child with Tiberius Caesar by Nero, and being specially eager to bear a baby of the male sex she employed the following method of prognostication used by girls—she cherished an egg in her bosom and when she had to lay it aside passed it to a nurse [*nutrix*] under the folds of their dresses, so that the warmth might not be interrupted; and it is said that her prognostication came true." In my view, Joshel (1986), 11, sees more in Pliny's letter on his nurse than the text justifies.

38. Pliny, *Letters* 4.21; Aulus Gellius, *Attic Nights* 10.2 The infant girls would obviously have needed nurses, but, not surprisingly under ancient conditions, the quintuplets did not survive.

39. Galen, *Hygiene* 1.9; cf. 1.7. Under extreme circumstances, goats could be used to nurse infants; see Calder (1983) and Guida (1985).

40. *Digest* 24.1.28.1. Gardner (1986), 242, comments that the nurse "is apparently not part of [the husband's] household and may be free. She sounds rather like a child-minder or fosterer, to whom the babies may have been farmed out, leaving the *ancillae* free to get on with their work." See further Bradley (1986), 210–13, 215–20.

41. Galen, *Hygiene* 1.7–10; for three years, see also Quintilian, *Institute of Oratory* 1.1.16, and for weaning, 2.4.5. Note that although Galen has much to say about recommending mother's milk for infants, he assumes constantly that it is a nurse, not the mother, who is doing the nursing. He also believed in feeding on demand. In contrast, as an example of a woman nursing her own child, in extreme conditions, observe the Christian martyr Vibia Perpetua in prison in Carthage in A.D. 203: Musurillo (1972), 108–9, 114–15.

42. *CIL* 5.3519, 8.1506.

43. On nurses and storytelling, see Scobie (1983), 16–30. Popular saying: Publilius Syrus, *Sententiae* 659. Phaedrus, *Fables* 3.15, is also apposite: when an abandoned Lamb tells a Dog that the bond to its foster mother is far stronger than any natural tie to the mother, the conclusion is reached, "facit parentes bonitas, non necessitas."

44. *Digest* 26.10.1.7, 40.2.11–13.

45. *Theodosian Code* 9.24.1.1; cf. 9.24.1.5 and the accompanying *interpretatio*. For the context, see Barnes (1981), 219–20; Grodzynski (1984).

46. Bradley (1986), 216. The modern debate is of relevance here, summarized as follows by Pollock (1987), 11–12: "The main thrust of the most influential works in the field has been to argue that good parental care has evolved through the centuries. It is

claimed that before the eighteenth century parents subjected their children to a strict, often severe, disciplinary regime; relations between parents and children were formal and distant, and parents were purportedly unmoved at the death of any of their children. . . . It has been argued, too, that parents were often indifferent to the death of their offspring because so many children died. They have been regarded as either so familiar with childhood death that they had become resigned to the situation, or as having taken steps to protect themselves by refusing to become too emotionally involved with their children. . . . There has recently been a volte-face in the historiography of family life. Historians, rather than insisting on the differences between modern and past techniques of parenting, emphasize instead the continuities in modes of parental care. Most parents, we are now told, did indeed love and care for their offspring to the best of their ability.''

47. Soranus, *Gynecology* 2.44, the import of which is exaggerated by Rousselle (1988), 46. The extent of wet-nursing in Roman society could be taken, quite straightforwardly, as an indication of the efficiency of the practice, but not in all cases. At times, no alternative was available.

48. Quintilian, *Institute of Oratory* 6, Preface. When that text was composed, Quintilian was clearly in the throes of bereavement. The elder of his sons had just died at the age of nine. The younger son had died earlier, at the age of five, and his death had been preceded, a few months beforehand, by that of Quintilian's wife. Quintilian himself was born around A.D. 35, and Book 6 of the *Institute* was written around A.D. 95. When the second son was born, his mother had not yet completed her nineteenth year. On a crude calculation, Quintilian had married a teenage bride in his late forties, had fathered two sons in his early fifties, but after scarcely more than a decade of conjugal life found himself a childless widower. See M. Clarke (1967).

49. Fronto, *On the Loss of His Grandson* 2 (Loeb 2.222–233), with Champlin (1974), 155.

50. Cicero, *Tusculan Disputations* 1.93.

51. For discussion, see Golden (1988b).

52. For children being sent to the country to be nursed, see Seneca, *Controversiae* 4.6; *Digest* 32.99.3, 50.16.210.

53. Apuleius, *Metamorphoses* 2.3.

Table Notes

1. A dedication to Diana by the *noutrix* (*sic*) alone.

3. The element ''Verna'' appears to be part of the nurse's name but may be used literally; in either case a servile origin is indicated. The inscription does not record the nursling's name.

5. Aste is styled ''Caesaris n. ser.''; for the form, see Weaver (1972), 54–56.

7. The nurse's nomenclature should be noted: ''Cantria P. fil. Paulla sacerd. Augustae Aeclano.''

8. I assume that *nu* in the inscription is to be understood as *nu(trix)*.

9. The inscription is fragmentary, the nurse's name irrecoverable, but she appears to have been a freedwoman, given the element *lib.*, and was the *nu]trix* of an *alumnus*.

10. The inscription is fragmentary, and while the nurse's name is certain, the identity of the nursling(s) is not. However, "Hyalissi Vic[. . .] Hyacinti Flaviaes Proculae ser." seems to indicate three nurslings, the second of whom might have been named Victor. The servile status of the nursling(s) is demonstrably clear.

11. Vibpsania Severa was commemorated by her uncle Vibpsanius Vales, as well as by her nurse.

12. The nomenclature of L. Laberius Lupus shows him to have been freeborn.

13. Halicia Severa's charge is not named by the inscription.

14. The inscription is fragmentary, the nursling's name completely lost.

15. Ediste appears as "nutrix dominorum suorum"; she had a husband, Caerellius Felicio.

17. The nurse appears as "Lucceia Herophil Balbi l. nutrixs," which may mean that she was the nurse of her patron.

19. On L. Burbuleius Optatus Ligarianus, see *PIR²* B 174; Birley (1981), 271–72; Syme (1984), 1113; Syme (1988), 41. The name of the daughter Procula is known from *AE* 1982.157, also from Minturnae. A Burbuleia Secunda is known from *CIL* 6.16238, and a son-in-law is identified by *AE* 1983.517 as M. Messius Rusticianus, belonging to a senatorial family from Baetica. Cf. Syme (1988), 101.

20. Musa was an imperial slave: "verna Caisaris"; cf. note 5 above. The nomenclature of Praesens shows him to have been freeborn.

21. The inscription is fragmentary, the nursling's name completely lost. But it is tempting to regard the nurse as a servile dependent of the well-known Egrilii of Ostia, on whom see Meiggs (1973), 196–98, 502–7.

22. The inscription is fragmentary. The nursling's name was perhaps Hypatianus, possibly a slave.

24. The inscription gives the nursling's name as *Viciorinu*.

25. On Casperius Aelianus, whose *familia* is probably represented here, see *PIR²* C 462; Syme (1984), 1277.

26. The inscription is fragmentary but appears to give a list of dedicatees, including the nurse Ammia. No nursling is evident.

27. The inscription gives no indication of the nursling.

28. The transcription of *AE* omits *ux* in "Pontiae L(ucii) f(iliae) Proculae ux(ori)"; but see *NS* 1913, 47–48.

32. Cf. Curchin (1982), 44, 58 n. 95. No nursling's name is recorded.

33. Cf. Curchin (1982), 44, 58 n. 95.

34. Cf. Curchin (1982), 44, 58 n. 95. But the women may have been the nurslings' mothers.

35. Cf. Curchin (1982), 44, 58 n. 95; probably libertine. No nursling's name is recorded.

36. Cf. Curchin (1982), 44, 58 n. 95. The inscription is fragmentary, the names of nurse and nursling lost.

37. The nurse appears as "nutrix et favia."

38. The unnamed nursling was the son of Romulla, and the *nutricius* of Epic(h)aris; the freedman L. Saloninus joined mother and nurse in commemorating him.

39. C. Desidienus Proculus was "dec(urio) col(oniae) S[a]loni[t]anor(um)"; cf. Wilkes (1969), 335.

40. The inscription is fragmentary, the nurse's name incomplete, the nursling's name lost.

41. *PIR*² s.v. "Flavia Prisca" reports that the *c.f.* following the name of Fl. Prisca is not to be taken to mean "c(larissima) f(emina)" but "C. f(ilia)" and compares *CIL* 3.12701. In the latter there is no ambiguity about the filiation: "Fl. C. fil. Prisca." But the form of the present inscription is quite different: "Fl. Prisca c.f." There should therefore be no doubt about the senatorial standing; cf. Wilkes (1969), 284 n. 3, 335.

44. The nurse was the "liberta et nutrix" of the nursling.

45. The nurse was the freedwoman of Aurelia Candida, perhaps the nursling's mother.

46. The age at death of Julia Pistrix is partially obliterated.

49. The inscription is fragmentary, the nurse's name partially destroyed, the nursling's name completely missing.

50. The inscription is fragmentary, the relevant names partially missing.

51. The inscription is fragmentary and gives no names at all.

55. The inscription is fragmentary, the nursling's name missing (though apparently an infant boy). The child was commemorated by his nurse and *collactius*—probably the nurse's own son; on *collactanei*, see Chapter 6, Appendix.

56. The inscription gives the name of Verina as the *conlactia* of the nursling; cf. note 55 above.

57. The nurse appears here as the "nutricula et liberta bona" of the nursling.

58. Burn (1959) suggests that the inscription originally came from a Roman colony in the Greek East.

Inscription References

1.	*CIL*	1.45	21.	*CIL*	14.952a
2.	*CIL*	5.3710	22.	*CIl*	14.1510
3.	*CIL*	5.3950	23.	*CIL*	14.1539
4.	*CIL*	5.7277	24.	*CIL*	14.2183
5.	*CIL*	9.226	25.	*CIL*	14.2336
6.	*CIL*	9.347	26.	*CIL*	14.2716
7.	*CIL*	9.1154	27.	*CIL*	14.2752
8.	*CIL*	9.1278	28.	*AE*	1914.276
9.	*CIL*	9.3009	29.	*AE*	1960.249
10.	*CIL*	9.3033	30.	*AE*	1972.203
11.	*CIL*	9.3040	31.	*AE*	1980.326
12.	*CIL*	9.3730	32.	*CIL*	2.545
13.	*CIL*	9.4864	33.	*CIL*	2.3190
14.	*CIL*	9.5552	34.	*AE*	1966.197
15.	*CIL*	10.30	35.	*AE*	1960.190
16.	*CIL*	10.2185	36.	*AE*	1972.277
17.	*CIL*	10.2669	37.	*CIL*	3.2377
18.	*CIL*	10.3112	38.	*CIL*	3.2507
19.	*CIL*	10.6006	39.	*CIL*	3.12916
20.	*CIL*	14.486	40.	*CIL*	3.12997

41. *CIL* 3.8350
42. *CIL* 3.10038
43. *CIL* 3.8196
44. *CIL* 3.10948
45. *AE*   1972.434
46. *CIL* 8.2889
47. *CIL* 8.2917
48. *CIL* 8.27988
49. *CIL* 8.13191

50. *CIL* 10.7038
51. *CIL* 12.312
52. *CIL* 12.757
53. *CIL* 12.3899
54. *CIL* 12.4797
55. *CIL* 13.2104
56. *CIL* 13.11397
57. *AE*   1969–70.584
58. *AE*   1960.193

3

Child Care at Rome: The Role of Men

*A*t the approximate age of three, the child who was later to become the emperor Nero found himself a virtual orphan. His father, Cn. Domitius Ahenobarbus, was dead of dropsy, and his mother, the younger Agrippina, was in exile from Rome on a political charge.[1] Thus it was, so Suetonius records, that the child was reared in the household of his father's sister, Domitia Lepida, supervised by two pedagogues, a dancer and a barber: "et subinde matre etiam relegata paene inops atque egens apud amitam Lepidam nutritus est sub duobus paedagogis saltatore atque tonsore."[2] The time Nero spent in his aunt's household was probably short, for Agrippina was not long in exile, and, once restored to the mainstream of Roman life, she remarried and provided a stepfather for her son in the person of C. Sallustius Passienus Crispus. Later still, a second stepfather for the young Nero emerged, when Agrippina subsequently married the emperor Claudius as part of her strategy to lead her child to the emperorship.[3] Nevertheless, despite Agrippina's marriages, Nero continued in early life to be served by other attendants, notably two men named Beryllus and Anicetus. Josephus records that the former was a pedagogue of Nero before he gained the administrative position of *ab epistulis Graecis* (which he was holding around A.D. 55 or 56, apparently not without influence on the emperor), while Suetonius and Tacitus, respectively, refer to the latter as Nero's *paedagogus* or *educator* before he similarly rose to become commander of the imperial fleet at Misenum early in Nero's reign.[4] The elevation of servants to posts of considerable governmental importance is striking, though it was not an unusual type of progression.

The precise functions fulfilled for Nero by the dancer, the barber, Beryllus, and Anicetus are not recorded in the sources, though perhaps Beryllus at least was one of the teaching pedagogues of whom Suetonius knew.[5] But for appreciation of the structures of upper-class Roman family life and for knowledge of how aristocratic Roman children were reared, it is of interest to note the existence of Nero's male attendants, men who were undoubtedly all of servile origin.[6] While the need for child care during Nero's "orphanage" is obvious, Suetonius implies that such work was not the primary responsibility of Domitia Lepida, Nero's aunt, so much as of servants at her disposal. And indeed, even when both parents were alive and not separated from their children, it was common to have underlings on hand, drawn from the *familia,* for the day-to-day tending of upper-class children. Agrippina herself, for instance, had at least two nurses for the infant Nero—Egloge and Alexandria—but a male *cunarius* ("cradle rocker"), the freedman Ti. Claudius Eunus, is also attested.[7] The appearance of female nurses in the service of aristocratic families is not really surprising, but the use of men is rather less predictable at first blush. Consequently, my object here is to compile, describe, and analyze evidence that refers specifically to male child minders at Rome—men, that is, described in literary and epigraphical sources as *nutritores, educatores,* and *paedagogi.* What can be learned of such men, and what was their social role?

II

As the case of Nero's boyhood attendants illustrates, Roman literary sources can reveal the names of various male child minders. Yet when such men as Sosibius, the *educator* of Britannicus, or Sphaerus, the pedagogue of Augustus, are encountered, the evidence tends to be skewed toward people in the service of the imperial family or other upper-class families.[8] Therefore, a potentially more illuminating guide to the range of families within society that used child minders can be found in inscriptional evidence, particularly in tombstones, since such material is by nature less partial than the literary record. The lists of *nutritores, educatores,* and *paedagogi* that follow have been compiled from the inscriptions of Rome, and the individual child minders on record there have been arranged in various categories to reveal both the upper- and lower-class contexts in which they operated. Because the epitaphs frequently provide little information beyond identities and attachments, the inscriptional evidence is of limited value. But it is an important body of information which needs to be set out in considerable detail.[9]

(A) First, there are four men in the service of children of the imperial family:

1. [L. Aurelius L. Caesaris l. Nicomedes] . . . divi Veri
    imp. nutritor   1598
2. Hymnus paedagogus [J]uliae Germanici filiae   3998
3. Malchio Drusi paedagogus   3999
4. M. Livius Augustae lib. Prytanis Liviae Drusi paedag.   33787

The name of Nicomedes (no. 1) comes from a literary source and can safely be restored to the acephalous inscription giving the cursus of the *nutritor* of the emperor Verus. He was given equestrian rank by the emperor Antoninus Pius and went on to hold administrative and military appointments. Such advancement from probable slavery was spectacular and, as with Beryllus and Anicetus above, is attributable to special imperial favor. Eventually, Nicomedes was buried with his wife, Ceionia Laena, whose *nomen* was obviously derived from Verus's family and who thus may have been an imperial freedwoman.[10] The status of M. Livius Prytanis (no. 4) as a *libertus* is certain, and he was presumably manumitted sometime before A.D. 14, when Livia became Julia Augusta, but was commemorated after that date. Since their inscriptions come from the Monumentum Liviae, Hymnus (no. 2) and Malchio (no. 3) should be considered at least to be of servile origin. Their single names could indicate actual servile status (though this criterion is not always a reliable guide), especially for Malchio, who is distinguished on his inscription from a *liberta,* perhaps his wife.[11]

The children associated with the four men are as follows. First, Lucius Verus was the son of L. Aelius Caesar and (perhaps) Avidia, a shadowy figure, who in A.D. 138 was adopted at the age of seven, on his father's death, by Antoninus Pius. Second, Julia Livilla, the last child of Germanicus and the elder Agrippina, who was born at Lesbos in A.D. 18, lost her father in infancy (Germanicus died in 19) and her mother in 33, when she was fifteen. Third, Drusus may be Drusus Caesar (13 B.C.–A.D. 23) the son of Tiberius and Vipsania, or Drusus Caesar the son of Germanicus and the elder Agrippina; there seems to be no way of firmly distinguishing between the possibilities. But Livia Julia (died A.D. 31), finally, was the daughter of Nero Claudius Drusus and Antonia Minor (and granddaughter of Livia); her father died in 9 B.C., but her mother outlived her, surviving until A.D. 37.[12]

(B) Next, the following men worked, certainly or possibly, in the service of children of upper-class families:

5.	Pao lib. nutritor	1332 (= 31632)
6.	Fufidius Amycus (nutritor)	1365
7.	Cursius Satrius nutritor	1746
8.	Cn. Cornelius Atimetus Cn. Lentuli.	
	Gaetulic. l. (nutricius)	9834
9.	[He]rculanius (nutritor)	31686 (= 37055)
10.	L. Fabius Ammianus (nutritor)	37078
11.	C. Mussius Chrysonicus (nutritor lactaneus)	1424; 1623; 21334
12.	Gemellus Messalinae Tauri f. paedagogus	6327
13.	Jassulus Philerotis lib. Sisennae paedagogus	6328
14.	Philocalus paedagogus	6329
15.	T. Statilius Zabda paedag. Statiliae	6330
16.	Soterichus paedagog.	9752
17.	C. Sulpicius C. l. Venustus (paedagogus)	9754

Three of the *nutritores* in this category are fairly straightforward cases. Pao (no. 5) appears in his inscription without *nomen* (he may have been set free by his nursling or his nursling's father, unless he was an independent *nutritor* who was hired), but his status as a freedman is clear enough. Fufidius Amycus (no. 6) seems to be a family *libertus;* he shares his *nomen,* that of his nursling's mother, Fufidia Pollitta, with his companion and probable wife, Fufidia Chrestina, a convention that can be taken to signify former servile status in the same household for both partners.[13] Cn. Cornelius Atimetus (no. 8), another family *libertus,* was set free by the father of his charge, Cn. Lentulus Gaetulicus, consul in A.D. 26.[14] The remaining *nutritores,* however, present some problems. [He]rculanius (no. 9), for example, might be assumed to be servile on account of his single name, but he was commemorated as "nutri-[tori clien]nti (*sic*) opsequentissmo," and *cliens* might connote freed or even freeborn status. L. Fabius Ammianus (no. 10) made a dedication to his charge, together with his wife Claudia Dia and their children. Neither spouse carries the *nomen* of the nursling, so they can only be described as free; but if originally servile, one of the pair might have taken the *nomen* of the nursling's mother, who is unfortunately unknown. Equally uncertain is the status of Cursius Satrius (no. 7), who made a dedication to his charge, calling him "patronus omnia praestantissimus," a phrase that could suggest freed status for the *nutritor*. But in another inscription, Cursius Satrius used the same phrase of his nursling's father.[15] Even if it were assumed that the nursling became patron of a man manumitted by his father, a problem would still persist, for the *nutritor*'s *nomen* is different from that of father and son; again, however, freedom could have come from the nursling's mother, who is also unknown. Finally, the *nomina* of Mussius Chrysonicus (no. 11) and his companion Aurelia Soteris similarly differ from the *nomina* of all three of their attested nurslings; the couple may have been a free husband-and-wife team, working independently, but this is no more than speculation.

The first four pedagogues in this category (nos. 12–15) are known from inscriptions belonging to the Monumentum Statiliorum, so it can be assumed that they were all originally slaves. Indeed, freed status for Jassulus (no. 13) is certain (he must once have been a *vicarius*), and likely for T. Statilius Zabda (no. 15), while the single names of the other two pedagogues point to actual servile status.[16] In the three remaining cases, Soterichus (no. 16) may also have been a slave, but C. Sulpicius Venustus (no. 17), and the Sulpicia Ammia who apparently worked with him and was perhaps his wife was clearly freed.

The children in the charge of these *nutritores* and *paedagogi* were all of senatorial or equestrian status. The senator T. Aelius T.f. Pal. Naevius Severus c.v., who belongs perhaps to the early third century, was commemorated by Pao (no. 5); C. Caerellius Fufidius Annius Ravus C. fil. Ouf. Pollittianus, commemorated by Fufidius Amycus (no. 6; and Fufidia Chrestina), was probably the son of C. Caerellius Sabinus and Fufidia Pollitta, daughter of L. Fufidius Pollio, consul in A.D. 166; and the nursling of Cn. Cornelius Atimetus (no. 8) was Cossus Cornelius Lentulus Gaetulicus, son of Cn. Cornelius Lentulus Gaetulicus, consul in A.D. 26.[17] Of Antonius Arrianus, "c(larissimus) i(uvenis)," who made a dedication to [He]rculanius (no. 9), nothing further is known; but L. Virius Lupus Julianus, who received a dedication from L. Fabius Ammianus (no. 10), was the consul of A.D. 232; and Naeratius Scopius, the charge of Cursius Satrius (no. 7), was a son of Naeratius Cerialis, consul in A.D. 358.[18] The three nurslings of Mussius Chrysonicus (no. 11) and of his companion Aurelia Soteris were Gellia Agrippiana, "c(larissima) p(uella)," Licinia Q.f. Lampetia Basilioflora, and her probable brother, Q. Licinius Q.f. Florus Octavianus, eq(ues) Rom(anus).[19]

It has been suggested that the pedagogues Gemellus (no. 12) and T. Statilius Zabda (no. 15) both cared for the same child, Statilia Messalina, who in A.D. 66 became the wife of Nero, whereas Jassulus (no. 13) is likely to have cared for Sisenna Statilius Taurus, son of Sisenna Statilius Taurus, the consul of A.D. 16.[20] But no specific Statilian child is associated with Philocalus (no. 14). Soterichus (no. 16) was responsible for a relatively fulsome dedication to M. Junius M.f. Pal. Rufus, who may be the man who was prefect of Egypt from A.D. 94 to A.D. 98 or the prefect's possible son, or adoptive son, M. Junius Mettius Rufus, consul in A.D. 128.[21] But the connection cannot be certain, and doubt also surrounds the identities of the two apparent sisters, Sulpiciae Galbillae, who set up the dedication to C. Sulpicius Venustus (no. 17), and Sulpicia Amma; however, they may have been the daughters of C. Sulpicius Galba, consul in A.D. 22.[22]

(C) The third category of child minders represents a complete break with the first two and introduces men associated with children who were of servile origin:

18.	Ti. Claudius Epaphas nutricius	5405
19.	Aurelius Glycon nutritor	8425
20.	Thamyrus nutricius	8486
21.	Ti. Claudius Symmachus Aug. lib. (nutricius)	8660
22.	Cointus Aug. lib. (nutritor)	8925
23.	C. Tadienus L.f. Secundus nutricius	10170
24.	Florentius nutritor	13151
25.	Sutius (nutritor)	11005
26.	T. Aelius Artemidorus nutritor	16446
27.	Eunus nutricius	27365
28.	Synhetus nutritor	38952
29.	Aurelius Augg. lib. Secundus (educator)	13221
30.	Artemisius paedagogus et lib.	8613
31.	Carus (regis paedagogus)	8980
32.	Q. Lollius Philargurus paedagogus	8989

A number of these men were imperial *liberti*. There is no doubt about Ti. Claudius Symmachus (no. 21), Cointus (no. 22), Aurelius Secundus (no. 29), or Artemisius (no. 30), while Ti. Claudius Epaphas (no. 18) and

Aurelius Glycon (no. 19) are associated with imperial slave nurslings and should themselves be considered imperial freedmen. Moreover, Thamyrus (no. 20) was probably an imperial slave, to judge from his single name and the post attested for him of *dispensator,* and Florentius (no. 24) and C. Tadienus L.f. Secundus (no. 23) also have connections with the *familia Caesaris.* Florentius, who appears in his inscription with only a single name, in contrast to the other individuals mentioned, may well be a slave, but C. Tadienus Secundus was freeborn—the only certain freeborn child attendant in the whole collection. The term "regis paedagogus" should probably mean that Carus (no. 31) was an imperial slave.[23] Of the others, Sutius (no. 25) and Synhetus (no. 28) both seem to be slaves, to judge from their single names, but Eunus (no. 27) was the *collibertus* of Ti. Claudius Panoptes, who may have been an imperial *libertus,* though his inscription does not say so. T. Aelius Artemidorus (no. 26) was free, as was the pedagogue Q. Lollius Philargurus (no. 32); freed status may be suspected but cannot be proved.[24]

It is important to emphasize that no longer in evidence here is the tending of upper-class children but that of children from the opposite end of the social scale, and, as would be expected from what has been seen so far, some of the children associated with the child minders in this category belonged to the *familia Caesaris.* Ti. Claudius Epaphas (no. 18) was commemorated by two slaves who belonged to Domitian, Euhodus and Ev(a)nder, and Q. Lollius Philargurus (no. 32) was commemorated by a certain Evenus, "Ti. Caesaris Augusti et Juliae Augustae servos" (it is not clear why the pedagogue of a slave belonging to Tiberius and Livia should bear a nonimperial *nomen,* unless he was hired by them). Epictetus, the nursling of Ti. Claudius Symmachus (no. 21), was perhaps an imperial slave, too. There are seven cases of nurslings who became imperial *liberti.* A dedication to the senior freedman official M. Aurelius Aug. lib. Isidorus, "melloproximus a rationibus," was made by three people, including his *nutritor* Aurelius Glycon (no. 19). The nursling of Cointus (no. 22) was Alexander Aug. lib.; that of Florentius (no. 24) was M. Aurelius Aug. lib. Marcianus, who died in his fifth year; that of C. Tadienus Secundus (no. 23) was Trophimus Aug. l., a gladiator; and that of Aurelius Secundus (no. 29) was Sabinus Augg. lib. The pedagogue Artemisius (no. 30) set up a dedication to the "puer rarissimus," Faustus Aug. lib., "adiutor ab epistulis," who died at the age of nineteen, by which time he had been set free and had also provided for the manumission of Artemisius. Finally, Carus (no. 31) set up a dedication to his *alumnus,* C. Julius Epaphra divi Augusti l., who died at the age of sixty.[25]

Some of these cases are of special interest, however, because the relevant inscriptions also reveal the names of the children's parents. For example, M. Aurelius Marcianus was survived not only by his *nutritor* Florentius (no. 24) but also by both parents, M. Aur. Aug. lib. Eutyches and Valeria Eutychia, who might be expected to have been able to take care of their own child.[26] The parents of Hymenaeus Thamyrianus, an imperial slave and the charge of Thamyrus (no. 20), are also on record.[27] Moreover, the same is true of children who were servile but not associated with the *familia Caesaris.* The *collibertus* of the *nutricius* Eunus (no. 27) was Ti. Claudius Panoptes, who, with his wife, Charmosyne, had two daughters, Thetis and Charis, who died at the respective ages of nine and fifteen. Supervision by a former slave of children born to parents of servile origin in the same *familia* is indicated, and since the parents survived their children, and indeed Eunus, they, too, must theoretically have been available to care for them. Likewise in the case of the apparent slave child Hylocharis Aemilianus: he was commemorated by his parents, Secundus and Successa, and by the *nutritores* Sutius (no. 25) and Sutia, all of whom seem to be slaves (the parents commented in their inscription that their son's charm had provided consolation in their toil). Clearly there had been no loss of contact between parents and child, despite the appearance in the boy's life of *nutritores.* But parents are not always on record. The nursling of T. Aelius Artemidorus (no. 26) was Cornelia Primitiva. She must have been a *liberta* because she described the Cornelia Romana to whom, together with Artemidorus, she dedicated as her *patrona* (but not her mother). As the owner of the slave girl Primitiva, Cornelia Romana seems to have provided an attendant for the child, as necessary. Finally, Synhetus (no. 28), described in his inscription as the ''nutritor Pardi liberti et alumni sui,'' received a dedication from two men, Julius Florentius and Julius Flosculus. Pardus may have been a foundling set free by the two Julii, who used another of their slaves to raise the child.

(D) Despite many uncertainties, the social status of the children associated with child minders, whether upper-class or lower-class, has been fairly easy to establish so far. There remains, however, a greater number of cases where problems of status attribution are more complicated. In order to avoid a mass of details which lead to few uncontroversial results, most of these cases are best consigned to an appendix for the sake of reference (see Appendix 3.1); but a select number of examples is worth direct consideration, to show the difficulties generally characteristic of the remaining evidence.

33. M. Aberrinus Philadespotus (nutricius)	10450
34. Licinius Meropymus liber. (nutritor)	21279
35. Tettienus Perilemptus lib. (nutricius)	27298
36. M. Ul(p)ius Primigenius (nutricius)	29191
37. C. Julius Hymetus (paedagogus)	2210
38. Diadumenus l. (paedagogus)	9747
39. L. Laevius Nicepo[r] Laeviaes l. (paedagogus)	9749

First, the freed status of L. Laevius Nicepo[r] (no. 39) is clear enough, but whose freedman and pedagogue was he? He may have been connected with an upper-class family. The suffect consul of A.D. 102, L. Antonius Albus, apparent grandson of the M. Antonius Albus known to have been priest of Artemis at Ephesus, was married to a certain Laevia Paula, and so the pedagogue could be associated with this woman's family. But nothing more than the possibility can be stated.[28] Secondly, inclusion of filiation in Roman nomenclature will normally signify freeborn status, and so freeborn children appear in connection with some of the men listed here. But they are not persons of identifiable upper-class families. The servile origin of the pedagogue Diadumenus (no. 38) is certain, but of the Julia L.f. Lucilla with whom he is associated nothing is known. Nor is anything known of the Claudia Ti. f. Quinta who set up a rather elaborate inscription to the pedagogue C. Julius Hymetus (no. 37). The latter had a brother, C. Julius Epitynchanus, and was Claudia Quinta's "tutor a pupillatu" as well as her pedagogue. Freed status for Hymetus seems likely (but is not provable), though Claudia Quinta herself remains a mystery.[29]

By contrast, thirdly, servile origins seem likely for children in some cases, though certainty is again elusive. Thus, for example, the free M. Ulpius Felicissimus received a dedication when he died at the age of four from four people: M. Ul(p)ius Primigenius (no. 36) and Capriola, *nutricii,* and M. Ulpius Aug. lib. Merop(s) and Flavia Phoebas, who look very much like the boy's parents but are not called such specifically. Felicissimus could have been the freeborn son of Merops, born after the latter's manumission, or his freed son, or a freed slave or *ingenuus* bearing no natural relationship to Merops and Phoebas.[30] Similarly, the *libertus et nutricius* Tettienus Perilemptus (no. 35) was commemorated by a woman named Tettiena Livilla, who can be connected with the family that produced consuls in A.D. 80 and about 99–100, and so regarded as either a family freedwoman or of freed descent.[31] M. Aberrinus Philadespotus (no. 33) received a memorial from his patrons M. Aberrinus Fortunatus and Aemilia Peiagia, for whose daughter he was *nutricius.* He must have been a *libertus,* but the precise status of the patrons, and hence of their daughter, is unknown; they could have been freed or the freeborn descendants of former slaves. Again, Licinius Meropymus (no. 34) was a freedman who acted as *nutritor* to the sons and *alumni* of Licinia Veneria. Presumably Veneria manumitted Meropymus, but her exact status cannot be determined; she, too, could have been a freedwoman or a freeborn descendant of former slaves, and so the position of her sons is incalculable. Thus, in cases where the children associated with child minders cannot safely be identified as the children of upper-class families, there may well be more evidence concealed in the inscriptions for the supervision of slave children. Alternatively, if children are considered or prove to be freeborn, it becomes necessary to postulate use of child minders for the children of free but modest family background, a kind of intermediate social group set off from both upper-class families and those still in or close to slavery.

This last possibility also arises from another group of inscriptions which, although inevitably full of awkward details, seems generally consistent in its main features with the observations made so far. Twenty-one men are attested in the role of *tata,* and they are listed in the final section of Appendix 3.1. They, too, must be regarded as child minders, in spite of the fact that the term *tata* can be used to signify a child's real father or a foster father, because their inscriptions contain the names of the true fathers, and sometimes mothers, of the children with whom they are associated. Essentially the word *tata* is not a functional term, like *nutritor, educator,* and *paedagogus,* but an informal term which connotes no more than an affective bond between a man and a child; obviously, therefore, the full body of inscriptions that disclose the identities of *tatae* cannot be drawn on for present purposes, since it is often impossible to decide whether an individual *tata* is a father, foster father, or something else. But in the twenty-one examples cited, it is certain that contact between the children and their real fathers was not lost, at least in most cases, so it is unlikely that the children on record were *expositi* raised by independent fosterers. Rather, it is preferable to think in terms of a familiar relationship between the *tata* and the child's parents.[32]

Positive status is available for only two of the *tatae*: C. Apisius C. l. Felix (no. 83) must have been a *libertus* or *collibertus* of his nursling's father, while Anthus (no. 95) was a slave who probably belonged to the owners of his nursling's father. As elsewhere, servile status is possible for *tatae* who have only one name. A number of men who have *nomina* different from those of the parents of their charges should be considered the parents' friends or neighbors.[33] None of the children in this category is of demonstrable upper-class background, though two are *ingenui*, the respective nurslings of C. Apisius Felix (no. 83) and Phoebus (no. 86), and instead most seem to be of servile status. To some degree, therefore, this material seems to indicate external of supervision of children at an intermediate social level.

III

If the inscriptional evidence is often scrappy and imprecise, certain facts emerge nonetheless. First, the evidence shows without doubt that child minding by men of servile background was a far from uncommon phenomenon at Rome. Of the attested individual *nutritores, educatores,* and *paedagogi,* only one can be seen not to be of possible or certain servile or freed status, although the possibility must remain open that a free, and perhaps freeborn, man such as the pedagogue Q. Lollius Philargurus (no. 32) was hired to work and did not remain in the *familia* to which he had belonged if once a slave. It must be allowed that within the juridical categories of slave and free there is likely to have been a great deal of variation in social status among the child minders, who should not be viewed as one homogeneous group. Slaves and freedmen who belonged to the *familia Caesaris,* for example, will have thought of themselves as socially superior to, say, men such as Crescentis (no. 46) or Hilarius (no. 70), but this does not affect the basic pattern as a whole.[34] Second, the inscriptions provide strong evidence of the range within society across which male child minders were used, not only, that is to say, for children of the imperial family and other upper-class families but for children, and especially slave children, of lower-class status, too. Moreover, child minders were put in charge of both boys and girls. The literary evidence tends mainly to refer to boys in the care of men, though occasional items refer to girls as well. Cicero has a record of Pilia's pedagogue, for example, and Pliny speaks of the pedagogues of Minicia Marcella.[35] The inscriptions, however, reveal a firm ratio of about one girl to every two boys attended by a child minder.[36] It should not follow that parents at all social levels constantly used child minders for all of their children, but it is clear that use of child minders was not a practice confined to the upper levels of society, as the literary evidence might seem at first to suggest, and this is a point that requires emphasis. Third, it appears from various commemorative texts that the tie formed between child minder and child lasted at times well beyond the child's attainment of maturity. Artemisius (no. 30), for instance, commemorated the "puer rarissimus" Faustus—the term of endearment is significant—when Faustus died in his twentieth year, long after he was beyond the practical need of an attendant and when he was himself already at work. The case of Nicephorus (no. 74) is similar. Further, many of the male child minders on record are definite *liberti,* but in view of the uncertainties of status attribution there may be many more, men such as L. Ciartius Hyperes (no. 68) and C. Cestilius Pasiphilus (no. 73).[37] What looks like a high rate of manumission for slave child minders is again suggestive of close personal connections between the men and their charges, or between the men and their charges' parents, and it is well known that imperial legislation on manumission provided for early release from slavery for slave *educatores* and *paedagogi.*[38] Perhaps, therefore, *nutritores* similarly benefited. However, close relations between child minder and child or child's parent cannot be assumed to have been generic; in situations where no tie was formed or endured, commemoration with a tombstone will not have occurred.

IV

The next step must be to try to put these facts into some sort of historical and social context so that the unarguably broad dimensions of male child-minding practices at Rome can be understood. To begin, the functions and conventional images of child minders can be surveyed, chiefly from the literary evidence, and then some aspects of the experience of childhood itself in Roman society can be outlined, as means of explaining the record already described.

For the *nutritor* and *educator* the literary evidence is less satisfactory than for the *paedagogus*. Indeed, the very meaning of the terms *nutritor* and *educator* is imprecise, and, as seen above, *nutritor* and *educator*, and *educator* and *paedagogus*, could be used of the same individual in the same job. From Varro's reference to Faustulus as the *nutricius* of Romulus and Remus, and Suetonius's reference to the *nutritor* of the grammarian M. Antonius Gnipho, who, Suetonius says, was exposed at birth by his parents, it is clear that these words can mean something like foster father, a man who reared a child in the absence of the child's natural parents.[39] However, a passage in the Augustan life of Severus Alexander names a certain Philippus as the boy's *nutritor* in childhood; and although Philippus is probably a fiction, the word *nutritor* here cannot mean the rearer of an orphan, or virtual orphan, since Julia Mamaea, Alexander's mother, was still alive when her son became emperor at the age of twelve or so in A.D. 222, and Gessius Marcianus, his father, survived until about the year A.D. 218.[40] Moreover, Philippus is spoken of in conjunction with a *nutrix,* Olympias, doubtless a fictitious person, too, but nurses are not generically associated with orphaned children. The word *nutritor* should thus be understood to mean primarily the male equivalent of the *nutrix,* not a foster father raising a child who had been separated from parents. The inscriptional evidence has already revealed some male child minders in the service of children whose parents outlived them; so *nutritor* must be considered for the most part to mean a male nurse, and not to imply that parents were unavailable to rear their own children.[41]

The term *educator* can also mean either a man who independently reared an exposed child for whom he was a true foster father or a man who was a family dependent responsible for early child rearing, someone who can be contrasted with parents and teachers.[42] As noted above, Tacitus specifically refers to Sosibius and Anicetus as the *educatores* of Britannicus and Nero. The parents of the children associated with the epigraphical *educatores* are all unknown, but it is not likely that the *educatores* themselves were true foster fathers, and in general the word *educator* is best understood as a synonym for *nutritor,* as just defined.

The literary sources are not terribly helpful in indicating when a child was entrusted to a *nutritor* or *educator*. Seneca is reported to have called himself Nero's *educator,* but perhaps with some exaggeration, since Nero was eleven years old when Seneca became his tutor; yet Britannicus was still surrounded by his *educatores* at the age of fourteen.[43] By contrast, it can be computed that Nicomedes became the *nutritor/ educator* of Verus before the boy was eight.[44] However, in a small way the inscriptional evidence makes up the literary deficiency, because memorials set up to deceased children occasionally include the children's ages at death. Eight ages are in fact available, as Table 3.1 indicates. Moreover, if the evidence of the *tatae* inscriptions is included, additional information on children's ages at death becomes available. (See Table 3.2.) The higher ages at death will not signify that the male attendant was still at work when the "child" died, only that an affective bond had been maintained after the nursling's childhood years. But the evidence as a whole establishes male involvement in child supervision for children's earliest years, and so lends credibility to Mussius Chrysonicus's description of himself as *nutritor lactaneus,* an attendant who fed milk to his charges.

The *nutrix,* besides fulfilling her obvious main function, is represented in literature as a comforter figure, telling stories to her nursling, rocking and singing the child to sleep, and so on. Yet the male nurse has no comparable conventional portrayal, a situation that could be taken to mean that the male nurse was less prominent a figure in Roman society, and it is certainly the case that more *nutrices* appear in the inscriptions of Rome. But the work must have been similar—Britannicus's *educatores* were still, it seems, in charge of feeding him as a teenager—and it is notable that several of the men are associated with women nurses (Mussius Chrysonicus again providing an example), so couples may not infrequently have worked together as teams.[45] When Soranus made his

Table 3.1. Age at Death of Nurslings (*Nutritor/Educator* Inscriptions)

| Child's Name | Age at Death | | | Reference |
	Y.	M.	D.	
M. Aurelius Aug. lib. Marcianus	4	8	3	13151
M. Licinius Hermes	2	—	38	15104
Geminia Agathe	5	7	22	19007
M. Terentius Paternus	18	—	—	27198
Thetis	9	—	—	27365
Charis	15	—	—	27365
M. Ulpius Felicissimus	4	—	5	29191
Manlia Niceph[oris]	5	—	—	38598

Ages 0–4 years: 1 case   Ages 5–9 years: 5 cases   Ages 10–14 years: 0 cases   Ages 15–19 years: 2 cases   TOTAL: 8 cases

Table 3.2. Age at Death of Nurslings (*Tata* Inscriptions)

Child's Name	Age at Death			Reference
	Y.	M.	D.	
C. Vibius Threptus	14	—	28	2334
Arminia Gorgilla	15	5	6	5642
Stertinia Maxima	3	10	9	6703
Aelius Primus	23	—	—	10873
Aelius Ingenuus	24	—	—	10873
Alexander	—	5	—	11395
Crescentilla	11	6	2	16578
L. Flavius L.f. Anien. Saturninus	5	6	—	18196
Hortensia Justa	8	—	18	19552
Justa	16	—	4	20930
C. Numisius Felicissimus	4	—	54	23113
C. Q(uintius) Hermias	4	4	8	25301
Terentia Spe(s)	3	—	—	27259
Victor	2	3	—	28906
T. Aconius Karus	21	3	—	34206
Ti. Julius [. . .]	3	—	30	35530
Silvia	3	2	9	36353

Ages 0–4 years: 6 cases   Ages 5–9 years: 4 cases   Ages 10–14 years: 1 case   Ages 15–19 years: 3 cases   Ages 20–24 years: 3 cases   TOTAL: 17 cases

recommendations on how to select a wet nurse, he assumed a plurality of women to be available in upper-class households.[46] But perhaps, in actuality, men sometimes assisted the wet nurses with various tasks; the *nutrix* and *nutritor* could be paired for rhetorical effect, at least, as if it were commonly understood that they often worked together.[47]

For pedagogues, the literary evidence is much clearer. Two functions are evident. First, in a narrow sense, the pedagogue, like the *educator,* was or could be an early teacher for a child, and in some discussions it is this educational function that receives most attention.[48] But, second and more important, the pedagogue was also a child minder, taking over the tasks of supervising the child's daily regimen which previously had been handled by nurses, whether male, female, or both. The appearance of the pedagogue in Roman society resulted from Rome's contacts with the Greek world in the age of overseas expansion in the third and second centuries B.C., and it is in Plautus's play *Bacchides* that the duties of the pedagogue are first articulated in a Roman context. Admittedly, there is some danger in relying on Plautus for historical evidence, given the

Greek literary tradition on which his plays depend. But in view of the specifically Roman elements detectable in the plays, there seems little reason to doubt that the portrayal of Lydus in *Bacchides* was consistent with popular conceptions of the pedagogue at Rome at the turn of the second century B.C. Lydus, called both *paedagogus* and *magister* in the play, is the chaperon of the *adulescens* Pistoclerus, and it is at once of note that he is in attendance on a grown-up child. This is not merely a dramatic convention, for later evidence shows that the pedagogue at times retained supervision of the child well beyond boyhood. Lydus appears to be a slave, and, disturbed by what he regards as contemporary moral laxity, he finds refuge in his vision of a more salubrious past.[49] In the old days, he says, it used to be common for a pedagogue to remain with his charge until the latter was twenty years of age or until he had begun to hold public office, and he obviously believes Pistoclerus still needs his presence, even though today the pedagogue receives far less respect and deference than in the better times past. His function has been to instill *disciplina* in Pistoclerus, discipline meaning both academic and moral instruction; and now that Pistoclerus is no longer a child, Lydus's job is to fortify the moral lessons of earlier days by continuing to serve as Pistoclerus's moral tutor and chaperon, counteracting current permissiveness as found even in Pistoclerus's father. Because of the nature of the play, it may be that more attention is given to the moralistic than academic aspect of Lydus's occupation; nevertheless, the pedagogue here emerges as something rather more than a simple servant entrusted with a child's earliest academic training. The shaping of a child's character from boyhood to manhood has been and still remains the dominant feature of Lydus's relationship with Pistoclerus.

In later times, both Cicero and Quintilian shared the opinion that it mattered to what sort of pedagogue children listened for the sake of their speech, and Quintilian was prepared to allow that well-educated pedagogues could function as teachers.[50] But when boys went to school, their pedagogues were expected, more commonly, not to teach but to chaperon them, to exercise *custodia* over their charges; and time and time again, it is this protective aspect that recurs in literary anecdotes about and allusions to the men. Thus, for example, in Petronius's *Satyricon,* Eumolpus at one point promises to become "paedagogus et custos" to Giton.[51]

Protectiveness could include the teaching of etiquette and decorum. Plutarch reports that what the pedagogue taught children was "to walk in the public streets with lowered head; to touch salt-fish with but one finger, but fresh fish, bread and meat with two; to sit in such and such a posture; in such and such a way to wear their cloaks''; and Seneca gave the following as examples of pedagogues' precepts: "Walk thus and so; eat thus and so. This is the proper conduct for a man and that for a woman; this for a married man and that for a bachelor.''[52] In literature, such directives could lend themselves to parody. When Lucius the ass is handed over to a freedman who teaches him how to recline at the table, Apuleius has Lucius say: "I learned to nod my head as a sign of approval, and to toss it back as a sign of rejection, also to turn toward the wine-waiter when I was thirsty and show that I needed a drink, by winking first one eye and then the other.''[53] Clearly enough, the freedman functioned as Lucius's pedagogue.

But beyond the practical level came moral protectiveness, for the pedagogue was to "train the child's character to take a first step, as it were, on the path of virtue.''[54] Thus, he physically guarded the boy against homosexual harassment and was in constant attendance upon him in public and private.[55] He had himself, therefore, to be of sound character, to display *probitas* and be "of quiet disposition.''[56] Preferably he was to be a man of some education, or at least aware of his short-comings, for the influence he could exert on his charge was profound, a fact of which Seneca, among others, was very much aware and one that points up strongly the question of why Roman upper-class parents were so consistently prepared to entrust their children's formative years to servants of considerably lower social status. "Every young thing," Seneca wrote, "attaches itself to what is nearest and grows to be like it: the character of their nurses and pedagogues is presently reproduced in that of the young men.''[57]

The ideal pedagogue, therefore, was a *bonus vir*.[58] But the ideal was not perhaps always realized. The servant, it was thought, might have a harmful effect on the character of his charge: "Nowadays, the common practice of many persons is ridiculous . . . ; any slave whom they find to be a wine-bibber and a glutton, and useless for any kind of business, to him they bring their sons and put them in his charge.''[59] Remiss performance ("neglegentia") was always likely.[60] Or the pedagogue might simply abuse a boy physically. It must be understood, of course, that the job of supervising children cannot always have been easy, and correction was doubtless necessary at times. Plutarch's praise of Sar-pedon, the pedagogue of the younger Cato, for avoiding corporal punishment suggests that such chastisement was indeed common, and Martial refers to the "sceptra paedagogorum" with which the beating was presumably done.[61] The way to excess was obviously open, and the emperor Claudius, for one, recalled his treatment by his pedagogue with bitterness.[62] It is not surprising, as a result, that the pedagogue could be stereotypically portrayed as stern in appearance, or as a target of children's resentment and displeasure.[63] He was, after all, the sort of person, if an emotional child were needed in court as a witness, who would pinch a boy to make him cry.[64]

Yet, despite the complaints of moralists, the literary evidence overall tends to leave a fond image of the pedagogue, which must be based, one imagines, on ties of intimacy between pedagogue and child that formed early in the child's life and were maintained over time. The manumission and public funeral of Augustus's pedagogue Sphaerus, for example, has to be understood on this basis.[65] More generally, the pedagogue can be set alongside the nurse and mother as a person devoted to the child's best interests, as one prepared to defend the child against physical attack, as a servant faithful until his mother's death; he might overindulge the child, but his name could never be forgotten.[66] Still, there could be no thought that the affective ties of childhood should lead to the formation in adulthood of a close and equal bond with the pedagogue: "As a rule decisions about friendships should be formed after strength and stability have been reached in mind and age; nor should men who in boyhood were devoted to hunting and games of ball, keep as their intimates those whom they loved at that period simply because they were fond of the same pursuits. For on that principle nurses and pedagogues will, by right of priority of acquaintance, claim the largest share of our goodwill. I admit that they are not to be neglected, but they are to be regarded in an entirely different way; under no other conditions can friendship remain secure."[67] Cicero's remarks are noteworthy on several counts, for besides illustrating again the potential for intimacy between child and pedagogue and for the maintenance over time of the close association, they also point up the social distance between child and pedagogue and imply dominance of the pedagogue over the parents in the child's early life. Once more, therefore, the problem is raised of why upper-class Roman parents entrusted the molding of their children's characters to men whose status made them, in Cicero's view at least, unworthy of equal association once the children reached maturity.

The literary evidence, in sum, shows beyond doubt that the pedagogue was a fixed element in the life of the upper-class child in Rome of the classical period. From the time when a *nutrix* or *nutritor* was no longer needed, or when extra help was required, the pedagogue was probably the child's most constant companion and focal point of reference through the early years, even as the circle of social contacts expanded to include, besides parents and relatives, teachers and fellow pupils. The pedagogue's job was to instill in the child the social graces and to provide rudimentary academic knowledge, but in addition, and more importantly, to guide the child through the early years in the capacity of moral custodian. As a child rearer, the pedagogue, always of servile status or background, it seems, was given responsibilities by the child's parents that they were either unable or unwilling to assume themselves, even though he might be a figure against whom a strong social prejudice was felt. In view of the time he spent with the child and the tasks he performed, the pedagogue, like the *nutritor* and *educator,* has therefore to be regarded as a surrogate parent, and few upper-class children can have remained immune from the formative influence he exercised upon them. The socialization of the Roman child was heavily dependent on the person of the pedagogue, as indeed on that of the *nutritor* and *educator.* For, although few details are visible in the literary record on the *nutritor* and *educator,* much of the material on pedagogues that has been surveyed must be understood to apply to them as well, given the sources' lack of precision on the terminology for male child minders. Throughout the child's life, from infancy to adulthood, one or a succession of child-minding figures provided a presence whose impact on the child may well have been as great as the influence of parents, and explanation of that presence is clearly needed. What were the factors, then, that prompted the reliance in Roman society on the child-minding figure?

V

Most easily, the use of child minders by upper-class parents can be regarded as a function of slave owning in a society marked by extremes of wealth, power, and status. Wealthy Romans customarily maintained large numbers of slaves and freedmen in their households. Hence the use of child minders from within the slave *familia* will to some degree have been a simple matter of aristocratic convenience. Moreover, the highly specialized jobs of Roman slaves and freedmen make it far from startling that care of children should have been delegated to particular individuals by parents, and perhaps especially by mothers, who did not consider the mundane aspects of child tending consistent with or appropriate to their social dignity.[68] But does the widespread use of male child minders imply among the Roman elite a general indifference to children, an attitude perhaps prompted by a relatively high rate of infant mortality and a consequent reluctance to overinvest emotionally in young children whose survival to adulthood was far from predictable? Frequent losses of young children may well have led to a degree of emotional detachment on the part of the parents, but sufficient examples of genuine parental grief expressed on the occasion of premature child death are available to offset any proposition of wholesale parental indifference. Further, the hopes invested in Roman children of extending and emulating the traditional accomplishments of their families in public life were considerable, and far more was involved than personal loss when children died. In consequence, generic indifference among the Roman upper classes is not to be expected.[69]

As the original example of Nero suggests, there may at times have been a very practical reason for parents' use of child minders, namely the unavailability of parents to do the job themselves. Maternal death in childbirth must often have compelled use of a wet nurse if an infant's survival were to be guaranteed, and subsequent progression from a *nutrix* to a *nutritor* to a *paedagogus* is thus explicable in terms of sheer necessity. However, the possibility of response to maternal death is only one of a sequence of conditions that can be summoned to suggest that stability in the life of the growing Roman child was not a natural prospect. Familiar details from the history of the Julio-Claudians serve to illustrate the point.

The pursuit of a public career at Rome frequently took a man away from the city for military or administrative service abroad. The result was that contact between father and children might be not only temporarily broken but sometimes completely ruptured. Augustus was only four years old when his father, C. Octavius, died at Nola, returning from the governship of Macedonia. Caligula was seven when his father, Germanicus, died in Syria, though in this case the child had accompanied the father on his eastern mission. Claudius can scarcely have known his father, Drusus, at all, for he was only one year old when Drusus died on campaign against the Germans. It happens, in fact, that all the Julio-

Claudian emperors lost their fathers while they themselves were children.[70]

In such circumstances the way was open for the child to form a new relationship with a stepparent once the surviving parent remarried. Thus, the young Augustus spent part of his childhood in the household of L. Marcius Philippus, whom Atia, Augustus's mother, married after the death of C. Octavius.[71] As the case of Nero illustrates once more, a new father figure might make only a relatively brief appearance in a child's life, but in view of the high incidence of divorce and remarriage among the Roman aristocracy in the central period of Roman history, the intrusion of a stepparent into a young child's life was a very common event. Tiberius was only nine when his father died, but he had known a stepfather since the age of three in the person of Augustus, whom his mother, Livia Drusilla, married after her divorce from Ti. Claudius Nero. Similarly, Julia, the daughter of Augustus by his second wife, Scribonia, was born on the very day of her parents' divorce and would have known Livia as her stepmother from earliest memory.[72]

Julio-Claudian history, indeed, is replete with examples of events which may be imagined to have made an impact on the emotional development of the family's children. Augustus's grandsons, C. and L. Caesar were, respectively, aged eight and five when their father, M. Agrippa, died, though five years earlier both had been adopted by, and thus had found a new father in, Augustus himself.[73] Since Julia, their mother, remarried the year after Agrippa's death, her sons will also have been presented with a *de facto* stepfather in the person of Tiberius, though her third son, Agrippa Postumus, never actually knew his true father.[74] When Julia was sent into exile, Postumus, aged about ten, came to regard Livia as his stepmother.[75] Again, Germanicus was no more than six or so when his father, Drusus, died, while at the moment of his own death the ages of his surviving children ranged from three to fourteen.[76] Later, the children of Claudius—Octavia and Britannicus—were still in their teens when their father died, while the appearance of a stepmother in their lives six years beforehand proved fateful for both of them.[77]

It is not surprising to learn, therefore, that several of the Julio-Claudian children passed from household to household as fortune affected their parents. Augustus lived for a time in the house of his grandmother Julia when a boy, Caligula in that of Livia and that of his grandmother Antonia, and Nero in that of his aunt Domitia Lepida. Caligula's sisters

Drusilla and Livilla were also for a time under the care of Livia and Antonia.[78] What becomes clear, consequently, is that the life of the upper-class Roman child was subject to a series of dislocating circumstances that rendered minimal the anticipation of a stable domestic environment during the actual years of childhood. The dangers from politics were certainly unpredictable, and the infant Tiberius was perhaps lucky to survive his parents', and his own, flight through Italy, Sicily, and Greece in the troubled years 39 to 38 B.C.[79] But in a society where parents did not necessarily expect to remain married to the same partners indefinitely, it was more predictable that parents might not at all constitute their offspring's essential domestic framework of reference.

Of course, it could be objected that the Julio-Claudians were an exceptional family and that the vicissitudes confronted by their children were caused only by the family's position of political primacy. But the objection can be easily countered. Consider, for example, the case of M. Junius Brutus, the assassin of Caesar. The son of M. Junius Brutus and Servilia (though even in antiquity the paternity of Brutus was questioned in view of Servilia's notorious association with Caesar), he was born in 85 B.C. and lost his father in 77 B.C. After her first husband's death, Servilia provided Brutus with a stepfather when she married D. Junius Silanus, by whom she had three daughters, all named Junia. But Brutus himself was adopted by his mother's brother, Servilius Caepio. It is difficult to understand how the child responded to the loss of his father, his adoption, his mother's remarriage and creation of a new family, or to the family of his mother's half-brother and half-sister, M. Porcius Cato and Porcia, though he was eventually to marry the daughter, another Porcia, of his mother's half-brother.[80] The family situation was complex but by no means unrepresentative of late Republican familial history. And under the Principate the tortuous marital life of senatorial families continued unabated, as Figure 3.1 illustrates for one particular individual, Vistilia, the mother of Nero's general, Cn. Domitius Corbulo. The information the figure contains is drawn from a reconstruction of Vistilia's personal history and is admittedly hypothetical in part. But it indicates a plausible set of circumstances for Vistilia and thereby helps to emphasize the lack of stability in the upper-class Roman family. Vistilia's seven pregnancies, by six husbands, extended over a period of twenty years, but only two of her children were full siblings. Presumably she created six new households over twenty years, but did she take her children with her on each successive occasion (on the assumption that all

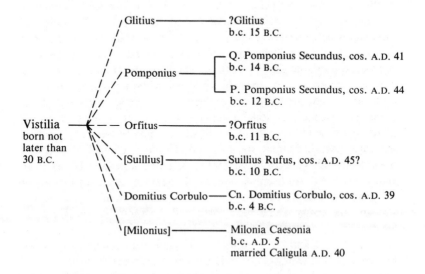

Figure 3.1. Vistilia's Husbands and Children
Based on Syme (1979), 805–14.

survived, though this is not certain for Glitius[?] and Orfitus[?])? What was the relationship between her children and their successive step-fathers? And what were the relationships among the children themselves, if indeed there was opportunity for such?

It is within this context of childhood spent in uncertain and frequently shifting parental marital circumstances that the role of child minders may perhaps best be appreciated. In contrast to the postulate of widespread familial dislocation in Roman children's lives derived from the evidence just described, the evidence on servile child minders, as noted already, shows that a relationship between the child and the attendant was often close and enduring over time. The information on manumission from the inscriptions, the very acts of commemoration which the inscriptions represent, and the occasional anecdotes surrounding men like Sphaerus all reveal constant maintenance of affective bonds between children and servants. Like the nurse, the male child minder could be materially rewarded for his services long after his child-rearing role had come to an end. A legal text, for example, speaks of a *nutritor* receiving a legacy of "maritime estates with the slaves who were there and all the *instrumentum* and the fruits which were there and the rents outstanding from tenants."[81] Certainly the limitations of the evidence have to be guarded against. But it should be possible all the same to imagine that the child minder provided an emotional and physical security in the life of the child which was not always present in the parent-child relationship. Moreover, that function was made possible by the existence of slavery, for the men who acted as child attendants can have had little choice about the jobs they performed, given that they were compulsorily appointed to tasks assigned to them by their masters. Servants were not likely to find themselves separated from their charges by the requirements of public careers or new marriages, and the potential for strong personal relationships which might follow in children's lives is reflected not least in Cicero's remarks, quoted earlier, on childhood friendships with them.

This is not to say that relations between upper-class Roman children and their parents could never be close and affectionate; plainly, such a gross generalization would be absurd. But the obtrusive presence of the child minders does indicate that views about the nature of the Roman family have to be flexible enough to allow for the incorporation within the family structure of more individuals than parents and children alone. Furthermore, the presence of child minders in the Roman family heightens understanding of the master-slave relationship at Rome. As the slavery system expanded through the central period of Roman history, the manipulation of slaves to the interests of the elite produced a relationship in which emotional factors offset the disparities of power and status between slave owner and slave and led to a dependence of the former on the latter that went far beyond the level of the material and the physical. Upper-class parents, that is to say, used surrogates under their control as a kind of compensatory mechanism for the essential lack of stability in Roman family life (to what degree of consciousness it is, of course, impossible to say) and to offset the far from remote possibility that they would have to face the loss of children before the latter achieved maturity. That mechanism was made possible by a system of wide-scale slave owning which upper-class parents were able to exploit to the full and which they continued to maintain over time.

Is it possible, finally, to explain why so many child minders were men? Perhaps the simplest solution lies in the general distinction that can be drawn in Roman society between the seclusive world of women and the more open world of men. The *nutrix* who catered to the upper-class infant would not have been obliged in the normal course of her work to appear beyond the confines of the household to which she belonged. But once children were old enough to dine in public, to attend public ceremonies, and to start a proper education, their chaperons and companions were more likely to be men for the reason that it was men who were allowed a greater degree of public mobility, even if of servile status. The existence of male child minders at Rome in all likelihood was predicated on general assumptions about male and female propriety which were deeply entrenched in the Roman mentality.

VI

The children of elite families embodied their parents' hopes for continuation of familial success in politics and statecraft, and to that extent upper-class children represented the future of Rome. But the situation was far different for children born into slavery. The achievement of renown—through military accomplishments and tenure of high governmental positions—and the contracting of spectacular marriage alliances were objects of ambition closed off by definition to the offspring of servile parents. Instead, and more modestly, slave children could aspire to the award of manumission, in return for faithful service, and the maintenance of a livelihood through skills acquired early in life. Yet the inscriptional evidence shows that it was not at all uncommon for slave children to be provided with child minders, so again the creation of a social context is required in order to account for that observable reality.

As with upper-class children, maternal death in childbirth may in some cases have made the use of the child minder unavoidable if an infant were to survive. As seen above, the parents of slave children are often unknown, and while a variety of factors could explain that fact, early maternal death must be one of them. In addition, children raised in slavery may have started their lives, like M. Antonius Gnipho, as exposed infants who were taken up and raised as the *alumni* of people sufficiently prosperous to provide for them; the *alumni* of the Licinia Veneria associated with Licinius Meropymus (no. 34) perhaps fall into such a category. Further, slave children may have been separated from their parents not by exposure but by the sale of their parents or themselves away from the *familia* into which they had been born. Evidence for the fragility of slave family life at Rome is unambiguous, and indeed disruption of slave families could and did occur not only as a result of sale but through bequests or gifts of individual slaves as well. No slave owner was obliged to respect the familial relationships his slaves had formed among themselves.[82]

Within such reasoning, however, it is implicit that slave children were considered worth rearing, and it has been seen in the inscriptional evidence that contacts between children and parents were not always lost despite the presence of surrogates. The provision of child minders for slave children by slave owners is best explained, therefore, by emphasizing the economic value of the children and, in cases where children and parents had not been separated, by slave owners' wishes to ensure that slave or ex-slave parents were not unduly diverted from their normal occupations by the requirements of tending their children. Sentiment does not have to be a factor of general relevance. The occasional slave owner may have believed that a *nutritor* or *paedagogus* was important for the emotional well-being of a slave child separated from parents, but the protection of property in his ownership will have been a more paramount concern. With the advent of the imperial age, and a corresponding decrease in the numbers of slaves available from wars of conquest, the rearing of slave children to adulthood became at Rome an important means of maintaining the level of the servile population. Slave owners provided female nurses for slave infants in their *familiae,* and again therefore progression to the *nutritor* and *paedagogus* marked a logical step. Although the material dependence of the politically and socially elite on continuing supplies of slaves from one generation to the next is self-evident, a clear demonstration of how young slaves were prepared for their adult roles is provided by the institution of the *paedagogium Caesaris,* interpretation of the epigraphical evidence on which suggests that imperial slaves, as boys, were trained by special pedagogues for court service and other duties in later life.[83] Yet what is visible on a relatively large scale in the imperial household was probably only a development of a principle in evidence in all elite households. The younger Pliny maintained a *paedagogium* in one of his villas, which quartered young slaves in his possession, and he is not likely to have been exceptional.[84]

It remains to consider briefly the use of child attendants at what I have termed an intermediate social level, that is, among people who seem to be free from slavery but do not belong to the upper levels of Roman society. The families of Julia Lucilla and Claudia Quinta come into play here, women known from the inscriptions of Diadumenus (no. 38) and C. Julius Hymetus (no. 37). But there are other kinds of complexity. For instance, a certain P. Aelius Placentius set up a dedication to his sons' *nutritor,* M. Aurelius Liberalis (no. 41). Both men are free, but whether freed or freeborn it is impossible to tell. Their *nomina* suggest connections with the *familia Caesaris,* but that is only a possibility. However, Liberalis is not likely to have been the *libertus* of Placentius, given their different *nomina* (unless on the unknown wife's side), but he could have been a hired man. If the free(d) father employed a free(d) *nutritor* for his sons, it would seem nevertheless that the child attendant was used by a family not far removed from slavery. Perhaps the most that can be said of examples such as these is that parents' transition from slavery to freedom left them with some child-minding resources from within the *familia* where they had once been slaves or, in the case of truly freeborn parents and children, that upper-class conventions were followed by people lower on the social scale, for reasons of social emulation, once moderate wealth or small-scale slave ownership had been secured.

VII

When Nero died in A.D. 68, his remains were deposited in his family tomb by his nurses Egloge and Alexandria. It is not known how they had spent their lives since the emperor's childhood, but in rather impressive fashion C. Caecina Tuscus, the son of one of Nero's nurses, had become prefect of Egypt in the mid-60s, though he was subsequently exiled, as was Anicetus, who spent the rest of his life in comfortable banishment in Sardinia following his role in Nero's divorce of Octavia in A.D. 62. Equally unknown are the fate of Beryllus and that of the barber and dancer whom Nero had known in his aunt's household.[85]

Nero's childhood attendants are on record principally because of Nero's notoriety, and in other circumstances even their very existence might well have gone unnoticed. Many names of other unimportant people have been collected here, for whom also no more than fragments of information are available. They are people whose impact on history in any conventional sense was minimal, part of the great mass of "the silent and the submerged" who will always remain little more than names, and yet the collocation of their identities and the establishment of a context in which they worked have resulted in information that allows greater awareness to emerge of the structure of the Roman family and of the experience of childhood in Roman society. From infancy to adulthood, the life of the Roman child was affected by the ubiquitous presence of child minders who were selected to provide children with basic wants and needs, and it is now evident that many of these people were men. Child care, as distinct from education, was not exclusively a concern of women at Rome, and that fact is of significance for the history of Roman childhood. But whether male or female, the child minders tended to be of servile stock, people at the disposal of the socially prosperous who were able to take advantage of Rome's slavery system for various reasons. Moreover, it would seem that childhood itself was subject to strains and tensions from the outset. The children of the elite were distanced from their parents by the demands of society upon the latter, and slave children had no guarantee of continuous contact with their parents at all. Within the uncertain world of childhood that followed, however, the child minders functioned as surrogate parents, providing a continuity and stability that went beyond the provision of material needs, and they themselves were able to benefit through acquiescence to the responsibilities to which they were assigned. Any definition of the Roman family, therefore, must recognize the largely silent contribution of the child minders, whose emotional importance can only be glimpsed but whose presence is unmistakable.

Notes

1. For the background, see M. T. Griffin (1985), 26–27.

2. Suetonius, *Nero* 6.3 The verb "nutritus est" should not have educational connotations, especially in view of Nero's age, but see M. T. Griffin (1976), 63, who regards the pedagogues as men "of scandalous incompetence," perhaps an exaggerated judgment. Geer (1931), 61, commented as follows on Suetonius's reference to the pedagogues: "this . . . is just the kind of picturesque but unimportant detail we expect from him." My disagreement with this view will quickly become apparent.

3. For the chronology of Nero's "orphanage," see Bradley (1978), 48–50. For Agrippina's marriages, see M. T. Griffin (1985), 28–29.

4. For Beryllus, see Josephus, *Jewish Antiquities* 20.182–184; and for Anicetus, see Suetonius, *Nero* 35.2; Tacitus, *Annals* 14.3. Cf. M. T. Griffin (1976), 63, 67 n. 3, 87–88; M. T. Griffin (1985), 32, 46.

5. Suetonius, *Nero* 22.1; cf. Bradley (1978), 285–86. There is no reason why the barber and the dancer should not have had two simultaneous jobs.

6. On Beryllus, see Millar (1977), 226, 378. Tacitus, *Annals* 14.3, specifies that Anicetus was a *libertus*. The dancer and the barber will have been slaves or freedmen in the household of Domitia Lepida.

7. Suetonius, *Nero* 50; *CIL* 6.37752. Cf. Treggiari (1976), 87: "Child care was mostly in the hands of women." For the general practice, see Bradley (1986).

8. For Sosibius and Sphaerus, see Tacitus, *Annals* 11.1, 11.4; Cassius Dio 48. 33.1. Note also Euodus, the *educator* of Caracalla; *PIR²* E 117. The identity of Britannicus's *nutrix* is also known: Claudia Phthonge; see Gordon (1958), no. 122.

9. The numeral provided with each name is the serial number of the inscription in *CIL* 6 in which the child minder's name is preserved. The attested title of each individual is included, sometimes in parentheses if it does not form part of the man's nomenclature. I have included *nutricii* with *nutritores* in the lists, since the terms are indistinguishable, and in the discussion that follows I have used the terms *nurslings* and *charge* for the child supervised by the child minder, even if the child was an adult by the time a particular inscription was set up. Most of the inscriptions date from the early imperial period. An additional *nutricius* is provided by *AE* 1946, 100; T. Flavius Diadumenus, who received a dedication from a woman named Coete, apparently the wife of a man named Sigerius. The commentary to the *AE* entry suggests that Sigerius is the *cubicularius* involved in the assassination of Domitian. Cf. *RE* II A, 2 col. 2277.

10. On Nicomedes, see Pflaum (1960–61), no. 163; Weaver (1972), 27, 237, 265, 283; Boulvert (1974), 65 nn. 384 and 385, 126 n. 74, 156 n. 285, 253–55, 265 (his wife), 326; cf. Barnes (1967), 68; Birley (1987), 90, 125. The literary text is *Historia Augusta, Verus* 2.9, "educatorem habuit Nicomedem."

11. Treggiari (1975a), 56.

12. For Verus, see *PIR²* C 606; Syme (1979), 325–32; Birley (1987), 48, 90. For Julia Livilla, see *PIR²* I 674; her *nutrix* and *medica* are also on record, *CIL* 6.8711. For the Drusi, see *PIR²* I 219, I 220. For Livia Julia, see *PIR²* L 303. Cf. Treggiari (1975a), 56, who believes that Hymnus, Malchio, and Prytanis were all provided by Livia herself.

13. Treggiari (1981), 56.

14. On whom see *PIR*² C 1390.

15. *CIL* 6.1745.

16. Boulogne (1951), 65, identifies Gemellus as Roman, Philocalus as Greek.

17. See *RE* I, 1 col. 525; *PIR*² C 157, C 161, F 507, C 1392, C 1390.

18. See *PIR*² A 814; *RE* IX A, 1 col. 238; Birley (1981), 150–51; *PLRE* I 810.

19. See *PIR*² G 137.

20. See Treggiari (1976), 89–90, suggesting also that the *paedagoga* Statilia Tyranis (*CIL* 6.6331) served Statilia Messalina. Support is available from Nero's example of a child being attended by a plurality of pedagogues, but other possibilities remain open; see *RE* III A, 2 cols. 2207–8. For Jassulus's charge, see *RE* III A, 2 col. 2199.

21. See *PIR*² I 812, I 374; *RE* Suppl. VII col. 313; Brunt (1975), 144.

22. See *RE* IV A, col. 758; Treggiari (1976), 90.

23. On these men, see Boulvert (1974), 82 n. 470, 114, 280 n. 114, 326 n. 331, 330. For the second-century date of Glycon's inscription, see Weaver (1972), 253, 256; and for the servile status of the *Augusti dispensator,* see Weaver (1972), 104, 250; the post is attested for Thamyrus by *CIL* 3.563, 12289.

24. Q. Lollius Philargurus may possibly be connected with the QQ. Lollii known from Cicero, *Verrines* 3.61–64; cf. *RE* XIII, 2 cols. 1387–88; or with M. Lollius, cos. A.D. 21; cf. *PIR*² L 311. Treggiari (1975a), 56, regards him as a freedman.

25. See Boulvert (1974), 280 n. 114, 326 n. 330. Faustus had been set free at a relatively early age. Cf. Weaver (1972), 69, 101, 103 n. 1, 238, 262; his inscription is not earlier than the era of Hadrian. Boulogne (1951), 65, considers Artemisius Greek.

26. See Weaver (1972), 101 n. 2, 157–69, for the nomenclature problems of this family group and their resolution through recourse to the *senatus consultum Claudianum.*

27. The parents' names were Herma and Sympherusa; the family group is also known from *CIL* 3.563, 12289; cf. Weaver (1972), 217.

28. See *PIR*² L 74; Syme (1979), 92 n. 16; Syme (1984), 1075.

29. *PIR*² I 675 is an entry for a third-century Julia Lucilla, but it seems unlikely that she is the same person. Hymetus, considered Greek by Boulogne (1951), 65, is further described on his inscription as "aedituus Dianae Plancianae." The name of Claudia Quinta's *mamma,* Julia Sporis, is also recorded.

30. Boulvert (1974), 326 n. 30, regards M. Ulpius Primigenius as an imperial freedman, but this cannot be certain.

31. For the consuls T. Tettienus Severus and Galeo Tettienus Severus Ti. Caepio Hispo, see *RE* V A, 1 col. 1106; Syme (1979), 708–9.

32. For further discussion of *tatae,* see Chapter 4.

33. See Appendix 3.1 nos. 78, 81, 85, 89, 90, 94, 96 for instances of *tatae* with different *nomina* from those of parents.

34. For the latitude that must be allowed in determining social status, see Demos (1982), 228–33, 288–91; Meeks (1983), 20–23.

35. Cicero, *Letters to Atticus* 269.2; Pliny, *Letters* 5.16.3.

36. In the total of ninety-seven cases recorded, thirty-two girls appear and at least sixty-two boys. The number of boys cannot be given accurately, since some inscriptions just refer to an unspecified number of sons.

37. Twenty-seven of the first seventy-six men have the element *libertus* in their inscriptions, but only one of the twenty-one *tatae*.

38. Gaius, *Institutes* 1.19, 39, mentions the *paedagogus* only, but *Digest* 40.2.13 and *Institutes* 1.6.5 add the *educator* (and *nutrix*).

39. Varro, *On Agriculture* 2.1.9; Suetonius, *Grammarians* 7. According to Suetonius, M. Antonius Gnipho was a freeborn child later manumitted by his *nutritor*. This implies that Gnipho became a slave after his exposure, though the implication has been denied on technical legal grounds; see Watson (1967), 171; Treggiari (1969), 114–15, 248. But in reality the technical situation may have been irrelevant, and Gnipho was probably "in statu servitutis" (Suetonius, *Grammarians* 21). Mohler (1940), 265, called the *nutritor* Gnipho's master. See also Christes (1979), 21–25. Boswell (1988), 63 n. 30, implies that the term *nutritor* is used generically of men raising foundlings as slaves in Pliny, *Letters* 10.66. In that text, however, the term does not appear at all. Sherwin-White (1966), 650–55, on Pliny, *Letters* 10.65–66, refers to "fosterers," reasonably enough; but note that Trajan's "quibusdam" is very vague.

40. *Historia Augusta, Severus Alexander* 13.4 (cf. also *Historia Augusta, Elagabalus* 13.8: Alexander in the care of his *nutritores* when orders were given for his murder). See Syme (1971), 146; Birley (1988), 221–22.

41. For other usages of *nutritor/nutricius*, cf. Caesar, *Civil War* 3.108, *Alexandrian War* 4; Martial, *Epigrams* 8.28.5; *Digest* 33.7.27; and see the discussion of Dixon (1988), 149–55.

42. See Cicero, *Pro Plancio* 81; Seneca, *Controversiae* 9.3.2, 9, 10, 10.4.3, 21; Seneca, *On Benefits* 3.17.4; Quintilian, *Institute of Oratory* 7.1.14; Ps.-Quintilian, *Declamations* 358, 372, 376; Tacitus, *Annals* 15.62; *Historia Augusta, Pius* 10.5. Cf. in general *TLL* s.v. "educator" and Maxey (1938), 55–56.

43. Tacitus, *Annals* 15.62, 13.15; cf. 12.8, 14.53.

44. See the references in n. 10 above.

45. The following couples are attested: Fufidius Amycus (no. 6) and Fufidia Chrestina; L. Fabius Ammianus (no. 10) and Claudia Dia; C. Mussius Chrysonicus (no. 11) and Aurelia Soteris; M. Ul(p)ius Primigenius (no. 36) and Capriola; Ti. Cl. Hermes (no. 45) and Cl. Paterna (?); C. Apisius Felix (no. 83) and *nutrix;* Julius Telesphor (no. 85) and Cornelia S(p)es, *mamma;* P. Farsuleius Isidorus (no. 90) and Quintia Parthenope, *nutrix;* Anthus (no. 95) and Rhoxane, *mamma;* Salonius Epictetus (no. 96) and Aphrodisia, *mamma.*

46. Soranus, *Gynecology* 2.20.

47. *Historia Augusta, Tacitus* 6.6.

48. Thus, for example, Boulogne (1951); Bonner (1977), 34–36.

49. Plautus, *Bacchides* 162, 419–434, 438–439.

50. Cicero, *Brutus* 210–211; Quintilian, *Institute of Oratory* 1.1.11, 1.1.8, but 1.2.10 implies that the pedagogue was not usually concerned with academic instruction.

51. Petronius, *Satyricon* 94.2; see also Quintilian, *Institute of Oratory* 1.2.25; Martial, *Epigrams* 3.58.30, 8.44.2, 9.27, 12.49.1. For the pedagogue accompanying the boy to and from school, see Cicero, *On Friendship* 20.74; Apuleius, *Metamorphoses* 10.5; Appian, *Civil Wars* 4.30. Note at *Historia Augusta, Firmus* 14.1, the phrase "paedagogus litterarius," which implies that the pedagogue was not normally an academic teacher. At Seneca, *Moral Epistles* 50.2, a pedagogue appears as the chaperon of a blind slave, the *fatua* of Seneca's wife.

52. Plutarch, *Moralia* 439F–440A; Seneca, *Moral Epistles* 94.8.

53. Apuleius, *Metamorphoses* 10.17.

54. Plutarch, *Moralia* 439F.

55. Martial, *Epigrams* 9.27.10–11. Cf. Suetonius, *Augustus* 44.2, Augustus assigning special seats at the games for young boys with adjoining seats for the pedagogues, in a passage emphasizing maintenance of decorum at the *spectacula; Galba* 14.2, the witticism that T. Vinius, Cornelius Laco, and Icelus were known as Galba's pedagogues because they lived with him in the palace and never left his side.

56. Cicero, *Letters to Atticus* 269.2; Seneca, *On Anger* 2.21.9. See also Quintilian, *Institute of Oratory* 1.2.5, for the advice that parents should "attach some respectable man or faithful freedman to their son as his friend and guardian, that his unfailing companionship may improve the character even of those who gave rise to apprehension."

57. Seneca, *On Anger*, 2.21.9; cf. also Seneca, *Moral Epistles* 25.5–6, 11.8–9, 89.13; Plutarch, *Moralia* 4A–B; *Cato the Younger* 1.5; Quintilian, *Institutue of Oratory* 1.1.8. Given this cluster of associations, it is worth noticing the way in which, toward the end of the second century A.D., Clement of Alexandria exploited the type of the pedagogue for Christian purposes in a work of moral and spiritual advice called, simply but significantly, *The Pedagogue*. Clement depicts Christ as the Christian's moral guide, mentor, and teacher, who will use any means possible, from punishment to cajolery, to instruct his "charge." But the advice given is not confined to matters of the spirit. It includes also practical instructions on how Christians should behave at table, how they should dress, how they should comport themselves in public, how they should conduct their relations with members of the opposite sex. Brown (1988), 126, comments on the work as follows: "At first sight, the *Paidagôgos* strikes us as egregiously fussy. We are spared few details. We meet the Christian at table: 'Keeping the hand and couch and chin free of grease-stains; possessing the grace of the countenance undisturbed, and committing no indecorum in the act of swallowing.' He must burp gently, sit correctly, and refrain from scratching his ears." The "fussiness," however, has to be understood in the light of the tradition represented by the quotations from Plutarch, Seneca, and Apuleius above: in effect, Clement's work is a prefectly logical development of conventional ideas long in evidence in the wider society to which he belonged.

58. Seneca, *Moral Epistles* 25.6.

59. Plutarch, *Moralia* 4A–B.

60. Quintilian, *Institute of Oratory* 1.3.5.

61. Plutarch, *Cato the Younger* 1.5; Martial, *Epigrams* 10.62.10.

62. Suetonius, *Claudius* 2.2.

63. Suetonius, *Nero* 37.1; Dio Chrysostom 72.10. Aurelian's firmness toward the senate, it is said, earned him the soubriquet "the senate's pedagogue" (*Historia Augusta, Aurelian* 37.3).

64. Quintilian, *Institute of Oratory* 1.3.5.

65. For Sphaerus, see above, n. 8.

66. Seneca, *Moral Epistles* 60.1, 27.5; *On Anger* 2.21.6; Valerius Maximus, *Memorable Deeds and Sayings* 1.8.12; Appian, *Civil Wars* 4.30.

67. Cicero, *On Friendship* 20.74.

68. On the specialization of slave jobs, see Treggiari (1975a) and (1976).

69. See the closing remarks of Chapter 2.

70. For Augustus, see Suetonius, *Augustus* 8.1, with Carter (1982), 92–93, 97–98 (and note also Augustus's *nutricula* at Suetonius, *Augustus* 94.6). For Caligula, see Tacitus, *Annals* 2.72; Suetonius, *Caligula* 10.1 For Claudius, see Suetonius, *Claudius* 2.1; Cassius Dio 55.1.4. For the full source material on the Julio-Claudian emperors as children, see *PIR*² I 215, C 941, I 217, C 942, D 129.

71. Cassius Dio 45.1.1.

72. For Julia, see Dio 48.34.3. For Augustus's marriage to Livia, see Carter (1982), 182. On the frequency of remarriage in Roman society generally, see Chapter 7.

73. See *PIR*² I 216, I 222.

74. See *PIR*² I 634, I 214.

75. Cassius Dio 55.32.1.

76. See *PIR*² I 221, I 223, I 220, I 641, I 664, I 674.

77. See *PIR*² C 1110, C 820.

78. Nicolaus of Damascus, *Life of Augustus* 3; Suetonius, *Caligula* 10.1, 24.1; *Nero* 6.3.

79. Suetonius, *Tiberius* 6.

80. On Brutus, see M. Clarke (1981), 9–12, and the analysis of Africa (1977–78).

81. *Digest* 33.7.27.1.

82. For the background of slave family life, see Bradley (1987), 47–80.

83. On the *paedagogium,* see Mohler (1940); cf. Boulvert (1970), 82, 177.

84. Pliny, *Letters* 7.27.13; cf. Maxey (1938), 57.

85. For Egloge and Alexandria, see Suetonius, *Nero* 50 (Nero's mistress Acte is also included); and observe Suetonius, *Nero* 42.1, for reference, in A.D. 68, to an anonymous *nutricula*. For C. Caecina Tuscus, see Bradley (1978), 215–16; cf. Brunt (1975), 143. For Anicetus, see Tacitus, *Annals* 14.62.

Chapter Appendix 3.1

(A) Nutritores/Nutricii

40. L. Passienus Caricus (7271; cf. 33249). He made a brief dedication to Passiena Proba, conceivably but not necessarily his daughter. The inscription comes from the Monumentum Passienorum, so both persons were probably freed or descended from freed members of the *familia* of L. Passienus Rufus, cos. 4 B.C. See *RE* XVIII, 4 col. 2098.

41. M. Aurelius Liberalis (10766). He was the *nutritor* of the unnamed sons of P. Aelius Placentius, who made the dedication. Both men are free, the sons perhaps freeborn. The difference of *nomen* stands out.

42. P. Antonius Zmaracdus (10848). The inscription records burial provisions made by Aelia Arsinoe, Aelius Hilarus, Aelius Timotheus Junior, P. Antonius Arsinous, and P. Antonius Marinus, for T. Aelius Timotheus, *pater,* the *nutritor,* themselves, and their *liberti/ae.* The *nutritor* could be regarded as the *libertus* of a full family group.

43. M. Antonius Tyrannus (12023). He made a dedication to his *contubernalis,* Antonia Arete, for both of whom servile origins are highly probable; cf. Treggiari (1981), 56, 68. They are described as "nutricii M. Antoni Flori."

44. Callimorfus (14083). The inscription gives only the name of a *nutritor*, for whom the single name suggests slave status.

45. Ti. Cl. Hermes (15104). He and Cl. Paterna made a dedication to their *alumnus*, M. Licinius Hermes. If the inscription is accurately transcribed, the *alumnus* was the son of M. Licinius Januarius and Licinia Agathe, and died at the age of two. The parents' shared *nomen* suggests servile origins, but because of the child's early age at death, he may have been freeborn. Ti. Cl. Hermes and Cl. Paterna may also have been former slaves.

46. Crescentis (16574). He was the *libertus* of Ti. Claudius Proculus Ceryllicanus and the *nutricius* of this man's unnamed son. Use of a family dependent for a freeborn child seems likely.

47. M. Publilius (19547). The inscription commemorates two free boys, L. Serbilius (= Servilius) Eutychanus sen. and L. Serbilius (= Servilius) Eutychanus iun., and their mother Hortensia Firmi [*sic*]. The mother's status is dubious; the father is unknown. But the *nutritor* must be free.

48. Zethus ser. Caesaris Semnianus (20433). He received a dedication from Junia Elate, his *contubernalis,* and his nursling, Cassia Blanda. Elate can be assumed to be a member of the imperial *familia;* cf. Boulvert (1974), 108 n. 108, 302 n. 214. But the *nomen* Cassia is odd for the *familia Caesaris.* Zethus's *agnomen* indicates that he had had another owner before entering the imperial household; cf. Boulvert (1974), 16–17, 37 n. 215; Treggiari (1981), 51, 65.

49. C. Marius C. l. Agathocles (21432). He received a dedication from his freeborn but illegitimate nursling, Livia Sp. f. Pelasgia.

50. Q. Quintius Eutyches (25302 = *CIL* 5.7188). He received a dedication from his nurslings Quintius Eutychianus and Quintia Victoria. The common *nomen* suggests membership in the same household, and the male *cognomina* suggest servile origins.

51. Verna Caes. n. ser. Neonianus (28593). His nursling, Memmia Tertulla, commemorated her *nutricius* and her mother, Memmia Panthera. Boulvert (1974), 326 n. 331, suggests that the *nutricius* was Memmia Tertulla's father, and Panthera could then be considered a freedwoman. But Neonianus could have been a slave in a Memmian household before entry to the *familia Caesaris.*

52. Apollonius (38598). He made a dedication to Manlia Niceph[oris] together with her parents, Helvius and Manlia Modesta. Since the daughter has her mother's *nomen,* the father is likely to be a slave, the mother perhaps a freedwoman. Apollonius appears to be a slave from his single name.

(B) Educatores

53. L. Do[mitius] Heliodorus (4871). He received a dedication from Domitius Philetus, "interpretes Aug. n."; cf. Weaver (1972), 82 n. 6. Both men are free, probably freed.

54. Aelius Germanus (10174). He received a dedication from Aelius Nicetes. Both men are free, probably freed.

55. Aelius Provincialis Augg. lib. (15983). Together with Aelius Viator (below, no. 56), this man was commemorated by three people: Memphius, Iraenaeus, and Renatus, the *alumni* of a woman named Coelia Palaestina, who was also commemorated. The *edu-*

catores were clearly imperial freedmen, and Coelia Palaestina was free(d). The *alumni* were Coelia's heirs and so would have been free, too, but they are likely to have originally been slaves.

56. Aelius Viator Augg. lib. (15983). See above, no. 55.
57. Licinius Polytimus libert. (27198). He was the freedman and *educator* of M. Terentius Paternus, who came from Spain and died at the age of eighteen.

(C) Paedagogi

58. [M.] Fulvinius M. l. Alexander (4718). His inscription comes from the Monumentum Marcellae but mentions no other people. Freed status is certain.
59. L. Maro[. . .] (7011). Only the existence of a pedagogue emerges from the inscription.
60. Felix (7657). No other persons are mentioned in the inscription. Felix was perhaps a slave. Boulogne (1951), 65, posits Roman nationality.
61. C. Gargilius Haemon (8012). From the information preserved in his inscription, it emerges that C. Gargilius Haemon—considered Greek by Boulogne (1951), 65—was the pedagogue and freedman of C. Gargilius Proculus, who in turn was the son of an imperial freedman, C. Julius Philagurus divi Aug. l. Agrippianus. According to Dessau (*ad ILS* 8486), Proculus seems to have entered a different *familia* from that into which he was born before Philagurus was set free, and Philagurus entered the *familia* of Augustus through the will of M. Agrippa. Agrippa died in 12 B.C., but given the element "divi Aug. l.," Philagurus cannot have been manumitted before A.D. 14. It is probable that Proculus was put under the supervision of a pedagogue in the household of the Gargilii while still a slave (the Gargilii in *PIR*² are of no help for household identification) and that Proculus manumitted his pedagogue once having been set free himself.
62. Pothus Aug. lib. (8988 = 33756). He was commemorated by his daughter. His status as an imperial freedman is certain.
63. [Sec]undius (8900). The inscription is too fragmentary to allow interpretation. Cf. Boulvert (1970), 178 n. 597.
64. Acratus l. (9741). The inscription gives only the pedagogue's name, but his freed status is certain. Boulogne (1951), 65, posits Greek nationality.
65. [Q.] Aemilius Diadumenus (9742). This man was commemorated by Aemilia Entrop[e], mother of his charge, Faustus, and whose own mother was Aemilia Cedne. The shared *nomen* suggests three freed persons in a common household, with Faustus still perhaps being a slave. Boulogne (1951), 65, regards the pedagogue as Greek.
66. Q. Caedius Q. l. Agatho (9743). The inscription preserves only the pedagogue's name and that of Caedia Q. l. Nice. The freed status of both persons is clear. Boulogne (1951), 65, posits Greek nationality.
67. [. . .]onis l. Charito (9744). The inscription is fragmentary, but the pedagogue's freed status is clear. Boulogne (1951), 65, posits Greek nationality.
68. L. Ciartius Hyperes (9745). He was the pedagogue of L. Ciartius Scyrus, the *collacteus* of P. Ciartius Helops. All three individuals are free, but the shared *nomen* (and the *cognomina*) suggests freed status, and there may be a connection with "the obscure

senator L. Clartius or Ciartius.'' Sherwin-White (1966), 511; cf. *PIR*² C 747; *RE* Supp. 1 col. 317.

69. Q. Cospius Q. l. Phyl (9746). He was commemorated by his wife, Cestia Epiphania, as was their son, Cestius Phylacio, who died at the age of nine. His freed status is clear. For upper-class Cestii, see *PIR*² C 686–692, but no clear association can be posited.

70. Hilarius (9748). He was the pedagogue of a certain Celer. The single names suggest slave status for both persons.

71. [. . .]stidius Philemo (9750). The inscription is fragmentary, but the pedagogue was presumably free. Boulogne (1951), 65, posits Greek nationality.

72. Phoebus (9751). The inscription gives only the pedagogue's name. He was perhaps a slave. Boulogne (1951), 65, posits Greek nationality.

73. C. Cestilius Pasiphilus (33392). He was the pedagogue of a Cestilia and was perhaps a freedman in charge of a freeborn girl. The inscription is from the Monumentum Cestiliorum.

74. Nicephorus (33894). He set up a dedication to his charge, Rufus, who died at the age of eighteen years, seven months, ten days. The single names suggest slave status.

75. Malchio Caesaris l. (37761a). The inscription gives minimal information, but the pedagogue's freed status is clear.

76. Sasa Lucian (37812a). The inscription gives only the pedagogue's name.

(D) *Tatae*

77. C. Vibius Tyrannus (2334). The *tata* and *patronus* of C. Vibius Threptus, the son of Vibia Epiteuxis and the public slave Threptus. The child died at the age of five and was commemorated by his parents and *tata*. Tyrannus and Epiteuxis were perhaps *colliberti*, or Tyrannus may have been the patron of Epiteuxis. But C. Vibius Threptus (named after his father?) is likely to have been born after Epiteuxis's manumission, given his early age at death.

78. C. Taurius Primitivus (5642). The *tata* of Arminia Gorgilla, the daughter of C. Arminius Aphrodisius and Valeria Gorgilla. The child died at the age of fifteen and was commemorated by her parents and *tata*. All the individuals are free, but *nomen* variation is apparent.

79. Arruntius Hermes (5941). The *tata* of Arruntia Hermione, who was commemorated by Hermes and her father, Arruntius Hermias. The inscription comes from the Monumentum Arruntiorum, so all three individuals can be assumed *liberti*, or descendants of *liberti*, of L. Arruntius, cos. A.D. 6 (*PIR*² A 1130). Hermione's mother is not on record.

80. Narcissus (6703). The *tata* of Stertinia Maxima, daughter of Acratus and Molpe. The child died at the age of three and was commemorated by her *tata*, who, like the parents, seems to have been a slave. It is possible in this case that the free child had become separated from her parents.

81. Cornelius Atimetus (10873). The *tata* of Aelius Primus and Aelius Ingenuus, the sons of Aelia Data and Fructus. The sons died at the respective ages of twenty-three and twenty-four and, together with Fructus, were commemorated by Aelia Data and Cornelius

Atimetus. They should be regarded as the freeborn sons of a freedwoman. Given Fructus's death, it is possible that Atimetus was a stepfather.

82. Anthus (11395). The *tata* of Alexander, the son of Marinus. The child died at five months and was commemorated by his father and *tata*. All three individuals look like slaves. Alexander's mother is not recorded.

83. C. Apisius C. l. Felix (12133). The *tata* of the freeborn L. Apisius C.f. Scaptia Capitolinus, the son of C. Apisius C. l. Epaphra and Oscia Ɔ. l. Primigenia. Felix could have been the *libertus* of Epaphra, or of Epaphra's own patron. Capitolinus also had a *nutrix*.

84. Epaphroditus (16578). The *tata* of Crescentilla, the daughter of Crescens and Soteris. The child died at the age of eleven and was commemorated by her parents and *tata*. All four individuals appear to be slaves.

85. Julius Telesphor (16926). The *tata* of Silvin[. . .], the daughter of Domitius Apollonius and Do(mitia) Fortunata. The girl was commemorated by her *tata*, parents, brother (Silvanus), *mamma* (Cornelia S(p)es) and *tatula* (Threptus). Free status is clear for the *tata* and parents, but *nomen* variation is apparent.

86. Phoebus (18196). The *tata* of the freeborn L. Flavius L. f. Anien. Saturninus, the son of (L.) Flav[ius Eu]hodus. The child died at the age of five and was commemorated by his *tata* and father. Phoebus was perhaps a slave. Saturninus's mother is not recorded.

87. Ofellio (19552). The *tata* of Hortensia Justa, the daughter of Q. Hortensi(us) Perpetu(us). The girl died at the age of eight and was commemorated by her *tata*, father, and brother (Communis). Ofellio appears to be a slave, but the father and daughter were clearly free. Justa's mother is not recorded.

88. Amphio (20930). The *tata* of Justa, the daughter of Hermes and Successa. The girl died at the age of sixteen and was commemorated by her parents and *tata*. All the individuals seem to be slaves.

89. [. . .]ius Fortunatus (23113). The *tata* of C. Numisius Felicissimus, the son of C. Numisius Theseus and Numisia Urbica. The child died at the age of four and was commemorated by his parents and *tata*. Fortunatus was free, but it is doubtful that he was a Numisius. The shared *nomen* suggests former servile status for the parents.

90. P. Farsuleius Isidorus (25301). The *tata* of C. Q(uintius) Hermias, apparent son of C. Q(uintius) Eufemus. The latter commemorated his wife, Aelia Tyche, who died at the age of fourteen, and Hermias, who died at the age of four. The *tata* and the *nutrix* Quintia Parthenope also participated in the dedication. Perhaps the best interpretation here is that Tyche was Hermias's mother and that she died in childbirth four years before her child. *Nomen* variation is apparent.

91. Ignotus (27259). The *tata* of Terentia Spe(s), who died at the age of three and was commemorated by her unnamed parents, grandmother, and *tata*.

92. L. Valerius Sabbio (27964). The *tata* of L. Valerius Capitolinus, the son of Pontia Veneranda and L. Valerius Acratus.

93. Hilarus (28906). The *tata* of Victor, the son of Myrsine and Mercurius. The child died at the age of two and was commemorated by his parents and *tata*. All the individuals appear to be slaves. The inscription should be regarded as a duplicate of the fragmentary 22802, the probability of which has not been noticed.

94. L. Mummius Onesimus (34206). The *tata* of T. Aconius Karus, the son of Flavia Hygia and T. Aconius Blastus. *Nomen* variation is apparent.

95. Anthus M.M. ser(vus) (35530). The *tata* of Ti. Julius [. . .], the son of Terminalis and Julia Euphrantice. The child died at the age of three and was commemorated by his parents, the *tata,* and Rhoxane, *mamma.* He was perhaps the freeborn son of a *liberta,* unless a slave manumitted very early. The father and *mamma* appear to be slaves, as Anthus certainly was.

96. Salonius Epictetus (36353). The *tata* of Silvia, the daughter of Claudius Protomachus and Claudia Damal. The child died at the age of three and was commemorated by her parents, *tata,* and Aphrodisia, *mamma.*

97. Onesimus (38694). The *tata* of Galatia, the daughter of Syntrophus and Acte. The child died at the age of three; she and her parents were commemorated by Onesimus. Galatia may therefore have been an orphan. All the individuals appear to be slaves.

Chapter Appendix 3.2

Male child minders are attested epigraphically elsewhere than at Rome, but for the purposes of this study a systematic collection of all Italian and provincial texts was not attempted. However, a number of details that complement points made above can be noted here.

1. According to Suetonius (*Claudius* 26.1), Livia Medullina (*PIR*[2] L 304) died from ill health on the day she was due to marry the future emperor Claudius. The circumstances recall those of Minicia Marcella (Pliny, *Letters* 5.16), particularly since Medullina was commemorated by her *paedagogus,* the freedman Acratus (*CIL* 10.6561, Velitrae). That the pedagogue regularly chaperoned adult female charges is implied by *CIL* 3.7316 from Edessa in Macedonia. The inscription commemorates Epictetus, the freedman and *nutricius* of Mulvia Placida (*PIR*[2] M 700), who made the dedication when her husband, Sex. Tadius Lusius Nepos Paullinus, was governor of Macedonia.

2. Three inscriptions refer to child minders who, like certain of Nero's attendants, went on to other jobs. M. Nummius Euhodus is called in *CIL* 5.4347 (Brixia) not only the *nutritor* but also the *procurator* (and freedman) of M. Nummius Umbrius Primus Senecio Albinus, cos. A.D. 206 (*PIR*[2] N 238). So, too, L. Roscius Eubulus, known from *CIL* 5.4241 (Brixia) was a *nutrit(or)* and *procurat(or).* Marianus, the *nutritor* of L. Didius Marinus (*PIR*[2] D 71), praetorian prefect in A.D. 223, appears in *CIL* 3.6753 (Ancyra) as an imperial freedman collecting the *vicesima libertatis* in Bithynia, Pontus, and Paphlagonia. Quite distinctive is P. Calpurnius Princeps, who is described in a text of A.D. 200 from Ostia as "equo publico donatus, omnibus honoribus functus, educator"; his charge may have been M. Umbilius Maximinus Praetextatus, "c(larissimus) p(uer) p(atronus) c(oloniae) (Ostiensis) et sacerdos geni col(oniae)"; *AE* 1977.151.

3. Child-minding couples continue to appear. A Dalmatian inscription, *CIL* 3.14261[1], shows Aurelius Trophimus and Prae[. . .]ia Thallussa as the *nutritores* of Atitianus, who died in his thirty-second year; from Italy, *CIL* 9.3252 (Corfinium) gives A. Vercius Auxiliaris and Adauta as the *nutritores* of Ostoria Felicitas, who died as an infant; and *CIL* 14.2828 (Ager Praenestinus) identifies Cn. Pomp(eius) Januarius and Pompeia as the *nutritores* of C. Julius Beronicianus, dead at five.

4. Freedmen are well in evidence, beyond those already mentioned: L. Aemilius Hippolytus, a Greek, *educator* and *collibertus* of L. Aemilius Euhodus (*CIL* 2.4319,

Tarraco); Arrius Celerinus, *nutritor* and freedman of Arria Luppula (*CIL* 8.3430, Lambaesis; cf. 8.332; 8.4021); Istoricus, a pedagogue (*CIL* 2.1482, Baetica; cf. 2.1981); L. Furius Lalos, pedagogue of Polla (*CIL* 5.3157, Vicetia); Sex. Cervius Jucundus, freedman of Cervia Psyche, *nutricius* of L. Jucundus Phota, *vilicus* of Cervia Psyche (*CIL* 9.3103, Sulmo); Hagnus, *nutricius* of T. Rubrius Nepos (*CIL* 14.3834, Tibur); Messiu[s] Priscus, a pedagogue (*CIL* 10.8129, Surrentum). M. Tullius Communis, *nutritor* of the *eques* M. Tullius Cicero, is taken to be a freedman by *RE* XXII, 1 col. 1250, though *CIL* 10.482 (Paestum) is not specific on this.

5. Judging from single names, the following men might be considered slaves: the pedagogue Atticus (*AE* 1985.169, Ostia); the *nutritor* Laberius (*CIL* 10.189, Potentia); the pedagogue Symphorus (*CIL* 10.1944, Puteoli); the *educator* Marcianus (*AE* 1972.337, Narbonensis).

6. Note, finally, that *CIL* 10.6561 (Velitrae) was found with *CIL* 10.6562, which also mentions a pedagogue named Acratus; he may be the same man as Livia Medullina's pedagogue, but Acratus is associated in the second text with an Elvia (= Helvia?) Scepsis. Note also that *CIL* 5.4400 (Brixia) gives P. Acilius Surus as *nutri(tor)* of L. Acutius Caecilianus, the *alumnus* of Caecilia Procula; and that *CIL* 10.648 (Salernum) shows the *liberta* C. Vettia Grata to have had a *nutritor* by the time of her death at the age of two.

4

Tatae *and* Mammae *in the Roman Family*

A recent study of the family in American history makes the point that the familiar words *dad* and *daddy* comprise "a relatively new term of address for fathers."[1] From a Roman perspective, however, that opinion tantalizes, for the Latin word *tata* comes immediately to mind as an obvious linguistic predecessor of the English term, just as the complementary word *mamma* anticipates the equally familiar *mom* and *mommy*.[2] But if the English form of address is not linguistically new, its popularity as a term of affection draws attention nevertheless to the question of whether the Latin words *tata* and *mamma* were used as widely and were as affectionate in their associations as their modern counterparts. In point of fact, *tata* and *mamma* are rarely found in Roman literature and occur most frequently in inscriptions commemorating the dead. Accordingly, my purpose here is to examine the contribution their appearance in the inscriptional evidence makes to knowledge of Roman family life, and in so doing I shall be concerned not only with adults, the *tatae* and *mammae* themselves, but also with the children—who sometimes were adults, too, when recorded in their inscriptions—associated with them. The focus will fall mainly on evidence from the city of Rome, but I shall also consider some material from other areas of the wider Roman world at appropriate points. Since the inscriptions are often elliptical, much will have to be speculative. Yet, despite the difficulties, it should be possible to integrate the information they furnish with other evidence on the history of childhood and the family in Roman society.

II

The starting point has to be usages of *tata* and *mamma* in extant Latin literature and above all a text from Varro—a fragment of a now lost work on the rearing of children—in which a predictable connection between *tata* and *mamma* on one hand and *pater* and *mater* on the other is established. Varro says that *tata* and *mamma* were simply children's words for father and mother, and it is this basic link that Martial exploits in a brief epigram on the "maxima mamma" Afra.[3] However, a discrepant usage appears in a line of Persius, who evidently took *mamma* to be comparable in meaning to the word *nutrix* in its sense of a nursemaid or nanny: "Why do you angrily reject your nurse's lullaby?"[4] Thus, a *mamma,* it seems, was not necessarily a mother in spite of Varro, and by extension a *tata* may not necessarily have been a father. The literary examples, however, are too modest in number to argue a single or even predominant meaning for *tata* and *mamma.* But the inscriptions quickly confirm that the words were used of men and women who were not the biological parents of the children connected with them, and in the majority of cases it happens that their meaning is essentially indeterminate. How, then, are the terms *tata* and *mamma* to be defined and explained? To answer that question, the inscriptions have to be examined in detail. Some of the basic information they convey is presented in Tables 4.1 and 4.2, where serial numbers preceded by T (for *tata*

Table 4.1. Tata Inscriptions*

	1	2	3	4	5	6	7
T1	F	m	L	X	S	X	L
T2	F	f	F			X	F
T3	F	f	F				
T4	F	m	S?				
T5	F	f	F	X	F	X	F
T6	F?	f	F	X	F?		
T7	—	m	L?				
T8	S?	f	F	X	S?	X	S?
T9	F	m f	S? S?				
T10	F	m m	F F	X?	S?	X	L?
T11	S?	m	S?	X	S?		
T12	F	f	F				

Table 4.1. *Continued*

	1	2	3	4	5	6	7
T13	L	m	I	X	L	X	L
T14	F	f	L				
T15	F	m	F				
T16	F	m	F				
T17	F	f	F				
T18	S?	f	S?	X	S?	X	S?
T19	F	m	S?				
T20	F	f	F?	X	F	X	F
T21	S?	f	F				
T22	F	m	F				
T23	S?	m	F				
T24	S?	m	I	X	F		
T25	F	f	L				
T26	S?	f	F	X	F		
T27	S?	f	F				
T28	F	m	F			X	F
T29	S?	f	S?	X	S?	X	S?
T30	L	m	F				
T31	S?	m	F			X	S?
T32	S?	f	S?	X	S?		
T33	F	m	F	X	F	X	F
T34	F	f	F				
T35	F	f	F	X	F	X	F
T36	F	f	F				
T37	F?	m	F				
T38	—	f	F	X	—	X	—
T39	F	m	F	X	F	X	F
T40	S?	—	S				
T41	F	m	F				
T42	S?	m	S?				
T43	F	m	F	X	F	X	F
T44	S?	f	—			X	S?
T45	S	m	F	X	S?	X	F
T46	F	f	F	X	F	X	F
T47	S?	f	F				
T48	S?	f	S?				
T49	F	—	—				

*See Table Notes at the end of this chapter.

Key: Column 1 = status of *tata*   Column 2 = sex of child (*male/female*)   Column 3 = status of child   Column 4 = child's father attested or inferable   Column 5 = status of father   Column 6 = child's mother attested or inferable   Column 7 = status of mother   F = free   I = *ingenuus/a*   L = *libertinus/a*   S = *servus/a*

Table 4.2. Mamma Inscriptions*

	1	2	3	4	5	6	7
M1	F	f	I			X	F
M2	F	m	S?				
M3	F	m	F				
M4	F	m	I			X	F
M5	F	m	F				
M6	L	m	L	X	L		
M7	F	m f	S? S?				
M8	—	m	I				
M9	F	f	S?				
M10	F	m	F				
M11	F	f	F				
M12	S?	m	F	X	S?	X	S?
M13	—	f	F				
M14	—	f	L				
M15	F	f	F				
M16	S?	f	S?				
M17	F	m	L				
M18	S?	f	F?				
M19	F	m	L				
M20	F	f	F				
M21	F	m	S				
M22	F	f	S?				
M23	F	f	F?	X	F	X	F
M24	F	f	F				
M25	F	f	F				
M26	S?	m	F				
M27	F	m	—				
M28	F	m	I				
M29	F	m	S?				
M30	F	m	F				
M31	F	m	F				
M32	F	f	L				
M33	S?	f	F				
M34	F	m	L				
M35	S?	m	F				
M36	I	m	F				
M37	F	f	F				
M38	F	m	F				
M39	F	m	I			X	F
M40	L	f	F				
M41	I	m	S	X	S		
M42	L	f	F				
M43	F	f	F				

Table 4.2. Continued

	1	2	3	4	5	6	7
M44	L	f	L	X	L	X	L
M45	F?	m f	L L				
M46	F	f	F				
M47	F	m	F				
M48	F	f f	S S	X?	S?		
M49	F	m	F?				
M50	F	f	F				
M51	F	f m	S S	X	S		
M52	S?	m	S?				
M53	F	m	F				
M54	S?	m	F	X	F	X	S?
M55	S?	f	S?	X	F	X	F
M56	L	m m	F F			X X	L L
M57	F	f	F				
M58	F	f	F?	X	F	X	F
M59	S?	f	F	X	F		
M60	F	m	F?			X	F
M61	S?	f	F				

*See Table Notes at the end of this chapter.

Key: Column 1 = status of *mamma*   Column 2 = sex of child (*male*/*female*)   Column 3 = status of child   Column 4 = child's mother attested or inferable   Column 5 = status of mother   Column 6 = child's father attested or inferable   Column 7 = status of father   F = free   I = *ingenuus/a*   L = *libertinus/a*   S = *servus/a*

inscriptions) or M (for *mamma* inscriptions) are used, as throughout, for the sake of convenience.[5]

In theory, the easiest way to proceed is to find cases where the meaning of the words *tata* and *mamma* as father and mother is not in doubt, though it soon emerges that the number of such cases is relatively small. There is no problem, for example, with a dedication to a girl (her name is missing from the stone) made by her *tata* Fortis and her *mat(er)* Caenis, since the girl is called their daughter, *filia* (T44).[6] Here *tata* in the sense of father is to be regarded as a familiar counterpart to the more formal *mater*, comparable to a reverse example (M60), a dedication to a *mamma* and a *pater* by their son, *filius*.[7] Again, an inscription from Sardinia uses *tata, mamma,* and *parentes* in conjunction, while another from Circeii honoring a *mammula* who is also a "vera mater" shows the diminutive form being used to indicate a parent.[8] However, since indications of parent-child connections of this sort are uncommon in the inscriptions as a whole, it is very difficult to find other instances where *tata* and *mamma* unquestionably mean father and mother, even though this might be the general presumption when the texts are first read. In a case (M56) where two sons, Ti. Julius Eunus and Ti. Claudius Deuter, commemorate their respective fathers, Ti. Julius Aug. l. Secundus and Ti. Claudius Aug. l. Eunus, together with their *mamma,* Claudia Aug. l. Cedne, the inscription seems to use the word *parentes* to mean all three latter individuals. It is probable that the *mamma* had married twice and that she was the mother of the two dedicants who were thus half-brothers.[9] But in practically all other cases there must be an element of doubt. This is because of examples where *tata* and *mamma* are differentiated from a child's biological parents. For instance, a girl named Silvia is commemorated by her parents Claudius Protomachus and Claudia Damal (use of the word *filia* makes this certain), and also by Salonius Epictetus, *tata,* and Aphrodisia, *mamma* (T46 = M55).[10] As examples of arguable situations that consequently arise, the following may be observed.

First is a dedication to an infant boy by his *tata* and *mamma* which runs in part thus: "Zetho Corinthus tata eius et Nice mamma f." (T42 = M52). It would be tempting to read the last letter as an abbreviation for *filio* ("to their son"), and it would then be certain that Corinthus and Nice were the boy's parents. But "f(ecerunt)" ("they set this up") would be just as epigraphically appropriate, and while Corinthus and Nice could still be regarded as father and mother, there would be no actual proof that this was so.[11] They might have been figures comparable to the *tata* and *mamma* recorded independently of the parents in the case of Silvia just mentioned. Second is a dedication (T2) to M. Gellius Helius by Gellia Nymphidia to her husband, and by Gellia Florentina to her *tata* (also by a public slave to his friend).[12] A *nomen* shared by spouses is often taken to mean that the couple were former slaves, manumitted by the same slave owner or in the same household. Thus, it could be thought here that Florentina was the daughter of servile parents, born after her parents' emancipation or set free with them. On the other hand, Helius could just as well have been a man, like Salonius Epictetus above, who for some reason had come to form a close relationship with Florentina but who was not her father. The inscription as it is provides no proof that he was Florentina's biological father. Third is a dedication (T31) to T. Minusius Eutyches by Primitiva, *mat(er)*, and Januarius, *tata.*[13] On the analogy of the inscription of Caenis and Fortis (T44), it would seem natural to take these individuals as a family group, with *tata* again understood as an affectionate complement to *mater*. Yet, because there is no use of the word *filius* in this inscription, it is impossible to say precisely what the relationship between Eutyches and Januarius was. Once more, Januarius could have been someone comparable to Salonius Epictetus, a *tata* but not a biological father.

It happens, indeed, that most of the inscriptions belong to a category where the meaning of *tata* and *mamma* is unclear, and no advantage would accrue from multiplying examples. In contrast, however, because biological parents are independently attested or inferable, *tata* and *mamma* demonstrably do not refer to fathers and mothers in a considerable proportion of the total evidence, some twenty of the *tatae* inscriptions and ten of the *mammae* inscriptions, with other possibilities.[14] It is from these cases, therefore, that progress is to be made.

At once it is the servile character of the personnel involved in the relevant inscriptions that stands out. That is, the individuals concerned tend for the most part to be slaves, former slaves, or people not far removed from slavery.[15] It is, of course, notoriously difficult to be sure of legal status when people are mentioned in inscriptions without positive status indicators (hence the use of question marks in the tables to signify uncertainty), but if criteria customarily accepted as guides to status are adopted, the general point is valid enough. So, if the appearance of single names alone is taken, as frequently, to mean that individuals using them were slaves, in a dedication (T29) to a girl, Justa, by her parents, Hermes and Successa, and her *tata*, Amphio, all four individuals can reasonably be judged slaves.[16] Again, since a shared *nomen* will signify a servile background for spouses, the parents of Silvia (T46 = M55) are likely to have been slaves at some stage of their lives.[17]

Some cases are of sufficient interest to warrant close description:

1. The boy C. Vibius Threptus was commemorated by his *tata*, C. Vibius Tyrannus, his mother, Vibia Epiteuxis, and his father, Threptus, a public slave (T1). The boy is clearly free, but because C. Vibius Tyrannus was his patron as well as his *tata*, he must have been *libertinus*, which would then mean that his mother was a freedwoman.

2. Arruntia Hermione, also free, was commemorated by two men whose names are given as "Arrunti Hermias pater et Hermes tata" (T6). It cannot be said with certainty whether this means "Arruntius Hermias and Arruntius Hermes" (making both men free), or

"Hermias, slave of Arruntius, and Hermes" (making one man a definite and the other a possible slave), though the former is perhaps more likely. However, because the inscription comes from the Monumentum Arruntiorum, all the individuals mentioned can safely be judged close to slavery, if not a combination of actual *servi* and *libertini*.

3. The free Stertinia Maxima was commemorated by the single-named *tata*, Narcissus, and is described as "Acrati et Molpes fil(ia)" (T8). That may conceivably indicate that she was *ingenua*. But given the parents' names, it is more likely that she was the freed daughter of a slave couple.

4. The monument of the freeborn L. Apisius C.f. Scaptia Capitolinus gives the names of his parents, both freed, his brother and sister, both freeborn, and his *tata*, a freedman sharing the family *nomen* (T13). There is no doubt of his servile extraction: he and his siblings had been born after their parents' emancipation.

5. The freedman M. Favonius ⊃. l. Stabilio is associated with two freedwomen, one his mother, the other his *mamma* (and perhaps his patron; the text is unclear on this), each a Favonia (M6).

6. The free boy Cn. Arrius Agapetus shared his *nomen* with his mother, Arria Agapete. But his father, *mamma,* and *nutrix* all had single names only (Bostrychus, Helpis, Fi[l]e[t]e) (M12). He is surely the child of a woman once a slave.

7. The Felicio who commemorated the freeborn Quintia C.f. Prima was a *verna* (M41); so his mother must have been an unrecorded slave woman, not Quintia Prima herself.[18]

In other cases a servile orientation is not so plain but cannot be altogether ruled out. Terentia Spes, a free girl, was remembered by *parentes, avia,* and *tata,* none of whose names was written down (T38). Pomponia Sabina and her daughter Petronia Sabina were both free, but Petronia's *mamma,* Januaria, was apparently a slave (M59).[19] The difficulty is that it is impossible to say whether persons free at the time their inscriptions were set up were freeborn or freed. Either point of view could be maintained. But it can be said, to look from a slightly different angle, that in none of the inscriptions discussed or referred to so far is there any trace of personnel from the upper reaches of Roman society, that is, from the senatorial and equestrian orders; nor is there any appreciable difference in status between *tatae* and *mammae* as a group and the children with whom they are paired. Whatever the truth about the status of those who have to be categorized only as free, the overall population seen so far is, in a general sense, completely lower-class.

Can anything be learned from the ages at death recorded in the inscriptions? The information available from the full corpus of material is set out in Tables 4.3, 4.4, and 4.5. The children's ages at death could be divided into four categories:

1. Cases where the attested *tata* was not the child's biological father (Table 4.3, column 2).
2. Other cases where a *tata* is attested (Table 4.3, column 3).

Table 4.3. Children's Ages at Death: *Tatae* Inscriptions

	Y	M	D	H	1	2	3	4
T1	14		28		m	X		
T5	15	5	6		f	X		
T7	7				m		X	
T8	3	10	9		f	X		
T10	23				m		X	
T10	24				m		X	
T11		5			m	X		
T15	4				m		X	
T18	11	6	2		f	X		
T22	25	6			m		X	
T24	5	6			m	X		
T26	8				f	X		
T29	16				f	X		
T31	3	10	24		m		X	
T32	2	3			m		X	X
T33	4		55		m	X		
T35	4	4	8		m	X		
T38	3				f	X		
T40	2	11			—		X	
T42	1		16		m		X	X
T44	3	4	4		f		X	
T45	3		30		m		X	X
T46	3	2	9		f	X		X
T47	5				f		X	X
T48	3	9	12		f		X	

Key: Column 1 = sex of child (*m*ale/*f*emale)   Column 2 = *tata* not father inscription   Column 3 = other *tata* inscription   Column 4 = overlap with Table 4.4

Table 4.4. Children's Ages at Death: *Mammae* Inscriptions

	Y	M	D	H	1	2	3	4
M5	25		22		m		X	
M10	4	6	27		f	X		
M11	16				m		X	
M12	3		45		m	X		
M16	5		20		f		X	
M18	6	5			f		X	
M27	6	5	26		m		X	
M28	7		1	10	m		X	
M29	2	10	6		m		X	
M35	10	4	13		m		X	
M36	3				m		X	
M42	15	3	11	7	f		X	
M46	7	3			f		X	
M52	1		16		m		X	X
M53	24				m		X	
M54	3		30		m	X		X
M55	3	2	9		f	X		X
M57	5				f		X	X
M58	6	6	22		f	X		
M59	3	10	9		f	X		

Key: Column 1 = sex of child (*male*/*f*emale)   Column 2 = *mamma* not mother inscription   Column 3 = other *mamma* inscription   Column 4 = overlap with Table 4.3

Table 4.5. Ages at Death: *Tatae* and *Mammae*

	Y	M	D	H	1
T3	40				T
M9	35	10	27		M
M19	65	3	10		M
M20	60	3	10		M
M38	50				M
M43	45				M

Key: Column 1 = T(*ata*)/M(*amma*)

3. Cases where the attested *mamma* was not the child's biological mother (Table 4.4, column 2).
4. Other cases where a *mamma* is attested (Table 4.4, column 3). But the numbers of ages then become too minuscule for any meaning-

ful inferences to be drawn from them (though it can be noted that the ages in the third category all fall under age seven). The fact is that only a small proportion of the total volume of inscriptions provides information on the age of death of those commemorated, and a division obviously has to be made between commemorated children and commemorated *tatae* and *mammae.* The ages of all children whose age at death is given tend to cluster in the years of infancy and early childhood, with just a sprinkling of ages in the teens and early twenties.[20] It can be said, therefore, and without any surprise, that *tatae* and *mammae* tended to be associated with young children and that the tie between child and *tata* and *mamma* could extend into the child's adulthood (as the few ages for deceased *tatae* and *mammae* confirm; Table 4.5).[21] But there is no particular significance attaching to the ages at death of children who appear in the inscriptions where *tatae* and *mammae* are not biological parents.

The same is true of the terms of endearment and the expressions of grief used in the inscriptions, which are not to be thought banal because of their conventionality. Epithets such as *infelicissimus/a, pientissimus/a, carissima, indulgentissima,* and *optima,* variously applied to the commemorated or commemorating *tatae* and *mammae,* suggest that their relationships with children were affectionate and intimate.[22] And at times, in their more elaborate forms, the sentiments of the bereaved still convey a strong sense of the loss that was experienced. The lament of the freedwoman Salvidiena Hilara, for instance, who set up a memorial to Salvidiena Faustilla, is heart-rending: "Salvidiena Hilara, freedwoman of Quintus, to Salvidiena Faustilla, her heart's delight, who was accomplished in all the arts. 'You have left your *mamma* to sorrow, mourning and tears.' She lived for fifteen years, three months, eleven days, seven hours. An evil fate has torn the girl from me. 'My precious darling, you have left your *mamma* in misery.' "[23] But the emotions expressed were equally keen, no matter who the *tatae* and *mammae.*

To summarize so far, then, the evidence of the inscriptions in which *tatae* and *mammae* are not the parents of the children associated with them presents a picture of lower-class men, women, and children bound together in intimate relationships that could begin in children's earliest years and persist until their maturity. In their duration and warmth, however, the relationships were no different from those attested in inscriptions where the meaning of *tata* and *mamma* is indeterminate and where the adults (in some cases, at least) may have been the children's parents. Yet the *tatae* and *mammae* were not parents, and at this point an effort needs to be made to establish their social identity. If they were not the children's parents, who were they?

III

One solution is to suppose that *tatae* and *mammae* were grandparents. There is support for such a view in the case where a *tata* follows *parentes* and *avia* (grandmother) in a sequence of dedicants ("fecerunt parentes pientissimi et avia et tata"), if *tata* is taken as the masculine parallel to *avia* (T38). One editor indeed took *mamma* elsewhere to mean grandmother without question, since the woman concerned was distinguished from *parentes:* "P. Mindius Vitalis et Mindia Zosime parentes et Mindia Charis mamma Galatiae filiae carissimae fecerunt" (M58).[24] But this is really a strategy of despair, because there is no obvious or logical reason why the equation with grandparents should be made and certainly no basis for it in the literary evidence, meager as that evidence is. Nor can it be thought that the meaning of grandparents should apply in the inscriptions as a whole, in a generic sense. In one instance, a *mamma* dedicates to her *alumna;* she cannot have been the girl's grandmother (M59).

Perhaps stepparents should be brought into consideration, on the assumption that remarrying parents regularly provided their offspring with nonbiological "mothers" and "fathers." Yet there are no clear examples of this to be found in the inscriptions. There is one situation where a *mamma,* Scetasia Musa, perhaps became the stepmother of a Scetasia Oecumene, but if so, she had already been her *mamma* beforehand, so this hardly constitutes compelling evidence (M44).[25] The solution cannot be dismissed utterly, but it can be no more than tentative.

Is it conceivable that *tata* and *mamma* were alternative words for *nutritor* and *nutrix,* as the evidence of Persius originally seemed to suggest? Should all the *tatae* and *mammae* who are distinguishable from biological parents simply be regarded as nurses, whether male or female? This, I think, is a more attractive solution, because it appears to make sense of the circumstances pertinent to some of the relevant inscriptions. For instance, there is no reason why Hermes, the probable slave *tata* known from an inscription from the Monumentum Arruntiorum (T6), should not have been a child minder provided by his aristocratic owner to take charge of a girl from the *familia,* a pattern determinable from separate evidence on *nutritores* and other male child minders.[26] Moreover, with inscriptions that identify *tatae* and biological fathers but no mothers, it could be assumed that the missing mothers were in fact dead or had been otherwise separated from their offspring, thus making substitutes to offer care desirable.[27] Likewise, in an inscription from Luceria, a teenage boy is commemorated by a *matertera* and a *tata;* perhaps the aunt had supplied the *tata* in the event of the parents' demise.[28] Again, the *tata* P. Farsuleius Isidorus is coupled in his inscription (T35) with a *nutrix*, Quintia Parthenope, in a situation where a mother appears to have died when her son was still an infant; the *tata* could well have been the nurse's husband, helping with the care of the boy in her charge.[29]

This solution will also fit the circumstances of some inscriptions in which parents are not attested independently of *tatae* and *mammae*. Consider the dedication to the *tata* Cn. Turranius Eutyches from the apparent slave Primulus (T4). It is a very simple inscription, mentioning only the two men, but its last line runs as follows: "n(atione) Hispanus is qui fecit." That is, Primulus had somehow arrived in Rome from Spain at a certain point in his life before he commemorated his *tata*. There is no proof, of course, that he was not Turranius's son (or that he was). But it would be plausible to imagine that Primulus had been separated from his parents in Spain as a child, brought to Rome as a slave, and entrusted there by his owner to a dependent to be reared. Or take the memorial of Stertinia Maxima, "Acrati et Molpes fil(ia)" (T8). I have already suggested that Stertinia may have been the daughter of a slave couple. But her parents, it can be noted, did not participate in the dedication to her, so that as a slave child she, too, may have been separated from Acratus and Molpe, by sale perhaps or parental death, and given over by her owner to a child minder to be raised; Narcissus, her *tata*, was himself in all likelihood a slave. Two inscriptions from the *monumenta* of senatorial families (M2 and T7) would suit the pattern supplied by the inscription of Hermes, and one makes explicit the connection between *mamma* (at least in its diminutive form) and *nutrix*. It is obvious that Ser. Cornelia Ser. l. Sabina, "nutrix et mammula" of Ser. Cornelius Dolabella Metillianus, the consul of A.D. 113, was not the consul's mother; *mammula* here is essentially a refinement of *nutrix*.[30] This in turn explains the inscription (M28) of Flavia Euphrosyne, "mamma idem nutrix" of the boy P. Flavius Crescens, son of P. Flavius Amarantus. Euphrosyne was not Crescens's mother and nurse, but only his nurse—with that fact communicated through a particularly tender form of expression.[31]

However, as those last items imply, *tata* and *mamma* cannot be held to be pure synonyms for *nutritor* and *nutrix;* otherwise there is no point to a phrase like "mamma idem nutrix." A distinction must be observed, and it can be straightforwardly stated: *nutritor* and *nutrix* are functional terms, designating people who carried out a particular kind of work assigned to them, whereas *tata* and *mamma* are personal terms, expressing the existence of a social relationship between adult and child. The terms *tata* and *mamma,* that is to say, imply an emotional tie between adult and child, not the performance of work by an adult on behalf of a child.[32] Of course, it may well have been the case that in reality *tatae* and *mammae* did the same jobs and tasks as *nutritores* and *nutrices,* but they did not have the functional status of the latter because they were not functionaries. Thus, there is no need to distinguish between paid *nutrices* and unpaid foster mothers, because *mammae* would not have expected to receive compensation for their work (nor is it correct to believe that all *nutrices* were paid).[33] Their work, like that of *tatae,* was undertaken voluntarily. The way to put it, I think, is that a relationship between a *nutritor* or *nutrix* and a child would develop from the work chosen by or imposed upon the functional child minder, whereas work voluntarily performed by a *tata* or *mamma* would be the natural consequence of the preexisting social or emotional link with the child. In the former case, the development of intimacy was incidental and derivative; in the latter, it was primary and fundamental. *Tatae* and *mammae* were not the exact equivalents of *nutritores* and *nutrices.*

A further observation can be made. To historians of the family working in a social and intellectual climate where the nuclear family dominates modes of thought and analysis, it is natural to view the reproductive unit of father, mother, and children as a narrow, almost exclusive social entity, virtually cut off from external influences except insofar as those of, say, other relatives (grandparents, aunts, uncles, cousins) or of hired help may be approved and promoted by the father and mother themselves. If the core unit is disrupted, through spousal death or divorce, and reconstitution occurs following parental remarriage, it is also natural to think in terms of antagonism or tension between stepparents and children, or between divorced parents who still have claims on their common children. However, factors of this sort may not be entirely appropriate for understanding the Roman family. In the inscriptions that identify *tatae/ mammae* and biological parents there is, as far as can be told, no suspicion of any antagonism between the two sets of figures. Instead, there is a sense that in some manner the two sets of figures complement one another, both chronologically and emotionally, and that they have come to form, as it were, a parental community. A view of child rearing is thus perceptible not in which a role played by an unrelated adult is seen as threatening or problematical to the natural parent but in which a collaborative ethic prevails. This could be accounted for by simply taking the *tatae* and *mammae* to be nurses (male and female), but in view of the distinction emphasized above I find this inadequate. Consequently, circumstances have to be sought to make feasible the emergence of what might be styled a collaborative style of child rearing, which means returning to the topic of status and then trying to visualize the physical living conditions of the people represented in the inscriptions.

IV

In inscriptions identifying *nutritores* and *nutrices,* it is not unusual to uncover connections between child-minding figures and aristocratic children, and literary sources, of course, supply other examples. However, it is striking that in the inscriptions recording parents and *tatae* or *mammae,* there is no evidence of upper-class children at all. Rather, as pointed out earlier, the population is overwhelmingly lower-class in disposition and of no social eminence.[34] In the main, therefore, this population must be composed of individuals who either were members of slaveholders' *familiae* (slaves and former slaves) or belonged to the amorphous category of the free urban poor—shopkeepers, artisans, and tradespeople, people with sufficient means to pay for commemorative monuments certainly and even to own slaves of their own at times, but who were well below the tier of the elite. Many would have lived in *tabernae* and the poorer quarters of the *insulae;* they would have been people from whom men like Cicero drew rents without too great a concern for the quality of the facilities they provided.[35]

The master's house was the physical center of the lives of the members of his *familia.* The size of an individual complement of slaves at Rome could, of course, vary greatly, the normal range perhaps being illustrated by the Augustan *lex Fufia Caninia* on testamentary manumission which speaks of holdings from less than ten to up to five hundred slaves (and beyond).[36] Freedmen, freedwomen, and *alumni/ae* could add further to the numbers of dependents in the overall household. A wealthy Roman's domestics might be scattered over several residences (though some traveled with him from house to house). But no matter what its size, the household of slaves and former slaves was a socially dynamic community in which members were brought into a complex series of interpersonal relations by virtue of the fact that all occupied the same physical, domestic space. Those in the *familia* who, at the master's discretion, entered into marital unions and had children might have enjoyed in the slave quarters a semblance of familial privacy if housed in small cells of the type known from the plans of excavated villas and even gladiatorial barracks.[37] But the degree of such privacy was probably minimal, restricted perhaps to the hours of sleeping for the most part. The norm assumed by Columella for rural slaves was that life was organized on a communal basis, and there is no reason to think that the situation was any different for the urban household.[38] If, for example, the House of Sallust at Pompeii is taken as representative of upper-class housing in the first half of the central period of Roman history, the following remarks become very significant for present purposes:

> The street-door-fauces-atrium-tablinum-garden sequence is normal . . . and marks a progression from public to private space. Yet the formal axial arrangement, and the tendency to keep the door open, gave a certain public access deep into the house. What happened in the atrium was visible to the street, and the atrium marked a characteristic intersection of public and private affairs. Here the paterfamilias received his clients, and the family displayed busts of ancestors and reminders of its importance. . . . The atrium was the center of the family's world: the shrine of the family gods stood here . . . , and the house faced inward to this space where, ideally, the women of the household did their spinning and the children played, under the authoritative and benevolent gaze of the paterfamilias. His office (originally also his bedroom . . .) was the tablinum, which because of its slightly elevated position on the main axis of the house dominated everything that happened within the home. . . . Subordinated to the semipublic domain of the paterfamilias in tablinum and atrium were the dark little cubicula that served as bedrooms and individual sitting rooms and could be closed off with doors or curtains. Even here true privacy was difficult to find, though, for the slaves who were all over the house would be aware of comings and goings.[39]

In the world of the Roman house, the slave girl (*ancilla*) could be found sleeping in the same room as her mistress, the slave boy lying at his master's feet.[40] There may, under the Principate, have been on the owner's part a tendency to secure greater residential privacy, but the internal population of the house did not alter, and privacy for the domestic staff remained minimal.[41]

Thus, the servile family—the family as the reproductive core unit and as represented in many of the inscriptions here—was not usually situated in a physical setting that reinforced its nuclearity by separating it from other reproductive units. Instead, it was one of a multiplicity of units that were constantly intersecting, so that for many of their members there can have been little sense of rigid, impenetrable familial boundaries. This was also true of residents of the rented apartments in the *insulae*, buildings that were notoriously overcrowded (and insanitary) and that, again, could not provide the individual core family of parents and children with a physical area that sequestered them from other groupings. It was probably common, in fact, for one apartment to house several families simultaneously. For these people, therefore, many of whom are again represented by the personnel of the inscriptions, life was also lived in a much more open manner than in societies where the style of housing is matched to a familial unit small in composition:

> The layout of the insula made privacy a hard thing to find. The apartment itself might well be full of neighbors, since several unrelated individuals or small *familiae* might share a *cenaculum*, taking turns cooking in the *medianum*, trying not to violate the law by throwing refuse out of the window, and retiring for privacy or sleep into an individual *cubiculum*. The rituals of insula life must inevitably have been different from those in the aristocratic domus. Street noises probably penetrated even to the interior *cubicula* and made sleep difficult. . . .
>
> Life had an inevitably communal nature in such surroundings. People leaned out the windows and looked into the street and into other apartments. The courtyard was a focus of socialization. The windows were perhaps the most important characteristic—they opened the residence to the world outside.[42]

In circumstances such as these, a correlation should be expected between the prevailing communal ethos and the nature of familial life. And it ought to be possible to recognize that the absence of rigid boundaries for the core family brought children into constant contact with a range of other adults within their living space—their parents' coresidents, coworkers, and neighbors—who at times came to play within their lives a quasi-parental role, even though unrelated, and who in consequence assumed the affectionate titles of *tata* and *mamma*. I do not intend to suggest as a result that the link between parent and child was unimportant or to deny that such a link may have been the most significant social bond. But the familial world of lower-class Roman children could not possibly have been confined to or dominated by the limits of the core unit and immediate kin connections. Rather, the familial world of such children had an openness that matched the openness of the physical setting in which they found themselves, and it is on the basis of this social reality that the existence of *tatae* and *mammae,* alongside biological parents, becomes explicable.

V

The *tatae* and *mammae* definitely known not to be biological parents can then be defined as quasi-parental but unrelated figures (and not functionaries) whose informal role in the lives of children grew out of lower-class living arrangements and complemented, without injecting strain or tension, the role of the parents proper. The question that remains is whether this characterization can apply to the *tatae* and *mammae* in the inscriptions whose relationship to the children associated with them is indeterminate.

It is indisputable that the social profile of all the personnel in all the inscriptions is essentially the same: the lower-class orientation prevails throughout. True, a few *ingenui* or *ingenuae* are to be found: Claudia Ti. f. Quinta, the ward of C. Julius Hymetus (M1); C. Allius C.f. Verus (M8); Maria C.f. Castricia, *mamma* of T. Livius Primigenius (M36); C. Papirius C.f. Col. Romanus (M39); Quintia C.f. Prima (M41); L. Flavius L.f. Anien. Saturninus (T24). But there is nothing to indicate that these are anything but socially undistinguished men and women. As their exemplar—and that surely of many of those who can only be designated free—L. Apisius C.f. Scaptia Capitolinus can be brought forward. His full citizen nomenclature is impressive, but the elaborate monument on which it appears also carries his father's name, and he, unmistakably, was a freedman, C. Apisius C.l. Epaphra (T13). It is true, too, that gradations of juridical status are evident (there are some individuals who are definite slaves and some who are definitely freed), and in the real world these distinctions will have translated into gradations of social status. But the differences are not to be exaggerated. For even when inscriptions reveal *tatae* or *mammae* who were the patrons of the children associated with them, showing thereby that the former had been responsible for the latter's release from slavery, there is still nothing to suggest that the social distance between the manumitting and the manumitted was all that great. C. Vibius Tyrannus, for example, was the "patronus ide(m) tata" of C. Vibius Threptus (T1), Claudia Alexandria the "mamma et patrona" of Ti. Claudius Faustinus (M19), Julia Filete the "mamma et patrona" of Julia Aephyre (M32). But the acts of manumission that terminology of this sort implies do not connote the same kind of social gulf between owner and slave as that apparent in the emancipation of a figure such as, say, Cicero's slave Tiro.[43] The only time an aristocratic figure appears, in the person of the consul of A.D. 113, his *mamma,* or rather *mammula,* is his *nutrix,* a functionary who has assumed the familiar title after her work as a nurse has begun. It is the exception that proves the rule. Consequently, all these people can be presumed to have lived in the same kind of communal mode described above, and nothing forbids the conclusion that many, perhaps most, of the *tatae* and *mammae* on record in the inscriptions were persons biologically unrelated, and only related by sentiment, to the children they commemorated or who commemorated them.

However, it was seen at the outset that *tata* and *mamma* can have the meaning of father and mother, both in the inscriptions and in the definition of the terms Varro supplied. It is obviously erroneous, therefore, to try to impose a single meaning on the words. A certain flexibility has to be granted, and each usage is best considered in isolation. In the end, to be honest, it is difficult to avoid subjectivity when trying to interpret the inscriptional examples of the words. Nevertheless there is something of value to be learned from the words themselves. It must be allowed, on Varro's evidence, that the words had parental associations: their usage implies a fatherlike or motherlike figure, distinct from functional child minders. But the evidence shows that they were not at all restricted to actual fathers and mothers: they could be attached to persons with whom the children concerned had no kin connection. When Romans used the words, therefore, it was not important whether the persons designated *tata* or *mamma* were related to those associated with them or not; what mattered was the sentimental attachment, not the presence (or absence) of a kin association. The problem of defining the terms—as parent, grandparent, nurse, foster parent, or whatever—can thus be recognized as a modern problem resulting from the domination of the nuclear family in conceptualization and analysis. But it was evidently not an ancient problem.

In sum, the evidence on the words *tata* and *mamma* can only lead to a view of the lower-class Roman family as a social unit that was conceptually different from the predominant modern form, one that could incorporate more extensive links to unrelated persons living in close physical proximity. Children themselves could expect in their early years to fall under the influence of a variety of parenting figures, whose simultaneous contributions to the child were not competitive but commonly supportive. Many doubtless used the words *tata* and *mamma* of their parents or of those who informally complemented or, at times, replaced them. But in a physical setting where the child was located among a plurality of reproductive units, there was no fixed equation between *tata* and *mamma* on one hand and father and mother on the other. Instead, the way in which the terms were used reflected the mingling of reproductive units that was natural to the communal setting. On this view, the inherent importance of the tie between parent and child is not necessarily minimized but simply set within the wider framework of the historical Roman family.

Notes

1. Demos (1986), 62.
2. See Howell (1980), 313.
3. Varro, in Nonius, 81M ("Cato vel de liberis educandis"): "cum cibum ac potionem buas ac pappas vocent et matrem mammam, patrem tatam"; Martial, *Epigrams* 1.100, with Howell (1980), 312–14.
4. Persius 3.18: "et iratus mammae lallare recusas."
5. Reference numbers for the inscriptions can be found in the concordance that accompanies the table notes. The inscriptions themselves have been gathered from *CIL* 6 and *AE* (as appropriate). Information on inscriptions from elsewhere than Rome that refer to *tatae* and *mammae* appears with the concordance.
6. " . . .] ann. iii mensib. iiii diebus iiii fecerunt Fortis tata et Caenis mat. filiae."
7. "d.m. M. Servilio Adelfo patri et Salviae Syntyceni mammae Servandus filius b. m. f."
8. *CIL* 10.7564, 10.6432.
9. See Wilson (1910), 29; Weaver (1972), 131 n. 5. Cf. in contrast Dixon (1988), 147.
10. "d.m. Silviae vix. anni. iii mens. ii dieb. ix Claudius Protomachus et Claudia Damal filiae et Salonius Epictetus tata et Aphrodisia mamma fec."
11. Cf. Dixon (1984), 11.

12. "d.m.s. M. Gellio Helio amico optimo Restitutus publicus et Gellia Nymphidia suo coniugi karissimo et Gellia Florentina tatae pientissimo fecerunt."

13. "d.m. T. Minusius Eutycheti vix. an. iii men. x dieb. xxiiii Primitiva mat. et Januarius tata fecer."

14. See Tables 4.1 and 4.2, column 4: approximately one-quarter of the evidence as a whole. (Cf. Chapter 3, Appendix 3.1, section D.) As for other possibilities, observe the following:

1. T10: Two free men, Aelius Primus (dead at twenty-three) and Aelius Ingenuus (dead at twenty-four), are commemorated by their mother, Aelia Data, and their *tata,* Cornelius Atimetus. Aelia Data also commemorates her husband, Fructus, who appears to be a slave. Given that and the name Ingenuus, it is likely that Data was a freedwoman and Primus a freedman. Fructus, it could be assumed, was the father of Primus and Ingenuus, thus making Cornelius Atimetus an independent *tata.* This is the most plausible interpretation of the case but cannot, of course, be proved.

2. M9: A free woman, Pedania Primigenia, commemorates her *verna,* Ampliata, dead at four. Pedania appears to be addressed by Ampliata ("noli dolere mamma"). But as *mamma* she could be *mater* only if a slave manumitted after Ampliata's birth. Alternatively, a separate slave mother (*ignota*) for Ampliata could be inferred.

3. M48: A similar case: two *vernae,* Januaria and Felicia, commemorate their *mamma,* Valeria Helpis. Perhaps mother and daughters are indicated, the mother alone having been set free. But a separate slave mother (*ignota*) for the *vernae* could be postulated.

In T35, a free boy, C. Q. Hermias (dead at four), is commemorated by a free nurse, Quintia Parthenope, and a free *tata,* P. Farseleius Isidorus. A free husband, C. Q. Eufemus, also commemorates his wife, Aelia Tyche (dead at fourteen). It is likely that Eufemus was Hermias's father, thus making Isidorus an independent *tata;* cf. Bradley (1986), 229. In T38, I assume that the father of the commemorated girl, Terentia Spes, is understood in the word "parentes" and is separate from the *tata:* "fecerunt parentes pientissimi et avia et tata." Note should also be taken of a Dalmatian inscription, *CIL* 3.9740, in which a *tata* honors his patrons, a father and two sons, who have died simultaneously.

15. See Tables 4.1 and 4.2, columns 1, 3, 5, 7.

16. For comparable cases, note T11: Alexander, Marinus *pater,* Anthus *tata;* T18: Crescentilla *filia,* Crescens *pater,* Soteris *mater,* Epaphroditus *tata;* T32: Victor *filius,* Myrsine *mater,* Mercurius *pater,* Hilarus *tata.*

17. Claudius Protomachus and Claudia Damal. For comparable cases, note T20: Domitius Apollonius and Do. Fortunata; T33: C. Numisius Theseus and Numisia Urbica; M58: P. Mindius Vitalis and Mindia Zosime.

18. The following can also be noted. In T45, the *tata* of a Ti. Julius (his name is incomplete) is certainly a slave, and both *mamma* (Rhoxane) and *pater* (Terminalis) have single names only; the mother, Julia Euphrantice, is free, but it is surely right to judge son and mother freed slaves or close descendants of such. In M51, the free *mamma* of two imperial slaves, each a *verna* and married to the other, is commemorated. Unless brother and sister, which is unlikely, they cannot both have been the *mamma*'s offspring. See also the information on M44 in the table notes.

19. Cf. also the personnel of T5, T24, T39, T43.

20. A few more ages are given in inscriptions from Italian centers other than Rome. First, commemorated children:

	Reference	Y	M	D	Sex	Location
1	*CIL* 9.899	13	9		m	Luceria
2	*CIL* 14.899		10	3	f	Ostia
3	*CIL* 14.1674	2	3	13	m	Ostia
4	*CIL* 14.1674	1	11	27	f	Ostia
5	*CIL* 14.3844	12	7	15	m	Tibur

In no. 1, the child is commemorated by *mater* and *tata;* in no. 2 with *mamma;* in nos. 3 and 4 with *mater* (dead at twenty-two) by *tata;* in no. 5 by *tata.* Second, commemorated adults:

	Reference	Y	M	D	*T(ata/ M(amma)*	Location
1	*CIL* 10.2104	75			T*	Puteoli
2	*CIL* 10.2283	54	—	7	M	Puteoli
3	*CIL* 14.4033	90	3	2	T	Ficulea

(Note: In no. 1, the *tata* is *tatula.*) An incomplete age is given in T36. Ages also appear in T43, M50, and M51, but meanings are far from clear.

21. Dixon (1988), 147, associates the *mamma* with the child "probably after it had grown beyond infancy." But note the ages in T11 and T42 (and see also *CIL* 14.899 in the previous note).

22. T5, M5, T2, M24, M26, M40, M45, M31, M38, *CIL* 10.7564.

23. "Salvidiena Q.l. Hilara Salvidienae Faustillae deliciae suae eruditae omnibus artibus, reliquisti mammam tuam gementem plangentem plorantem, vix. an. xv mensib. iii dieb. xi hor. vii, virginem eripuit fatus malus, destituisti vitilla mea miseram mammam tuam."

24. Wilson (1912), 178 n. 101.

25. See M44 in the table notes. An *alumnus* commemorating his *mammula* is found in *CIL* 6.14347.

26. See above, Chapter 3.

27. T6 has Hermias *pater* and Hermes *tata;* T11 has Marinus *pater* and Anthus *tata;* T24 has Fl[. . .]hodus *pater* (= Flavius Euhodus?) and Phoebus *tata;* T26 has Q. Hortensi(us) Perpetu(us) *pater,* Communis *frater,* Ofellio *tata.*

28. *CIL* 9.899, a dedication to L. Vitorius Fortunatus, dead at thirteen, from Vitoria Briseis *matertera* and P. Tamullius Eros *tata.*

29. On T35, see above, n. 14.

30. M2 is from the Monumentum Marcellae, a dedication to his *mamma,* Flavia Zosime, from Agathermer[us]; T7 is from the Monumentum Statiliorum, a dedication to a boy aged seven by an anonymous *tata.* Note also from the Monumentum Marcellae a dedication to a *mammula, CIL* 6.4850; and on *CIL* 6.16450, cf. Bradley (1986), 227.

31. Cf. Bradley (1986), 228.

32. The assumption that *tata* and *mamma* were functional terms, comparable to *nutritor* and *nutrix,* dominates the discussion of Dixon (1988), 146–49.

33. Cf. Dixon (1988), 124.
34. This may simply be an accident of the evidence.
35. On Cicero, see Brunt (1974), 86; Shatzman (1975), 409–14.
36. On the size of slave holdings, see Bradley (1989b), 128.
37. See Bradley (1989b), 52–53, 87. Observe in this connection *CIL* 6.10057: "d.m. Aurelio Heraclide agitatori factionis venetae et doctori factioni s.s. et prasinae fecit M. Ulpius Apolaustianus tatulae b.m."
38. Columella, *On Agriculture* 12.3.8 (communal eating).
39. Stambaugh (1988), 164–65. See also on the House of Sallust, Richardson (1988), 109–11.
40. *Digest* 29.5.1.28, 29.5.14. Cf. Richardson (1988), 111, on the "houses of the rich" typified by the House of Sallust: "their deficiencies must have been made up for by a large number of servants, but for these there is no more place provided than there is for the animals. If they did not simply bed down on pallets wherever there was a convenient corner, the personal servants in the rooms of those they attended, the rest as best they might, then these, too, must have found their place in sheds in the hortus."
41. On increasing privacy, see Stambaugh (1988), 168–72.
42. Stambaugh (1988), 178. See also Frier (1977).
43. Note also the Dalmatian inscription *CIL* 3.9740 (above, n. 14). On Tiro, see Treggiari (1969), 259–63.

Table Notes

The following notes are intended to point out features of interest (or difficulty) in the inscriptions not brought out in the main text. The emphasis is on brevity.

T3. The commemorated *tata* C. Antonius Antoninus is described as a soldier "ex classe praetoria Misenatium." Cf. *CIL* 14.3632 (Tibur), where the commemorated *tata* L. Vibius Crescens is described as "vet. coh. iiii pr."

T9. Herennius Fortunatus *tata* and Herennia Rhodine *mamma* share a common *nomen* and were thus probably of servile background. The commemorated boy Primitivus was a *discens* of Q. Attius Hermes; on apprentices, see Chapter 5.

T12. The *tata* C. Considius Alcis was patron of the dedicant G. Considius Alcimus.

T14. The inscription is phrased a little oddly, but Aufidia Veneria, patron of Aufidia Favor, is probably to be understood as her *mamma* also.

T22. A fragmentary inscription, restored "A. Egrilio Fausto [alumno] carissimo A. Egri[lius] Hilario tata . . ." *CIL* 14.935 does not have "[alumno]."

T25. The *nomen* of Flavia Trophime is the same as that of her *tata* but differs from that of her patron (Ummidius); she was undoubtedly a freedwoman, but perhaps in actuality set free by a putative wife of the patron.

T27. A fragmentary inscription, but *tata* and *mamma* were both of servile status apparently, to judge from the single names as restored: "[Obseq]uenti [mam]mae [Aba]scanto tatae . . ."

T30. The *tata* M. Metilius Eupor dedicates to his patron Metilius Eros.

T31. A dedication to T. Minusius Eutyches, dead at three years, ten months, twenty-four days, from Primitiva *mat(er)* and Januarius *tata*. This must be the same dedication as

CIL 14.3355 (Praeneste), but note the reading: "d. m. L. Manusio Eutucheti vix. an. iii mens. x diebus xvi, Primitiva mat. etiam Arius tata fecer."

T47. The commemorated girl Manlia Niceph[oris] is described as "agens annum v" which I have simply taken as age five in Tables 4.3 and 4.4. She was commemorated by Helius *tata,* Manlia Modesta *mamma,* and Apollonius *nutricius.*

M4. The inscription simply gives two names: "C. Hostilius C.f. Chronius, Hostilia Philematio mamma." I take the latter as *mamma* of the former.

M17. Ti. Claudius Zosimus commemorates his patron Ti. Claudius Verecundus as well as his *mamma.*

M24. The *mamma* Domitia Palestrice (of Domitia Anicetiana) was also patron of Onesimus and Hermeros, who joined in the dedication to her.

M34. The inscription reads: "M. Junius Phepsi l. Philotecnus Juniae mamme contiber(n). suae"; it may be preferable to read "con[l]iber[tae]" and to take Junia as a freedwoman.

M44. The inscription identifies the following personnel:

1. Scetasia L.l Oecumen(e), the dedicant.
2. Scetasia L.l. Musa, *mamma* of 1 (commemorated).
3. [L. Scetasius, patron and former owner of 1 and 2].
4. L. Scetasius Sp. f. Celer, son of 1 (commemorated).
5. Larnia C. et Musa(e) l. Thais, mother of 1 (commemorated).
6. [C. Larnius, patron and former owner of 5].
7. C. Larnius C.f. Ste. Aquilia, heir of 1.

The separate identities of *mamma* and *mater* are clear, as too the servile background of most of the persons named. However, a difficulty is caused by the need to account for the particular *nomina* of the three women: the *nomen* of Oecumene is the same as that of her *mamma* but different from that of her *mater.* The following sequence of events can be hypothesized:

1. C. Larnius (6) and L. Scetasius (3) own the slaves Thais (5) and Musa (2), respectively (and separately).
2. Thais has a daughter, Oecumene (1), who is transferred (e.g., by sale) to the household of L. Scetasius.
3. Musa, manumitted by L. Scetasius, becomes the *mamma* of Oecumene, who is also manumitted by L. Scetasius.
4. C. Larnius marries Musa.
5. Musa has a son, C. Larnius C.f. Ste. Aquila (7).
6. C. Larnius manumits Thais.
7. Oecumene has an illegitimate son, L. Scetasius Sp. f. Celer (4).

On this reconstruction, Oecumene's heir will have been the son of her *mamma,* with whom she could have spent part of her childhood. But, as a variation, it might also be that C. Larnius was Oecumene's father (by a first marriage to Thais), which would make Aquila her half-brother and Muso her eventual stepmother.

Concordance of Inscriptions

T1	= *CIL* 6.	2334
T2	=	2371 (= *AE* 1980.93)
T3	=	3098
T4	=	5337
T5	=	5642
T6	=	5941
T7	=	6443
T8	=	6703
T9	=	10016
T10	=	10873
T11	=	11395
T12	=	11690
T13	=	12133
T14	=	12840
T15	=	13997
T16	=	15009
T17	=	16316
T18	=	16578
T19	=	16854
T20	=	16926 (= 26594)
T21	=	17046
T22	=	17133 (= 14.935)
T23	=	17217
T24	=	18196
T25	=	18450
T26	=	19552
T27	=	20632
T28	=	20863
T29	=	20930
T30	=	22460
T31	=	22564 (= 14.3355)
T32	=	22802 (+ 28906)
T33	=	23113
T34	=	23792
T35	=	25301
T36	=	25532 (= 19506)
T37	=	25636
T38	=	27259
T39	=	27964
T40	=	28592
T41	=	29424
T42	=	29634
T43	=	34206
T44	=	35323

M1	= *CIL* 6.	2210
M2	=	4567
M3	=	5040
M4	=	5425
M5	=	7726
M6	=	8021
M7	=	10016
M8	=	11487
M9	=	11592
M10	=	12019
M11	=	12321
M12	=	12366
M13	=	12771
M14	=	12840
M15	=	13831
M16	=	14720
M17	=	15326
M18	=	15345
M19	=	15439
M20	=	15507
M21	=	15585
M22	=	16043
M23	=	16926 (= 26594)
M24	=	17026
M25	=	17223
M26	=	17439
M27	=	17800
M28	=	18032
M29	=	19473
M30	=	20318
M31	=	20578
M32	=	20603
M33	=	20632
M34	=	20823
M35	=	21405
M36	=	22227
M37	=	23350
M38	=	23556
M39	=	23801
M40	=	25276
M41	=	25324
M42	=	25808
M43	=	26001
M44	=	26008

T45 =	35530		M45 =	27208
T46 =	36353		M46 =	27827
T47 =	38598		M47 =	27844
T48 =	38694		M48 =	28206
T49 = *AE*	1973.21		M49 =	28241a
			M50 =	28447
			M51 =	29116
			M52 =	29634
			M53 =	33538
			M54 =	35530
			M55 =	36353
			M56 =	37752
			M57 =	38598
			M58 =	38638a
			M59 =	38769
			M60 =	38891
			M61 = *AE*	1988.89

OVERLAPS

T9 = M7
T14 = M14
T20 = M23
T27 = M33
T42 = M52
T45 = M54
T46 = M55
T47 = M57

Tatae and *Mammae*
Attested Elsewhere Than at Rome

Tatae			*Mammae*		
CIL	9.899	(Luceria)	*CIL*	9.1314	(Aeclanum)
	9.5228	(Asculum)		9.4881	(Trebula)
	10.2156	(Puteoli)		9.5228	(Asculum)
	10.2918	(Puteoli)		9.5341	(Cupra Maritima)
	10.3026	(Puteoli)		10.2283	(Puteoli)
	14.1143	(Ostia)		10.3942	(Capua)
	14.1674	(Ostia)		14.577	(Ostia)
	14.3384	(Praeneste)		14.899	(Ostia)
	14.3632	(Tibur)		14.1046	(Ostia)
	14.3844	(Tibur)		14.1118	(Ostia)
	3.9740	(Dalmatia)		8.23060	(Africa)
	10.7564	(Sardinia)		8.27696	(Africa)

	12.452	(Narbonensis)		10.7564	(Sardinia)
	12.884	(Narbonensis)	AE	1971.206	(Spain)
			AE	1975.463	(Sardinia)

	Tatulae			*Mammulae*	
CIL	6.9818		CIL	6.4850	
	6.10057			6.14347	
	6.16926	(= 26594)		6.16450	
	6.21854			6.20909	
	6.25636			6.21910	
	10.2104	(Puteoli)		6.24329	
	12.3518	(Narbonensis)		3.3601	(Pannonia)
				3.12896	(Dalmatia)
				8.15699	(Africa)
				10.6432	(Circeii)
				14.1729	(Ostia)
			AE	1946.140	(Rome)

5

Child Labor in the Roman World

*W*hen a son was born to parents of aristocratic status in Rome of the central period, it can be assumed that the child's early years were spent in relative ease and comfort. By definition, as the boy was educated and groomed to take his eventual place among the ranks of his social peers in the public life of the community, his material needs were automatically met, so that economic hardship and deprivation were largely unknown to him. The same was true for a daughter, though for the most part all she had to look forward to as an adult was marriage to a man of appropriate standing and the bearing of children for him. By contrast, the vast majority of children in Roman society were denied the benefits of upper-class life, and while their early years may also have been a preparation for adulthood, the nature of that process was very different. My purpose here is to examine some of the circumstances under which children outside the aristocracy were prepared for adulthood, particularly through analysis of information on child labor in Roman society. But first, to clarify the upper-class situation and to provide a point of comparison for the experiences of less privileged children, I begin with a synopsis of the early life of Cicero's son Marcus, a case history that is well documented because of the survival of Cicero's private correspondence.[1]

After the joyful announcement of his birth, probably in the late summer of 65 B.C., little is heard of the young Marcus in Cicero's letters until 58, when Cicero was in exile and Marcus became an object of increasing reference.[2] At that time Cicero evidently missed his son and was full of self-recrimination over the abandonment of his family.[3] But in the event

Cicero's enforced absence from Rome and the confiscation of his property it entailed had no significant impact on Marcus's upbringing. Consequently the various stages of Marcus's education and entry into the public world can be clearly seen.

As early as April of 59 B.C., before he was six years old, Marcus had been taught by Aristodemus of Nysa, a man who had also acted as tutor to the son of Cn. Pompeius; but three years later it is likely that he was under the supervision of the learned scholar Tyrannio of Amisus, who was in Cicero's household in 56 and who certainly then tutored Marcus's cousin Quintus.[4] Cicero himself could take a personal hand in his son's education when opportunity allowed, though by 54 a third tutor is in evidence in the figure of Atticus's freedman M. Pomponius Dionysius.[5] Dionysius served as teacher to Marcus and Quintus for several years, and he accompanied father and son during Cicero's governorship of Cilicia in 51–50. The eastern expedition, it may be presumed, must have been something of an event for Marcus, then about fifteen, including visits to, among other places, Athens and Ephesus and a winter sojourn with the princeling Deiotarus of Galatia.[6] After the return to Italy, the early months of 49 were a difficult period for Cicero. He contemplated sending Marcus to Greece but abandoned the idea, and instead Marcus assumed the toga of manhood at Arpinum in April of 49 (it was impossible then for Cicero to enter Rome). A letter written to Atticus the following month betrays an affection on Cicero's part perhaps occasioned by the event as well as the crisis in the political world.[7]

When Cicero left Italy in June of 49 B.C. to join Pompeius's forces in Greece, he was again accompanied by Marcus, who now experienced military service for the first time.[8] Two years later Cicero considered sending Marcus to Caesar in order to intervene in a dispute with his brother Quintus, caused by the latter's vilification of him, but again he changed his mind.[9] In 46, Marcus became aedile at Arpinum, doubtless through his father's influence, and although toward the end of the year he wished to join Caesar in Spain, by 45 he was journeying eastward once more, to resume his studies at Athens.[10]

Thus, by the time he was twenty, Marcus had been exposed to the finest of private teachers for the initial stages of his education, a direct result of Cicero's concern for his son's upbringing and of his ability, despite the vicissitudes of politics, to draw consistently on the services of tutors of established reputation. Marcus had also traveled extensively in the Mediterranean, and through holding municipal office and his involvement in the war between Pompeius and Caesar, he had made something of an entry into the world of public events. Even if the military command Marcus held under Pompeius when he was only sixteen was little more than honorific, the dangers and excitement of Pharsalus can scarcely have failed to make an impression.

Cicero's personal concern for his son's development is easily detectable in his correspondence, but it is difficult to measure the degree or nature of the sentiment he felt for Marcus. There are hints that the attachment was strong. Little should be made of two references to the boy in Cicero's speeches, where the orator drew on family relationships for rhetorical effect.[11] But in a letter to Atticus from 60 B.C., Marcus is called "my darling," and in letters to his brother Quintus and his wife Terentia from the exile period, Cicero styles his son "my charming, darling little boy" and "my darling child."[12] In spite of Cicero's frantic state of mind at that time, there can be no doubt about his feelings for Marcus when separated from him. Cicero could see in Marcus a worldly awareness—"Too wise for his years, the poor child already understood what was going on" (words written in 58)—an awareness perhaps more imagined than real, for Marcus was only five when the observation was made; while by 51 the child could be described as "a model of good behaviour and engaging manners."[13] On the other hand, Cicero was not blind to the growth of a tendency in Marcus toward what looks like laziness or rebelliousness when they were in Cilicia.[14] But all in all, it seems safe to say that Cicero was devoted to his son. Indeed, the letters to Atticus that belong to the period when Marcus was studying in Athens illustrate Cicero's overindulgence of Marcus, for whom as a student no expense was spared; and when mixed reports came in of his academic progress, Cicero's affectionate response was to believe the best of his son regardless and to contemplate no more than a personal visit by way of correction.[15] Late in 44, when Cicero wrote the *De Officiis,* it seemed appropriate, he said, to address the work to Marcus, for whom in the following summer, a few months before his death, he was looking to secure a priesthood.[16]

In spite of his educational opportunities and preparation for public life, all set in the context of great wealth and parental commitment, Marcus ultimately was never to emulate his father's achievements. But there is no need to follow Marcus's career further beyond his father's death, for the aim has simply been to sketch the style of life he enjoyed as a boy and young man. Although one may wonder about his emotional response to growing up in the shadow of the consul of 63 B.C., Marcus's lack of distinction cannot be attributed to any lack of material advantage in early life.

Material ease also surrounded the lives of girls and young women in upper-class Roman society, though the prospects they faced as adults were far more restricted than those of upper-class boys. The portrait of Minicia Marcella given by the younger Pliny illustrates the norm.[17] Minicia was the daughter of Pliny's close friend C. Minicius Fundanus, consul in A.D. 107, and of Statoria Marcella.[18] She died prematurely, in her early teens, but it is evident that she spent her life in comfort and security. Pliny makes clear that as a child she had been attended by a retinue of nurses, pedagogues, and teachers, and when she was sick private doctors had been at her disposal. When she died, Minicia was on the point of marrying a young man of suitable social rank, and an elaborate wedding had been anticipated. As it happened, "the money . . . intended for clothing, pearls and jewels" had "to be spent on incense, ointment and spices" for Minicia's burial.[19] But, despite the tragic outcome, the girl, as a child, had been properly prepared to enter the adult mode of life appropriate to her station.

Paradigms of upper-class childhood can thus be safely established. But what of childhood in other sectors of Roman society? One method of investigation is to examine evidence on work performed by children outside the aristocracy, because by its nature such activity suggests a set of experiences totally distinct from those of Marcus Cicero and Minicia Marcella. Various items of information can be pieced together from literary, legal, and inscriptional sources, but a significant body of evidence to which attention is worth directing first consists of apprenticeship documents from Roman Egypt, for this material provides a coherent body of information on several themes. The observations that follow derive from a survey of some thirty documents, covering the first three centuries of the imperial period, in which, typically, a child is handed over for a specific interval of time to a master craftsman in order to learn the craftsman's trade. The information they contain is summarized in Table 5.1.[20]

Table 5.1. Apprenticeship Summary*

	Apprentice	Trade	Reference	Provenance	Date	Duration
1	Free male	Nail making	BGU 1124	Alexandria	18 B.C.	6 mos. (?)
2	Male slave	Flute playing	BGU 1125	Alexandria	13 B.C.	1 yr.
3	Female slave	Weaving	P. Mich. V 346a	Tebtunis	A.D. 13	2 yrs. 6 mos.
4	Free male	Building	P. Mich. V 346b	Tebtunis	16	6 yrs.
5	Free male	Weaving	P. Oxy. 322 descr.	Oxyrhynchus	36	2 yrs.
6	Free male	Weaving	P. Mich. II 121 R II 8	Tebtunis	42	5 yrs.
7	Free male	Linen weaving	P. Fouad 37	Oxyrhynchus	48	2 yrs.
8	Free male	Weaving	P. Mich. III 170	Oxyrhynchus	49	—
9	Free male	Weaving	P. Osl. III 141	Karanis	50	—
10	Free male	Weaving	P. Wisc. 4	Oxyrhynchus	53	1 yr.
11	Free male	Weaving	P. Mich. III 171	Oxyrhynchus	58	—
12	Free male	Mat weaving	PSI 1132	Talei	61	—
13	Free male	Weaving	P. Mich. III 172	Oxyrhynchus	62	—
14	Free male	Copper smithing	PSI 871	Oxyrhynchus	66	—
15	Free male	Weaving	P. Oxy. 275	Oxyrhynchus	66	1 yr.
16	Free male	Weaving	P. Oxy. 2971	Oxyrhynchus	66	2 yrs. 6 mos.
17	Free male	Weaving	P. Tebt. 442	Tebtunis	113	2–3 yrs.
18	Free male	Weaving	P. Tebt. 385	Tebtunis	117	2 yrs.
19	Female slave	Weaving	SPP XII 40	Soknopaiou Nesos	150	1 yr. 2 mos.
20	Male slave	Shorthand	P. Oxy. 724	Oxyrhynchus	155	2 yrs.
21	Free male	Weaving	P. Vars. SN7	Tebtunis	170	3 yrs.
22	Free male	Weaving	P. Oxy. 725	Oxyrhynchus	183	5 yrs.
23	Male slave	Weaving	P. Grenf. II 59	Soknopaiou Nesos	189	1 yr. 8 mos.
24	Female slave	Weaving	P. Oxy. 1647	Oxyrhynchus	C2nd	4 yrs.
25	Female slave	Weaving	PSI 241	Antinoopolis	C2nd–C3rd	1 yr.
26	Male slave	Wool carding	P. Oxy. 2977	Oxyrhynchus	239	5 yrs.
27	Free male	Linen weaving	P. Oxy. 2586	Oxyrhynchus	253	4 yrs.
28	Female slave	Weaving	P. Mich. Inv. 5191a	Karanis	271	1 yr.
29	Free male	Building	P. Oxy. 2875	Oxyrhynchus	C3rd	3 yrs.
30	Male slave	Wool carding	BGU 1021	Oxyrhynchus	C3rd	3 yrs.

*See Table Notes at the end of this chapter.

II

One of the most frustrating features of the evidence is that it is difficult for the most part to fix the ages of the apprentices when they began to be trained. Obviously the very fact that the material concerns apprentices implies the training of young people, but it is unfortunate that a precise age is given in only one example, that of a fourteen-year-old slave girl, Nike, who was apprenticed to a weaver in Antinoopolis.[21] Since Nike was to be trained only for one year, it might be expected that by the age of fifteen she would be able to work independently though still, by modern standards, young for full-time work. Estimates of ages, however, can be obtained in various ways. For example, when a certain Tasooukios apprenticed her son for five years to a weaver in Tebtunis in A.D. 42, she agreed to pay the required poll tax on the boy; since the poll tax was levied only once boys in Egypt reached the age of fourteen, it must be assumed that Papontos, the son, was near his fourteenth birthday (when guardianship usually ended) at the time his mother made apprenticeship arrangements for him.[22] Moreover, some of the documents specify that the apprentice was a minor when the period of training began, a fact that is usually taken to mean that the apprentice was younger than fourteen, though how much younger it is impossible to tell.[23] All but one of the apprentices on record have their arrangements made on their behalf by a third party (a parent or slave owner most commonly), which again suggests for free apprentices at least that they were too young to enter into contractual obligations independently. The exception is provided by the case of Aurelios Zoilos, a building apprentice who engaged himself to his instructor in his own right and who presumably was no longer a minor.[24] Yet his mother gave her approval to the terms he made, as if she were negotiating for him, and in all probability Zoilos was not much older than fourteen.[25]

It seems safe to say, therefore, that apprentices generally began their training at about the age of twelve or thirteen, perhaps earlier at times. Variations are, of course, to be expected. More importantly, however, given the fact that the child when apprenticed was usually not acting independently, it seems likely that the choice of an occupation was a decision made not by the child but by the person who legally contracted on his or her behalf. A certain compulsion in children's lives can thus be glimpsed, of which other signs will appear later.

Within the documents three categories of apprentices can be distinguished: males who were freeborn, males who were slaves, and females who were slaves. Freeborn girls do not appear at all, and that is a detail of some significance, for it implies that daughters in artisanal families, like their counterparts in upper-class society at Rome, may not normally have been trained for work other than that of a traditional, domestic sort, but were instead prepared only for marriage and childbearing in the seclusive manner typical of women's life in antiquity as a whole.[26] In a broader Roman context, there is evidence of women working in jobs, particularly wet-nursing and midwifery, but when free women are seen in trades or crafts or shopkeeping, it is usually as assistants to men engaged in the same pursuits or as substitutes for husbands who had died.[27]

As prospective heads of families, it was essential that free boys be provided with the means to guarantee themselves a livelihood in their maturity, and in the short term their earnings might supplement their parents' income. In this context, the circumstances of Pausiris, a weaver from Oxyrhynchus who lived in the middle of the first century A.D., are especially interesting, because again they suggest a coercive element in the lives of children as far as choice of occupations is concerned. Pausiris had three sons—Ammonios, Dioskos, and Pausiris—all of whom became apprentice weavers.[28] Presumably the father himself could have taught his sons his trade, and indeed he is known to have had at least one apprentice of his own.[29] But there must have been something to be said in favor of the sons being instructed by other teachers, for Ammonios and Dioskos both went to the weaver Apollonios, and the younger Pausiris went to the weaver Epinikos, who, it happens, was the uncle by marriage of the elder Pausiris's own apprentice. The typicality of this family's arrangements is hard to judge, but something of an hereditary quality to job selection is indicated, a factor that can only have impeded any possibility of real social advancement in young boys' lives.[30] The case of a boy named Fuscus, who was apprenticed to a linen weaver but whose father was a Roman legionary veteran, seems highly unusual.[31]

If they were to become profitable commodities for their owners, slaves of both sexes might well expect to be trained in a craft. But the kinds of work performed by attested slave apprentices were not peculiar to their servile status. It happens that all the recorded female slave apprentices were engaged in weaving, but that is probably an accident of the documentary information, for adult slave women did not work exclusively as weavers.[32] Nevertheless their training in a specific occupation, when contrasted with the absence of apprenticeship training for free girls, is an important confirmation that slave children were regarded very differently from free children. Since their servile status denied them any of the considerations that applied to free girls, slave girls, as workers, could find their lives subject to manipulation just as much as slave boys.

The range of occupations attested by the documentary evidence is fairly extensive, but most of the records concern engagement of apprentices in the textile industry. It is doubtful that the information available is copious enough to allow for statistical inferences to be drawn, but the high proportion of cases involving weaving, linen weaving, and wool carding (24 out of 30) must reflect the prevalence of textile work in Egypt generally.[33] However, all the occupations on record—weaving and related jobs, nail making, copper smithing, music, shorthand, building—comprise what can be called skilled work. It will appear later that children elsewhere could be put to work in unskilled jobs, but predictably evidence of such is not to be found in the records of apprenticeship.

The documents tell little of the physical conditions under which the apprentices worked. They give information on the provision of food and clothing and at times payment of wages, even to slave apprentices, as in this example:

> And for the first two years and for seven months of the third year Heraklas shall pay no wages for the boy, but in the remaining five months of the third year said Heraklas shall pay as wages of the said apprentice 12 drachmas a month, and in the fourth year likewise for wages 16 drachmas a month, and in the fifth year likewise 24 drachmas a month; and Heraklas shall furnish to the said apprentice in the current twenty-fourth year a tunic worth 16 drachmas, and in the coming twenty-fifth year a second tunic worth 20 drachmas, and in the twenty-sixth year likewise another tunic worth 24 drachmas, and in the twenty-seventh year another tunic worth 28 drachmas, and in the twenty-eighth year likewise another tunic worth 32 drachmas.[34]

Details of this sort imply that the material lives of the apprentices were well worth favorable consideration, not least perhaps because of their potential future value as skilled workers. But one detail suggests that the period of apprenticeship was rather rigorous in some respects, namely the occasionally found stipulation that the apprentice is to work all day long, "from sunrise to sunset." The stipulation appears, for example, in the records for three slave apprentices—Thermuthion, Didymos, and Ptolemaios—and for two free apprentices—Thonis and the son of Aurelios Hermias.[35] By any standards, to work from sunrise to sunset is to work a long day, so perhaps for those children beginning their terms of apprenticeship the transition from childhood to the adult world of work came abruptly. Yet, as with other kinds of contractual evidence, it is difficult to tell how strictly provisions were enforced.

On the other hand, some documents specify that apprentices are to be given holidays, eighteen days a year, twenty days a year, three days a month.[36] In one instance, it has been suggested that an apprentice was given holidays at festival times because of his relatively high social standing. The son of Aurelios Hermias, a linen-weaving apprentice from

Oxyrhnchus, was the grandson of an *agoranomos,* and his teacher, Aurelios Dioskoros, used the more impressive title *epistates* rather than the commonplace *didaskalos.*[37] But such factors are not in evidence in other cases. Indeed, holidays might be completely excluded if a contract specified that days lost to illness or for any other reason had to be made up by the apprentice.[38]

The recorded periods of apprenticeship extend from a minimum of perhaps six months to a maximum of six years. The length of the training period was presumably controlled by several considerations. If an apprentice had already acquired some expertise in a craft before formal training began (as might be imagined for the sons of Pausiris) or if a parent or slave owner judged that an apprentice could be expected to learn quickly, then a short period of instruction may have been all that was necessary. Conversely, a longer period may have been needed for a slower child or for specialized instruction such as in linen weaving. It may be possible, too, to posit a connection between the age of a child when apprenticeship began and the duration of the training period. The slave girl Nike was apprenticed only for one year, perhaps because she was at the relatively advanced age of fourteen when she became an apprentice.[39] It is difficult to see why longer periods were required to acquire similar skills—if a generally standard rate of aptitude among children is assumed—unless apprentices were much younger than fourteen when instruction began. But the evidence as a whole is too fragile to substantiate this guess; and, as seen already, the apprentice Papontos, who was to train for five years, was close to fourteen when he began to learn weaving [40]

All in all, the documentary evidence on apprenticeship from Roman Egypt offers a very different picture of childhood life from the upper-class paradigms outlined earlier. At the age when Marcus Cicero, accompanied by his personal tutor, was traveling in the eastern Mediterranean, anticipating further periods of leisured study abroad and entry into the mainstream of Roman politics, slave children and boys of the artisanal class in Egypt could expect to undergo training in a job that would probably occupy them for the rest of their lives. Economic constraints dictated that they should begin to work, at about the age of twelve or so, in trades and even in places not necessarily of their own choosing, and while the skills they acquired may have been economically beneficial, they were not likely to lead to significant social improvement.[41] The pursuit of a craft, which could involve a long working day, may admittedly have given apprentices an advantage over other children in lower-class society who were not considered suitable for or capable of formal apprenticeship. But the process of learning, in the preteen and teenage years, effectively closed off to apprentices other kinds of "educational" experiences enjoyed by the children of the socially elite.

III

The evidence on apprenticeship from Roman Egypt is localized, in a very obvious sense. To what extent, therefore, can it be taken to represent the lives of children outside the elite sector of society in the Roman world at large?

One source of information that displays a great deal of consistency with the impressionistic picture just given is provided by the *Somnium* (*The Dream*) of Lucian of Samosata, supposedly an autobiographical account of how Lucian, toward the middle of the second century A.D., came to choose a life of serious literary study over an artisanal craft.[42] When Lucian left school in his teens, his father and his father's friends discussed Lucian's future, and, since the family's means were too modest to support a period of higher education, they decided to have Lucian trained in a handicraft. The advantages were that the young apprentice's immediate income would relieve the family budget and allow him some independence. Because sculpture, or stonemasonry, was a family trade—Lucian had two uncles and a grandfather in the business—this was the craft Lucian was to learn. But he spent only one day as an apprentice. Having been handed over to one of his uncles for instruction, he broke a slab of stone with a chisel, suffered a beating as a result, and ran home for comfort to his mother. There followed a vision, after which Lucian devoted his energies to culture rather than sculpture.[43]

"Lucian's painful and abortive experience as an apprentice sculptor . . . is credible and unimportant," it has been said.[44] But perhaps that remark should be amended to credible and of considerable importance, because the similarity of detail between Lucian's account and the Egyptian documentary record is striking. The concern in a family of modest wealth to increase its income through setting a child to work; the lack of choice available to the child as his life's occupation is selected for him; the child's subordination to parental authority; the decision to train the child in an hereditary craft; and the hint of severity accompanying apprenticeship are all details that either confirm or complement the Egyptian material, suggesting, albeit in a small way, that the prospects for a child of nonaristocratic status in second-century Syria were essentially the same as those of the apprentices in Egypt.[45] The only unusual aspect of Lucian's experience—and there is no way of judging its typicality—is his rejection of the norm.

Moreover, there are isolated pieces of evidence in a variety of Roman sources that, while being less detailed that Lucian's account, also imply that children, and especially boys, were regularly trained for specific occupations.

The evidence from Roman law can be noted first. Several texts from the *Digest* refer in broad terms to the training (*disciplina*) given to slaves, sample occupations being those of painter (*pictor*), copyist (*librarius*), and dresser (*ornatrix*).[46] Presumably these slaves could be of any age when they were taught, since some—those acquired as war captives, for instance—might well have been adults by the time they learned a trade. So, in the hypothetical but surely realistic legal example of the smith who bought and trained a slave and then sold him for double the purchase price, it is impossible, strictly speaking, to tell whether the apprentice was young or old.[47] But other items leave no doubt. The law allowed claims for *operae* against a freed child, "if he happens to be a copyist [*librarius*] or someone who calls out names [*nomenclator*] or if he is an actor or some kind of entertainer."[48] The *nomenclator* and the actor (*histrio*) could be expected to be below the age of puberty (*impubes*).[49] And both boys and girls were commonly put in charge of shops (*tabernae*).[50] The *discipuli* of the launderer (*fullo*) who might be left to supervise the laundry in the master's absence can then be reasonably regarded as children, as can those taught the cobbling trade by the cobbler (*sutor*).[51]

The literary evidence is equally suggestive. Vitruvius, for example, early in the age of Augustus, looked back on a long tradition of children being taught the artisanal skills of architecture within the craftsman's family, and Cicero mentions the *discipuli* of the slave engineer Cillo, who was in charge of an irrigation project at Quintus Cicero's house at Bovianum in 54 B.C.[52] Apprentice cooks appear in the plays of Plautus.[53] Martial gives a lament for a slave barber named Pantagathus who died, fully trained, as a boy (doubtless he would once have used a blunted training razor of the sort known to Petronius).[54] Apuleius has boys and girls appearing as dancers in his depiction of a ballet in Corinth.[55] Aulus

Gellius tells of an Attic slave boy, no more than eight years old, who waited at table in the house of the philosopher Taurus in Athens and ran errands (to buy oil, for instance).[56] When speaking of practices in the Centumviral court, the younger Pliny complains that his *nomenclatores* had been offered cash to serve as claqueurs; they would only just have attained the age of majority had they been citizens, he says, which means that they were probably around the age of fourteen.[57] Plutarch wrote, finally, of the elder Cato that he "used to lend money . . . to those of his slaves who wished it, and they would buy boys with it, and after training and teaching them for a year, at Cato's expense, would sell them again. Many of these boys Cato would keep for himself."[58] They could always be used meantime as messengers.[59]

This evidence shows children associated with a broad range of handicrafts and services. But children's occupations can be extended further still if rural work is taken into account. Training for farm work may not have required a great deal of formal apprenticeship. But, again, odd items of information, chiefly from the Roman agricultural writers, bolster the impression that children commonly began to work at an early age. Varro says that both boys and girls were capable of tending animals, and at one point he refers to a *servulus* in charge of donkeys.[60] Columella, in making recommendations on how to choose a *vilicus,* says that the bailiff should be a man inured to hard work since childhood, and as specific jobs for children he mentions supervision of poultry, trimming and pruning in the vineyard, and cutting down ferns with a sickle.[61] Lucius the ass, in Apuleius, is at one stage of his adventures assigned to the charge of a slave boy whose job it is to chop wood and bring it down from the mountainside.[62] Perhaps, therefore, the simple task of gathering apples can be added as a job appropriate for a girl, to judge from a poetic text; and there should, of course, be no doubt about the presence of female slave children on farms, so that again it is only freeborn girls who do not clearly emerge in work contexts.[63]

The literary evidence has the particular benefit that it shows children at work across time. Throughout the central period of Roman history, from Plautus early in the seond century B.C. to Apuleius and Aulus Gellius late in the second century A.D., writers of both imaginative and practical forms of literature took it for granted that their readers would find nothing disturbing or incredible in their allusions to children at work. Inscriptions, however, provide the most authentic evidence on child labor, for it is in epitaphs commemorating the dead that actual children and the jobs they did can be seen. The diversity of jobs attested in inscriptions is again great. Boys appear, variously slave or free, apprentices (*discentes*) or fully trained, as stonemasons, mirror makers, smiths, gold and silver workers, painters, mosaicists, bakers, stewards, accountants, ornamental gardeners, shopkeepers, and entertainers; there is even someone who seems to have been an apprentice shipping merchant.[64] Slave girls appear mainly in domestic roles, as maidservants (*ancillae*), attendants (*pedisequae*), and dressers (*ornatrices*).[65] The evidence on child entertainers provides a convenient illustration of the geographical range of the inscriptional evidence. From Rome there is the dancer (*saltator*) C. Asinius Olympus, who died at the age of eleven; the dancer (*saltatrix*) [J]ulia Nemesis, who died at the age of nine; the mime Adaugenda, who died at the age of ten; and the interlude artist (*emboliaria*) Phoebe, who died aged twelve. Phoebe may have originated from Gallia Narbonensis and doubtless grew up in slavery. Most of the child entertainers, whether kept by private owners or belonging to traveling companies, were slaves or of slave stock. The inscriptions disclose them in Centuripe in Sicily, Carthage in North Africa, Antipolis in Gallia Narbonensis, Corinth in Greece, Ephesus in Asia, Side in Pamphylia. Thyas, for example, was a *saltatrix* who was commemorated at Carthage; she died at the age of fourteen and had been the slave of a prosperous owner, Metilia Rufina. The person who commemorated her was her fiancé, a certain Thalamus. Another dancer, Septentrio, known from Antipolis, died at the age of twelve.[66]

Such ages at death are typical of many child workers. The *calculator* Melior, a home-born slave, had acquired great expertise in his job by the time of his death at thirteen.[67] The slave boy Pagus, who died at twelve, was similarly distinguished as a jeweler; he was fondly remembered by his owner and his parents.[68] The silver engraver C. Valerius (Dioph)-anes, known from an epitaph from Spain, died at eleven; the painter C. Vettius Capitolinus, from Rome, died at thirteen.[69] Among girls, the *pedisequa* Logas died at sixteen, the *ancilla* Theotime at fifteen, the *ornatrices* Sperata, Anthis, and Pieris at thirteen, twelve, and nine.[70] Also nine when she died was the gold worker (*auri nextrix*) Viccentia.[71] A passage in the *Code of Justinian* indicates that slaves were often working by the age of ten, and one in the *Digest* suggests that children could generally be at work at the age of five.[72] That may seem incredibly young. But the child entertainer Paridion, known from Pamphylia, was precisely five when he died, while three brothers commemorated at Rome as acrobats (*gymnici*) died when two were five and the third was seventeen months.[73]

Altogether, then, it seems inescapable that lower-class children in Roman society were set to work from the earliest moment they were considered capable of acquiring skills and becoming productive. Children were regarded as a precious commodity.[74] Once stated, such a conclusion may seem virtually self-evident. But the fact, or posited fact, of widespread child labor is a facet of Roman social and economic history that, as far as I know, has received scant attention. However, the impact of children on the labor force as a whole must have been great, and, from the viewpoint of the children themselves, exposure to the adult world of work must have arrived quickly in the lives of the majority. The period of apprenticeship or training may at times have led to the formation of a close bond between master and apprentice, to judge from epitaphs set up one to another, and such a process would perhaps have tempered the child's entry into the world of adulthood. One inscription, commemorating the dead apprentice Florentius, records that his master had loved the boy more than if he had been his own son.[75] Certainly, horror stories of the type familiar from the age of the Industrial Revolution in England, when children of both sexes were often brutishly treated, are not rampant in the Roman record.[76] But it should not be quietly assumed that working conditions were always benign. After all, the overall information is negligible in volume and quality, the case of Lucian has to be recalled, and the detail noted that lawyers could debate the liability of a cobbler who blinded his incompetent apprentice by striking him with a last.[77] At the least, the constraints imposed on children by the demands of labor and the kinds of work they did meant that their futures were generally fixed from very early stages of their development.

IV

When any generalization about economic behavior in the Roman world is made, it has to be remembered that many regional variations appeared in the sundry areas of which that world was composed.[78] Nevertheless it would seem reasonably safe to explain the prevalence of child labor by the simple expedient that lower-class families had to provide themselves with supplemental income through their children as quickly as possible or, in the case of labor expended by slave children, that slave owners wished to capitalize on property at their disposal as quickly as possible. However, it may be possible to appreciate such simple needs better by placing them within a social context broad enough to have general applicability throughout the Roman world, even as the dangers of easy generalization are kept in mind.

One point that deserves emphasis is the fact that throughout Greco-Roman antiquity there existed a convention of reciprocal obligations between parents and children: "it was natural that parents should beget, rear and educate children, and it was natural that children in return should honour and obey parents, give them material and psychological support, including grandchildren, comfort in old age, and burial."[79] Among Roman authors, the notion of children fulfilling obligations to parents is visible, for example, in Cicero and Seneca.[80] But perhaps the clearest expression of the material aspect of such obligations is to be found, for Roman society in a broad sense, in Plutarch's essay *On Affection for Offspring,* where Plutarch argues that human affection for children is a natural emotional response and (contrary to the view of Epicurus) that human procreation is not dictated by hope of material return.[81] The argument presupposes that a significant proportion of parents did indeed look to their children for material return, as well as for general consolation, especially in old age. For the rich, dependence on children for support in later years is never likely to have been crucial, and it was with the rich that Plutarch was chiefly concerned. He has little to say, both here and in the essay *The Education of Children,* about the poor, simply advocating that poor children should receive something of an education, but recognizing, too, that poverty was an inducement to infanticide.[82] However, at the levels of society represented by the apprentices and other working children described earlier, it has to be understood that many parents were compelled, through their children, to provide themselves with some prospect of financial support in old age when they themselves, devoid of the resources of the more affluent, were no long able to ensure their own livelihoods.

Furthermore, the rigors of old age itself in antiquity require some thought. Although in Roman poetry old age can sometimes be romanticized, as for instance in Virgil's portrait of the old Corycian or Ovid's idyllic picture of Baucis and Philemon (who, notably, did not have children), other literary sources can suggest the harsher aspects of later life.[83] It was a time when peace and quiet were necessary, though not perhaps guaranteed, and most men, according to Cicero, would consider old age loathsome; if the fearful ant's example of ensuring against destitution had not been followed, old age could be a time of sadness; and in the grip of a powerful imagination, Old Age in the underworld could be portrayed as the companion of Disease, Fear, Hunger, and Poverty.[84] The philosophically minded, men such as Cicero and Seneca, were able to compensate the onset of advancing years with retreat to abstract contemplation made possible by the contentment of material security.[85] But for the majority such relief was not possible. The contrast in this respect between the absentee landowner Seneca, visiting in old age one of his estates and complaining about its upkeep, and his coeval dependent Felicio, unrecognizable as the companion of Seneca's youth, is both strong and pathetic.[86] Old age combined with poverty was a double burden to bear, but a burden little worth the intellectual's attention.[87]

In view of the social conditions surrounding the dependence on their children of the less affluent, it becomes easier to understand why children began to work at relatively young ages in Roman society. Here, as in other premodern societies, ''childhood was a preparatory stage for adulthood, to be traversed as rapidly as was biologically reasonable, and nothing more.''[88] To judge from the case of Marcus Cicero, flexibility in preparation might be possible at the upper levels of society; but if upperclass children had to be prepared for careers in Roman civic life, children elsewhere in society had to be trained in jobs in order to preserve the essential well-being of their families. Child labor was a function of people's basic struggle for survival, a means of acclimatizing children to the common realities of material life around them.[89] Consequently it is not difficult to see why a physician such as Soranus could recommend a set of criteria by which to judge if a newborn child was physically worth rearing or not.[90] When parents chose occupations for their children, they were able to maintain control over their offspring in a society fundamentally patriarchal in character and to limit the emergence of individual independence inimical to the interests of familial cohesiveness. Therefore, the grief experienced by parents in the crisis of premature child death, the common occurrence of which is vividly illustrated by Virgil's description of the inhabitants of the underworld, was conditioned not simply by natural sentiment but also by reaction to the diminution of prospects for material security at later points in their own lives.[91] By modern standards, to reemphasize, children in Roman society were introduced through the medium of labor to the adult world at early stages of their physical development and were conditioned to fulfill obligations that could be discharged fully only when their parents died. At the lower levels of society especially, the result was that the adult pattern of life was established under strong constraints. Whereas the paradigms for the children of the socially elite were predicated on the continuous enjoyment and exploitation of wealth, those for the children outside the ranks of the elite were governed by the expectation of constant hardship from which there was little respite. It was only at a time of general holiday, after all, that Minucius Felix depicted a group of boys skimming pebbles across the water's edge at Ostia.[92]

Notes

1. For a full account of Marcus's life, see *RE* VII A, 2 cols. 1281–86. The relationship of Cicero and Marcus is made more comprehensible once the inadequacy of the image of the Roman father as a stern disciplinarian is brought out; see Saller (1986) and Saller (1988).

2. Cicero, *Letters to Atticus* 11.1.

3. Cicero, *Letters to Quintus* 3.3, 3.10; *Letters to Friends* 6.3, 8.1, 8.5; *Letters to Atticus* 68.5. On the dates of Cicero's exile, see Stockton (1971), 189, 193; from "about 20 March 58" to "4 August 57."

4. Cicero, *Letters to Atticus* 27.5; *Letters to Quintus* 8.2. On Aristodemus and Tyrannio, see Treggiari (1969), 116; Bonner (1977), 27, 28–30, 139; Christes (1979), 27–38.

5. Cicero, *Letters to Quintus* 17.2, cf. 24.6; *Letters to Atticus* 90.10, 92.5. On Dionysius, see Treggiari (1969), 119–21; Bonner (1977), 30–32; Christes (1979), 107–15.

6. Cicero, *Letters to Friends* 119.1; *Letters to Atticus* 102.3, 110.3, 116.10, 122.5.

7. Cicero, *Letters to Atticus* 141.1, 189.1, cf. 186.1, 172.1, 200.2; *Letters to Friends* 146.6.

8. Cicero, *De Officiis* 2.45; cf. Stockton (1971), 259.

9. Cicero, *Letters to Friends* 166, 167; *Letters to Atticus* 229.1, 230.1. For the return after Pharsalus, cf. Stockton (1971), 262.

10. Cicero, *Letters to Friends* 278.3; *Letters to Atticus* 244.1.

11. Cicero, *Against Catiline* 4.3; *Post Reditum* 8.

12. Cicero, *Letters to Atticus* 18.1; *Letters to Quintus* 3.3; *Letters to Friends* 6.3.

13. Cicero, *Letters to Quintus* 3.3; *Letters to Friends* 8.1; *Letters to Atticus* 102.3.

14. Cicero, *Letters to Atticus* 115.12.

15. Cicero, *Letters to Atticus* 361.2, 365.2, 367.4, 370.3, 391, 393.4, 394.2, 409.5, 413.2, 413.4.

16. Cicero, *Letters to Atticus* 417.2, 420.4; *Letters to Brutus* 9.3, 22. When Marcus joined the army of the Liberators, Cicero's love for him was politely acknowledged by M. Brutus (*Letters to Brutus* 2.6, 5.6). For Cicero's death, cf. Stockton (1971), 332. It might perhaps be said that Cicero's feelings for Marcus were not as strong as those for his daughter Tullia, but it seems incontrovertible that Cicero was actively concerned to foster

and to promote his son's development, and there is little point in denying sentiment as one of the motivating influences.

17. Pliny, *Letters* 5.16, on which cf. Sherwin-White (1966), 346–48. For the prospects of upper-class Roman women in general, see Pomeroy (1975), 148–89.

18. Pliny does not mention Minicia's mother, but for her identity see Syme (1988), 53, 305, 442, 468; she was perhaps still alive when her daughter died.

19. Pliny, *Letters* 5.16.7.

20. Apprenticeship documents have been studied many times in the past, and I have drawn freely from Westermann (1914); Zambon (1935); Zambon (1939); Herrmann (1958); and Wipszycka (1965), 57–74. But the emphasis of earlier studies has tended to fall on juridical or papyrological problems in the material rather than on its social significance, and child labor as a topic has generally been given little attention, though see Brunt (1958), 166, and the remarks of Wiedemann (1989), 153–56; cf. Forbes (1955), 331–34. In the notes that follow, I use the serial numbers of Table 5.1 for reference. It can be observed at once that in no. 28 the apprentice's teacher is named Aurelia Libouke—a craftswoman, therefore.

21. Table 5.1, no. 25.

22. Table 5.1, no. 6. See Taubenschlag (1955), 102; cf. Zambon (1935), 33; Bagnall (1968), 135–36; Lewis (1983), 169.

23. Table 5.1 nos. 5, 7, 8, 10, 11, 14, 21. Minority is signified by use of the terms ἀφῆλιξ or μηδέπω ὢν τῶν ἐτῶν, though their precise meaning is disputed; cf. Zambon (1935), 33.

24. Table 5.1, no. 29.

25. See Bagnall (1968), 136. Another apprentice weaver was thought to be precisely thirteen when he began to work, but this cannot be certain. See Westermann (1914), 313, on Table 5.1, no. 5, misidentifying the name of the apprentice; cf. Biscottini (1966), 209–13.

26. See Finley (1969), 129–42. Such, at least, was the ideal, but the reality might be different; see MacMullen (1980); and A. H. M. Jones (1974), 357: "Egyptian census returns show families in which both parents and children [of both sexes] are registered as wool or linen weavers."

27. See Treggiari (1976) and Treggiari (1979a).

28. Table 5.1, nos. 8, 10, 13.

29. Table 5.1, no. 11.

30. Cf. Lewis (1983), 134–35. See also Biscottini (1966), 209–10, and the commentary to P. Mich. III 170.

31. Table 5.1, no. 7. The father's name was L. Pompeius Niger, on whom see Gilliam (1971).

32. See Straus (1977), 75, 79–80; and cf. Biezunska-Malowist (1977), 73–108. P. Aberd. 59 (C4th—C5th, Panopolis?) records the apprenticeship of a girl in embroidery; see A. H. M. Jones (1964), 861, on apprenticeship in late antiquity. Domestic jobs, however, would not usually require formal apprenticeship.

33. For the wider background, see Wipszycka (1965); A. H. M. Jones (1974); Lewis (1983), 134–35.

34. P. Oxy. 725. See Zambon (1935), 55–61; Cohn Haft (1957).

35. Table 5.1, nos. 24, 26, 30, 22, 27.

36. Table 5.1, nos. 24, 22, 7.

37. Table 5.1, no. 27; see the commentary to P. Oxy. 2586.

38. Table 5.1 no. 28; see Pearl (1985), 258.

39. Table 5.1, no 25.

40. Table 5.1, no. 6.

41. Pearl (1985), 255, observes that the female apprentice of Table 5.1, no. 28, was sent from Karanis to Arsinoe, sixteen miles away, for her one-year apprenticeship. On the workshops in which weaving was done, note Wipszycka (1965), 56: "les artisans dans la majorité des cas, travaillaient dans le même logement où ils dormaient et mangeaient—dans de petites pièces d'habitation ou, quelquefois, dans une cour, sur un toit plat, dans une exèdre."

42. Cf. Westermann (1914), 312.

43. Lucian, *Somnium*, passim.

44. Baldwin (1973), 13–14. Cf. Bowersock (1969), 114–16.

45. Cf. Heichelheim (1938), 198. C. P. Jones (1986), 8–10, accepts also the plausibility of Lucian's evidence, pointing out that "sculpture could be highly paid, and when discussing the skills that a young man may honorably pursue Galen puts the figurative arts only slightly lower than the purely intellectual ones."

46. *Digest* 6.1.27.5, 7.1.27.2, 13.7.25, 19.1.13.22, 19.1.43, 19.2.13.3, 21.1.17.3, 25.1.6, 32.12, 6.1.28, 32.65.3 (*ornatrix* "apud magistrum").

47. *Digest* 17.1.26.8

48. *Digest* 38.1.7.5–6.

49. *Digest* 40.12.44.2.

50. *Digest* 14.3.8.

51. *Digest* 14.3.5.10, 9.2.5.3, 19.2.13.4.

52. Vitruvius, *On Architecture* 6, Preface 6; Cicero, *Letters to Quintus* 21.3; cf. Treggiari (1969), 99.

53. Plautus, *Aulularia* 409; *Pseudolus* 865, 886.

54. Martial, *Epigrams* 6.52. Note that use of *puer* in the sense of "slave" is very common in Martial, and that the word may sometimes mean "slave boy." Generally, however, it is difficult to tell whether the "boy" is a boy. For the usage, and on slave occupations in Martial, see Garrido-Hory (1981), 99–103, 135–46. Petronius, *Satyricon* 94.14.

55. Apuleius, *Metamorphoses* 10.29–32; see Millar (1981) on realism in Apuleius.

56. Aulus Gellius, *Attic Nights* 17.8.

57. Pliny, *Letters* 2.14.6; cf. Sherwin-White (1966), 106, 183. Note also Ammianus Marcellinus 26.3.3, the son of a charioteer apprenticed to a *veneficus*, scarcely at the age of puberty.

58. Plutarch, *Cato the Elder* 21.7; cf. Astin (1978), 261–62.

59. Petronius, *Satyricon* 29.7. According to Suetonius, *Grammarians* 23, Q. Remmius Palaemon was a weaver before he became a pedagogue and acquired an education; presumably, therefore, he had been apprenticed in weaving, as a slave boy, on the Egyptian pattern; cf. Christes (1979), 98–102. For weaving outside Egypt, specifically at Pompeii, see Moeller (1976) and Jongmann (1988), 155–86. And for instructive representations of various crafts, see Zimmer (1982).

60. Varro, *On Agriculture* 2.10.1, 3.17.6. See also Pliny, *Natural History* 13.132, gathering fodder for livestock.

61. Columella, *On Agriculture* 1.8.1, 2.2.13, 4.27.6, 11.2.44.

62. Apuleius, *Metamorphoses* 7.17–27; cf. Millar (1981), 73.

63. Virgil, *Eclogues* 8.37–40; but for the poetic antecedent, picking hyacinth, cf. Theocritus, *Idylls* 11.25–28. On slave girls in the country see Treggiari (1975b), 400; Ste. Croix (1981), 234–37. Note that in *CIL* 6.10010 (= 33820), a certain Aurelia Alciste makes a dedication, with M. Aurelius Sari, "discenti suo." Was she a teacher or simply a teacher's wife?

64. *CIL* 10.7039, 6.8659, 13.2036, 6.9437, 13.5154, 2.2243, 6.6182, 13.3225, 12.4052, 6.9249, 14.472, 5.5316, 13.5708, 3.14206, 21, 13.5826; cf. Burford (1972), 87–91; on entertainers, see below. Social status, to some degree of probability, can be inferred from nomenclature. Thus, in a group of inscriptions from *CIL* 6 that record apprentices (*discentes*), those in *CIL* 6.9249, 10012, 10013, 10014, 10015, 10016, 10017, and 10018 are probably slaves; those in *CIL* 6.10008, 10010 (= 33820), 10011, and 10011a are either freed or freeborn. Clear status designations, however, are given for none of these boys.

65. For example, *CIL* 6.27360, 6335, 9728, 9726, 9731, 9.3318. Treggiari (1979b), 191, shows that women probably trained in or outside the households to which they belonged according to the nature of the job; midwives, for instance, would need more formal training than readers and secretaries. According to *Digest* 15.1.27 pr., an *ancilla* or a *filiafamilias* could be a *sarcinatrix* or *textrix*; but according to *Digest* 2.13.12, women were banned altogether from becoming *argentarii*.

66. For all these cases, see Prosperi Valenti (1985).

67. *CIL* 14.472. Melior may have been his master's special favorite, a suggestion consistent with the practice in some Roman households of acquiring slave children as *delicia,* for which see Slater (1974); see Kinsey (1979).

68. *CIL* 6.9437; cf. Frank (1940), 212.

69. *CIL* 2.2243, 6.6182. Among the *discentes* known from Rome, one died at thirteen, another in his thirteenth year; *CIL* 6.10013, 10014. The ages at death of twenty-three and twenty-seven are given for apprentices in *CIL* 6.33930 and *CIL* 9.4437. Both men were commemorated by their teachers, but it is unlikely that they were still in training when they died; rather, it must be imagined that they had maintained close contact with their masters into maturity, once their periods of apprenticeship had ended.

70. *CIL* 6.6335, 27360, 9728, 9726, 9731. It can be presumed that individuals who died in their late teens had several years of work experience behind them: e.g., a *libraria* dead at eighteen and already married, *CIL* 6.9301; an *ornatrix* dead at nineteen and married, *CIL* 6.9732; *ornatrices* dead at eighteen and nineteen, *CIL* 6.5539, 33784.

71. *CIL* 6.9213.

72. *Code of Justinian* 6.43.3.1; *Digest* 7.7.6.1.

73. Prosperi Valenti (1985), 78–80; *CIL* 6.10158; cf. Nielsen (1987), 163–64; and note *Digest* 7.1.12.3: the *infans* had no work capability at all.

74. From evidence on the stealing and kidnapping of children, Boswell (1988), 75, 97, 105, 112, recognizes that they were valuable, not least because they could be put "to labor at any age" and might be "useful on farms or in shepherding." However, apart from *Digest* 14.3.8 (where "tabernas" should probably be taken as shops, not taverns), no corroboration is attempted. Nielsen (1987), 166–68, believes that *alumni* were sometimes "apprentices or assistants" of the people who commemorated them, "rather than fosterchildren or

that part of the fosterage consisted in teaching the *alumnus* a craft''; cf. earlier, B. Rawson (1986b), 196–97.

75. *CIL* 6.10013. For dedications to apprentices by masters, see *CIL* 6.9249, 10010 (=33820), 10011, 10012, 10013, 10014, 10015, 10016, 10017, 10018, 33930, 5.82, 9.4437; to masters by apprentices, *CIL* 6.10008, 10009, 10011a, 5.5316, 13.5826, 12.4502, 9.3721; cf. above, n. 69.

76. On England, see Thompson (1968), 366–84.

77. *Digest* 9.2.5.3, 19.2.13.4 (and note 21.1.17.3); Robertis (1963), 161–62; Birks (1981), 174–79.

78. Millar (1984).

79. Lambert (1982), 53–54.

80. Lambert (1982), 21. Observe Cicero, *Letters to Atticus* 176.2: "To refuse to maintain one's parents is wicked"; cf. also Quintilian, *Institute of Oratory* 7.6.5; *Digest* 25.3.5.1–2.

81. Plutarch, *Moralia* 493–497. Plutarch would presumably have approved the ideal image evoked by Musonius Rufus, in which children might form "a guard of honor for their father or mother . . . leading their parents by the hand or dutifully caring for them some other way." Lutz (1947), 99.

82. Plutarch, *Moralia* 8E, 497E. Again, Musonius believed, idealistically, that even poor parents should rear all their children. Lutz (1947), 99–101.

83. Virgil, *Georgics* 4.125–138; Ovid, *Metamorphoses* 8.611–724.

84. Horace, *Carmen Saeculare* 46; Cicero, *On Old Age* 2.4; Virgil, *Georgics* 3.67, 1.186; *Aeneid* 6.275–276.

85. Cicero, *On Old Age* 3.8; Seneca, *Moral Epistles* 12.

86. Seneca, *Moral Epistles* 12.

87. Cicero, *On Old Age* 3.8, 5.14.

88. Finley (1981), 159.

89. Observe Segalen (1986), 176, on work as a form of socialization in preindustrial societies; and Klapisch-Zuber (1985), 106–8, on child labor in fifteenth-century Tuscany as "true economic exploitation."

90. Soranus, *Gynecology* 2.79.

91. Virgil, *Aeneid* 6.426–429. On the topic generally, see Golden (1988b).

92. Minucius Felix, *Octavius* 2.3, 3.5–6. For the conventional elements, see G. Clarke (1974), 171–72, 178–79, not excluding "personal observations."

Table Notes

A similar list was compiled by Zambon (1935), 14–15, and a catalogue of references is given by Herrmann (1958), 119 n. 1, and by Pearl (1985), 255–56. I have omitted from this list a few items of very late date and items too fragmentary to be of much use.

5. P. Oxy. 322 descr. = Biscottini (1966), 186–92 = SB 10236.

7. See Gilliam (1971).

9. See Zambon (1939), 101–2.

10. See particularly the comments of P. J. Sijpesteijn, editor of P. Wisc. 4, on the connections between this text and P. Mich. III 170, 171, 172; cf. also Zambon (1939), 100–101.

15. P. Oxy. 275 = Hunt and Edgar (1932), no. 13.

17. P. Tebt. 442 = Shelton and Keenan (1971), 173–75. A gap in the text allows for restoration of two or three years for the duration of the apprenticeship period. The weaver in this document, Heron, also appears in no. 18.

20. P. Oxy. 724 = Hunt and Edgar (1932), no. 15.

21. P. Vars. SN 7 = SB 9374.

22. P. Oxy. 725 = Hunt and Edgar (1932), no. 14.

23. On the history of the restoration of P. Grenf. II 59, see Zambon (1935), 4–5; Forbes (1955), 331.

26. For discussion of κτενιστής, which has been rendered "wool carder" and "hairdresser," see Zambon (1935), 38–39; and Biezunska-Malowist (1977), 86–87, in favor of "wool carder," which I follow; contra, Forbes (1955), 332–33.

27. See Bagnall (1968), 135–39.

28. See Pearl (1985).

29. See above on no. 26.

6

Dislocation in the Roman Family

The question directly addressed both here and in the next chapter is that of how the upper-class family in the central period of Roman history is to be characterized. In sociological terms it has been stated that "the normal Roman family seems to have been a 'nuclear family' like our own," a view that commands considerable assent.[1] But while the nuclear model may well be valuable for elucidating some aspects of Roman family life, insufficient attention has been devoted to examining how it may accommodate apparently inconsistent inferences that can be drawn from the primary evidence. For instance, in a treatise called *On Brotherly Love*, dedicated to two Roman senators who were brothers, Plutarch assumed that it was not unusual in the society of his day for brothers to occupy the same living space, and he spoke indeed of "many examples of brothers using the same house and table and undistributed estates and slaves."[2] One could be forgiven, accordingly, for thinking that in the Greco-Roman world of A.D. 100 the *frérèche* was a common family form.[3]

In this chapter, then, I specifically ask whether the individual nuclear family, the reproductive triad, in upper-class society of the central period of Roman history was a firm and cohesive unit, and whether, as the nuclear construct seems to imply, it constituted the essential point of emotional reference for its members. The issues raised are enormous. But one means by which progress might be possible is by trying to locate the "emotional address"[4] of children in the family circles into which they were born and in which they grew up—in other words, by asking whether the range of children's emotional contacts was generally restricted to or generally extended beyond the father and mother who had produced them and the siblings who were their immediate peers. As a preliminary, however, a clear statement must first be made about the nature of marriage in upper-class Roman society, without which the creation of legitimate offspring and the formation of the core unit could not occur. Marriage, in fact, was not an institution upper-class Romans necessarily regarded as permanently binding until dissolved by spousal death. Divorce and remarriage were common. For questions of familial stability and children's emotional attachments, such a situation suggests a set of negative implications, the exploration of which may lead to a fuller appreciation of how the structure of the Roman family is to be properly understood.

II

Toward the end of his biography of Sulla, Plutarch describes the circumstances under which Valeria, a member of the patrician house of the Valerii Messallae, became the dictator's fifth and final wife:

> A few months later there was a show of gladiators and since at this time men and women used to sit all together in the theatre, with no separate seating accommodation for the sexes, there happened to be sitting near Sulla a very beautiful woman of a most distinguished family. Her name was Valeria; she was the daughter of Messalla and a sister of Hortensius, the orator; and it so happened that she had recently been divorced from her husband. As she passed behind Sulla, she rested her hand on him, pulled off a little piece of wool from his toga and then went on to her seat. When Sulla looked round at her in surprise, she said: ''There's no reason to be surprised, Dictator. I only want to have a little bit of your good luck for myself.''
> Sulla was far from displeased by this remark; indeed it was obvious at once that his amatory propensities had been stirred. He sent someone to ask discreetly what her name was and inquired about her family and past history. After this they kept glancing at each other, constantly turning their heads to look, and exchanging smiles. And in the end negotiations began for marriage. This was all innocent enough, perhaps, on her part; but, however chaste and worthy a character she may have been, Sulla's motive in marrying her was neither chaste nor virtuous; he was carried away, like a boy might have been, by a good-looking face and a saucy manner—just what naturally excites the most disgraceful and shameless sort of passion.[5]

It is evident from this passage that Plutarch felt some discomfort over the fact that the union between Sulla and Valeria was based on a mutual sexual attraction, an attitude consistent with the view that what would now be called romantic or passionate love was not a suitable basis for marriage between members of the Roman upper classes.[6] The context in which upper-class marriages occurred precluded any such notion, for at the time of a first marriage, as is well known, there was usually a considerable age difference between the principals—with the woman often being no more than a sheltered teenage bride and the man, by contrast, in the early stages of a public career—and a match was typically arranged for the couple by their respective families with little opportunity allowed for the satisfaction of personal inclination (whatever the legal technicalities concerning consent).[7] What mattered was the principals' character, their status and background, their respective families' wealth and political affiliations, whereas the principals themselves "were handled . . . more or less like chattels."[8] For the Romans, therefore, "Marrying because of physical attraction was irresponsible," and in an account of how families organized betrothals for their children one is struck by the singularly emotionless, businesslike character of the entire operation, together with the relative absence of courtship rituals as a prelude to marriage.[9] To marry for love at Rome was to engage in a socially deviant form of behavior.

The object of marriage for the Romans, and its most important function, was the procreation of children. Under the Republic indeed the censors are said to have required an oath when a man married that reproduction was the purpose in mind.[10] Not, however, that children were sought for their own sake by married couples: "A man must marry in order to have legitimate offspring—*sui heredes* to continue his estate and his cult, and to provide that worship necessary to the peace of the spirit which survived his death."[11] Beyond the sphere of such private concerns, moreover, children, once born, promised the future greatness of families already distinguished in the public domain or of families who aspired to such eminence. "Thus while for the man of the present age," it has been unambiguously observed, "marriage is the consummation of human happiness, for the Roman it was a practice dictated by necessity," a condition that imposed burdens on the husband but a civic obligation that could not be evaded if the well-being of the state were to be preserved.[12] Even a successful marriage, therefore, one that produced children, still had no need for the partners to share romantic sentiment of the ideal modern kind.

To be sure, there was in Roman society a concept of conjugal love, of which Valerius Maximus was able to find some examples (very few in number, one might note): a husband giving his life for his wife, spouses taking their own lives when their partners had already died, a wife miscarrying at the thought that her husband had been murdered.[13] Such stories may well have provided edifying *exempla* to a contemporary audience, and the element of devotion they contain should not be slighted. But there is nothing in them to suggest that marriage for the Romans normally began from the premise that a couple had first fallen in love, and the same is true of even such a tender image as that of Propertius's Arethusa pining for her soldier-husband away on military service in the East.[14] It would be foolish, of course, to say that love matches never occurred. The possibility was in fact admitted by Augustus (so it seems), when he allowed men who had not yet become senators to marry former slave women with whom they were in love.[15] Augustus's action, however, was clearly a concession, a significant departure from conventional standards. For the danger was that to allow individuals their own choice of marriage partners was to threaten families' control of property and power. Consequently it was the Roman ideal that affection between husband and wife should develop after marriage, not before, and that when it did so it was to have nothing of the *coup de foudre* about it. Rather, conjugal love was something that should be calm and nondisturbing, something to be quietly nurtured and cultivated.[16] The lawyers' phrase "bene concordantia matrimonia" suggests what was sought: marriage that contained a "proper state of moderation."[17]

Accordingly, one can agree that "a strong ideal of conjugal love and fidelity developed by the very late Republic and coexisted with arranged marriages and easy divorce within the upper classes."[18] But one must also insist that there was a constant tension between the ideal and reality, in the sense that the former could not be guaranteed in view of the unimportance of affection and emotional compatibility in the latter, especially when from the outset of a marriage the probability was high that loyalty between husband and wife would not necessarily entail sexual fidelity, which was perhaps not even always expected. The wife of Scipio Africanus was commended for her *fides* because she turned a blind eye to her husband's dalliance with an *ancillula* whom she set free after his death; and Augustus's wife, Livia, is said to have procured for her husband despite the strength of the bond between them.[19] Adultery, at least by a woman, was reproved by the Romans because if discovered it brought shame upon her family, particularly upon her husband; and it was the element of dishonor, not the sexual infidelity itself, that controlled the quality of the immoral in adultery. The arranged marriage, in which sentiment was no more than a subsidiary factor, thus provoked discord between the needs of families and the desires of individuals, and so the success of marriage was jeopardized from the beginning by the likely prospect of the appearance of dishonor dependent on the revelation of adultery. Lacking the sacramental pressure of Christian marriage which developed in the early medieval era, the Roman arranged marriage could not even ensure that mild form of conjugal love the Romans constructed as an ideal, and it is difficult in consequence to see how there can have been much emotional investment in the kind of marriage represented by that, say, between Cicero and Publilia.[20] Indeed, one commentator has been impressed by the "extreme boredom of marriages contracted without any mutual affection" at Rome.[21] It is not an acceptable inference, therefore, that the Roman ideal of conjugal love actually created, on a broad scale, marriages that by today's standards could be regarded as emotionally satisfying.

The importance of this point lies in recognizing that the absence of emotional investment in Roman marriage was one of the factors that contributed to the high incidences of divorce and serial marriage in Roman society. For the upper classes of the central period, there is an abundance of evidence to show that serial marriage was an omnipresent reality, if not a prescriptive norm, and it follows that individuals might expect a succession of marriages in the course of their adulthood.[22] Literature might well have promoted the fiction that marriage was a union for life.[23] But in actuality the number of women who could be described at death as *univira* was always small, and one husband of the late first century B.C. reflected the true situation when commemorating his wife of forty-one years, by remarking on the rarity of such long-lasting unions.[24] The Augustan legislation on compulsory remarriage after spousal death consequently should not be regarded as a radical measure but only as an open recognition and formalization of a well-established social practice.[25] But this means, in turn, that any attempt to characterize the upper-class Roman family must proceed from the perception that marriage for the Roman elite was not a permanently binding institution, and that as a result the families brought into existence by the procreation of children after marriage were subject to a high level of impermanence and flexibility as the parents of children sequentially, and in some instances cavalierly, changed spousal partners and established new households. In other words, the generally unromantic nature of Roman marriage should prepare for a very different context for children's emotional development than that associated with the modern affective nuclear family.[26]

III

The transitory aspect of Roman family life is easily demonstrable. But its full significance can only be appreciated in the context of the recent demonstration that the nuclear family—that is, what has been termed "the mother-father-children triad"—was the "primary focus of certain types of familial obligation" in Roman society. An impressive quantitative survey of funerary inscriptions from the western Empire has, indeed, revealed the importance attached to nuclear family ties in Roman commemorative practices, except in the case of certain military groups where there was no apparent opportunity for the establishment of such bonds, given that the overwhelming majority of dedications to deceased individuals were made by members of the triad.[27] The tendency is undeniable. Yet it is important to notice here that the evidence examined is pertinent only to one precise moment in families' lives, when one of its members had died, a moment when the religious constraints to mark the end of life were very pronounced. True, literary evidence lends weight to the conclusions drawn from the inscriptions, especially Cicero's "quasi-historical hierarchy of family bonds" in the *De Officiis,* in which the tie between husband and wife and that between parents and children receive prime positioning.[28] But this is a statement of theory only and fails to take into account the consequences of serial marriage, and one might wonder especially what Marcus, to whom the *De Officiis* is addressed, made of his father's remarks, knowing, of course, that his own mother had been divorced. So, if the hypothesis that "the nuclear family . . . was characteristic of many regions of western Europe as early as the Roman empire" is to be descriptively useful, it must be tested, to see if refinement is necessary, by being exposed to other moments of family history than those when death affected its behavior and motivated solidarity.[29] Further, on the assumption that commemoration of the dead was conditioned by affection as well as duty, an effort must be made to penetrate the emotional or affective life of the triad while all or most of its members were living.

To show the complications of Roman familial organization over time that followed from serial marriage, a certain amount of bald (and familiar) factual information is unavoidable. First, therefore, I summarize the matrimonial career of L. Cornelius Sulla Felix, who was born in 138 B.C. and died in 78 B.C. at the age of sixty (see Figure 6.1). In all Sulla married five times, his choice of wives in some instances obviously being dictated by political interests, and issue resulted from three of the unions. As a very young man, Sulla married Ilia (or Julia), who produced a daughter, Cornelia. The marriages to Aelia and Cloelia were barren. But by his fourth wife, Caecilia Metella, Sulla had three children, a son who probably bore the same name as himself and who died in childhood, and the twins Faustus and Fausta, who were still young when Sulla himself died. The marriage to Metella took place in 89 B.C., but she was dead by 81, when Sulla encountered Valeria at the games. The latter subsequently gave birth to Sulla's last child, Postuma, appropriately named since her father was dead before she was born.[30]

Consider the ramifications of Sulla's marriages from the point of view of his children. It can be assumed that the oldest child, Cornelia, remained with Sulla when the marriage to Ilia was over. This would be the natural expectation if the union ended as a result of Ilia's death (which is not known), but if divorce were the cause, the convention was in any case that children continued to reside in the father's household.[31] So, before her own marriage to Q. Pompeius Rufus, perhaps in 89 B.C., Cornelia is likely to have grown up under the partial influence of successive stepmothers, Aelia and Cloelia, each of whom in a sense "replaced" or was an adjunct to her natural mother.[32] Moreover, when Cornelia's children were born (a son and a daughter), they belonged in reality to the same generation as her half-siblings, Sulla's three children by Metella; and Cornelia would herself have been at a relatively advanced age indeed when her last half-sister, Postuma, was born.[33] It seems implausible consequently to imagine that Cornelia had any "normal" sibling relationship (in the modern sense) with Sulla's other children, especially with Postuma, who was considerably younger than her father's grandchildren. As for Faustus and Fausta, since their mother Metella predeceased their father (she was in actuality divorced by Sulla for religious reasons shortly before her death), they, too, may have had to contend with a stepmother in the person of Valeria.[34] But Faustus was

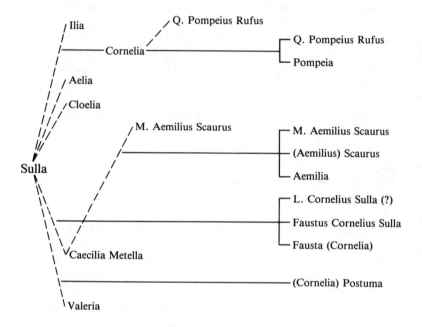

Figure 6.1. The Family of Sulla

entrusted under the terms of Sulla's will to the guardianship of L. Licinius Lucullus and so may have entered the latter's household in 78 B.C. or so.[35] At any rate, the twins lost both parents at an early age and must have undergone some transference.[36] As children, however, their family circle was not confined to parents and an older half-sister, but incorporated on their mother's side three other half-siblings, Metella's children by her previous marriage to Q. Aemilius Scaurus, *princeps senatus,* in whom apparently Sulla took a strong interest: Metella's daughter Aemilia was already married and pregnant in 81 B.C. when she was compulsorily divorced and remarried to Cn. Pompeius. Sulla also seemingly provided some support for one of Metella's sons.[37] What emotional bonds, if any, were formed between, say, Faustus and Fausta on one hand and Metella's children on the other, or between Cornelia and Postuma on one hand and their stepsiblings (Metella's children) on the other, cannot be determined.[38] Yet merely to pose the question is to point up how questionable in descriptive terms the simple model of the nuclear triad may be for covering all the individuals who in one way or another made up Sulla's family of children. Any notion that the children formed a cohesive group, given the range of their ages and experiences, is unlikely, and all the indications suggest instead that Sulla's sequence of marital alignments brought into existence a very diffuse set of personal relationships, with attachments spreading over from one narrow circle to another as the children's circumstances changed.

A second case history, that of the triumvir M. Antonius, leads to an identical conclusion. Antonius also married five times, and each union produced children, though the final marriage to Cleopatra was not recognized as lawful at Rome (see Figure 6.2). Little is known of Fadia, the first wife, other than that she was the daughter of a freedman, Q. Fadius, and that she bore Antonius an indeterminate number of children. The usual view is that mother and offspring were all dead by 44 B.C. at the latest. Antonia, the second wife, who was also Antonius's first cousin, produced one daughter, Antonia (1), in the eight years or so of their marriage. She was divorced in 47 B.C. so that Antonius could marry Fulvia, with whom he may have begun a liaison much earlier. The new marriage lasted until Fulvia's death in 40 B.C., by which time she had given Antonius two sons, Antyllus and Iullus. Meantime, however, Antonius was involved with Cleopatra, who gave birth to his twins in 40 B.C. But after the Pact of Brundisium, Antonius took another Roman wife, Octavia, the sister of Octavian, who produced Antonia (2) in 39

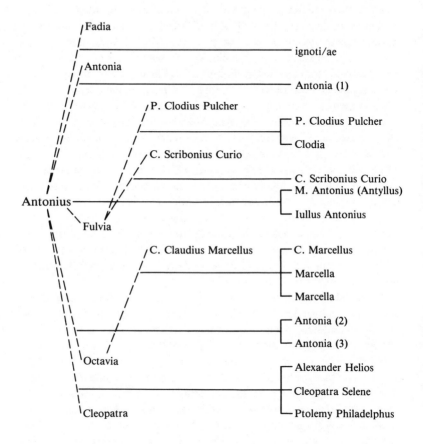

Figure 6.2. The Family of Antonius

B.C. and Antonia (3) in 36. In addition, by the time of Antonius's death in 30 B.C., Cleopatra had borne him another son.[39]

Consider again the childhood experiences of Antonius's children. Like Cornelia, Antonia (1) will presumably have had some contact with a pair of stepmothers, Fulvia and Octavia, before she reached maturity, although contact with her own mother, Antonia, was not necessarily lost, since the latter was apparently alive when Antonius married Octavia. But Antonia (1) came to know both half-siblings, through her father's third and fourth marriages, and stepsiblings, through her stepmothers' previous unions. For before becoming Antonius's wife, Fulvia was twice married, first to P. Clodius Pulcher (tribune of the plebs in 58 B.C.), and secondly to C. Scribonius Curio (tribune of the plebs in 50 B.C.), each marriage producing offspring (a son and a daughter, and a son, respectively); and Octavia had been married to C. Claudius Marcellus (consul in 50 B.C.), a union that had produced three children (a son and two daughters). Since Fulvia was widowed twice and Octavia once before marriage to Antonius, each mother will have kept her children with her on remarriage. Octavia in particular is definitely known to have cared for Fulvia's children by Antonius.[40] Eventually Antyllus and Iullus and the two other Antoniae all had half-siblings on both parents' sides and stepsiblings from their father's wives' earlier marriages. The lines of familial contact are clear. But what is visible ultimately from one individual's marital career is the gradual formation of a complex network of connections among the children in which the degree of emotional attachment is likely to have varied greatly. Another variable element was the amount of exposure of Antonius's children to their father. While Antyllus was old enough to be with Antonius in Egypt late in his father's career (Antyllus received the toga of manhood shortly before Antonius's death), it was simply impossible for Iullus and the two younger Antoniae to have known him at all.[41] Immediately after Antonius's death, the household of Octavia included her own children by Marcellus and by Antonius; Iullus; and Antonius's three children by Cleopatra.[42] Several triads had, of course, once been responsible for the development of this particular ménage at one moment in time, but the final product was far from nuclear in any straightforward sense.

It might be objected that the two matrimonial histories examined so far concern exceptional figures in Rome's political history and so are not representative of social behavior in the Roman upper classes at large. But the objection is not compelling, for the evidence on remarriage at large is firm enough to suggest that the shifting developments observable in the relatively well-documented families of Sulla and Antonius were widespread among Rome's upper classes.[43] Indeed, in prospographical reconstruction, historians often find it necessary to assume frequent remarriage as a standing social convention in order to make sense of the scattered data still extant, with the same, but not always explored, implication.[44] To give one example, it now seems to be accepted that the father of the notorious Clodia Metelli, Ap. Claudius Pulcher (consul in 79 B.C.), at some point remarried after his daughter's birth, his new wife in due course providing him with five other children (three sons and two daughters). Pulcher's two wives remain *ignotae,* but the second was apparently married twice apart from her union to Pulcher and gave birth to three other children as a result (two sons and a daughter, respectively).[45] If an effort is made to imagine the familial structure under which Clodia grew up as a child, it is again one in which exposure to a stepmother and a sequence of half-siblings and stepsiblings is evident, with the culmination, perhaps surprising, perhaps not, that the man she eventually married, Q. Caecilius Metellus Celer (consul in 60 B.C.), was her stepbrother, a man she had presumably known from a very early age.

Another pair of stepsiblings who married were Auria and the younger Oppianicus, members this time not of the Roman upper class in a strict sense but of locally prominent families at Larinum in Apulia in the first century B.C., whose history is known from a court speech made by Cicero in 66 B.C. Their marriage took place in 69 B.C. But their previous experiences seem to fit anything but a nuclear pattern.[46]

Oppianicus's father was married six times in all, his last wife being the notorious Sassia whom Cicero vilified in his speech (see Figure 6.3). Three of the elder Oppianicus's wives—Magia, Papia, and Novia—each produced a son, two of whom were killed by their father while they were very young. The exact order in which Oppianicus married his wives is indeterminable (though Sassia was certainly the last). But the younger Oppianicus was probably the oldest of the boys. Obviously he had no opportunity to develop any sense of enduring intimacy with his half-brothers; nor would this have been likely with both of them had they lived, because before his death the son of Papia was being raised by his mother at Teanum, eighteen miles from Larinum, and was normally visiting his father only on holidays. The sons of Papia and Novia, that is, belonged to completely separate households as a result of divorce and remarriage. Moreover, the younger Oppianicus lost his mother, Magia,

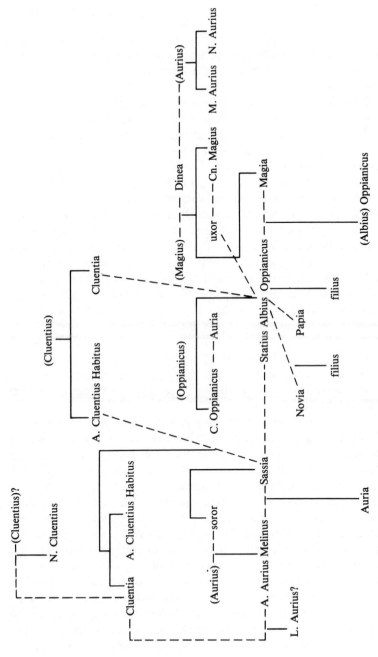

Figure 6.3. The Family of Auria and Oppianicus

while still a child and subsequently had to contend with a sequence of temporary stepmothers, perhaps four in all. The influence of the last, Sassia, was great enough for her to be able to compel Oppianicus to marry Auria when he was a young adult.

Auria herself was Sassia's daughter by her second husband, A. Aurius Melinus, who happened to be both Sassia's nephew and her former son-in-law. As a result of her first marriage, Sassia had two children, A. Cluentius Habitus, Cicero's client in the court case of 66 B.C., who was fifteen when his father died, and Cluentia, the one-time wife of Melinus, who was somewhat older than her brother. To judge from Cicero, the relationship between brother and sister was close enough, but any possibility that their half-sister Auria might share the intimacy was precluded by the age difference between them, for Auria in fact belonged to the same generation as N. Cluentius, Cluentia's son by another marriage. Nor did Auria have an opportunity to establish an enduring tie with her father, since Melinus was murdered by the elder Oppianicus, who subsequently became her stepfather. When Sassia and Oppianicus married, each had one living child whose other parent was dead and who therefore presumably formed part of the new household established by the marriage. It cannot be known how long they spent together as stepsiblings or how they responded to each other. But Cicero says that the younger Oppianicus married Auria against his will, suggesting that their past relationship had been difficult. In the event, Oppianicus's wishes proved irrelevant.

Despite case histories of this kind, however, it remains a fact that little direct information is available concerning the childhood lives of individual members of the Roman elite from the emotional and affective point of view. For the most part, no more than inferences are possible from suggestive texts, one being, for example, that children regularly lost their fathers before themselves reaching adulthood.[47] It would be dangerous, therefore, to try to offer sweeping conclusions about the emotional experience of childhood at Rome in any dogmatic way. Nevertheless, from the material so far described—in which the constant dissolution and reformation of familial triads cannot be mistaken, as fragments of triads melded and remelded to give rise to extensive familial connections through the process of remarriage—a proposition at least can be stated, namely that from the moment of birth the life of the upper-class Roman child was potentially subject to a high degree of emotional uncertainty and dislocation, the product of such factors as early separation from a natural parent by death or divorce, periodic separation from a father because of the demands of a public career or political crisis, the abrupt organization of new households, and conjunction with stepparents and stepsiblings occasioned by parental remarriage. Stated differently, the high incidence of remarriage in upper-class Roman society—which was, on the one hand, a natural sequel of the absence of any realistic idea that marriage was a permanently binding love bond to one partner, and which led, on the other hand, to a lack of clustering among descendants— helped create the prospect of a profoundly unsettled beginning to life for the offspring of the elite. This is not to claim that all relationships with stepsiblings and stepparents were automatically harmful, despite the literary topos of the *noverca,* or to maintain that strong affective bonds between parents and children (or stepchildren) did not exist or were not possible.[48] Instead, the proposition emphasizes only that the mother-father-children triad that came into existence after marriage and procreation was not at all a social unit likely to remain compact and stably composed until the offspring achieved maturity, and that parent-child relationships were exposed to constant strains and pressures as new marital alignments occurred.

IV

One of the clearest ways in which parental affection for children can be seen is in the inscriptions, often very moving, set up to commemorate those who had died prematurely. "What a cruel day dawned for my parents, that ninth day which carried me off from the laments of my wretched mother and father alike. What great expectations had been mine, if my destiny had allowed"—so, in part, the epitaph of the seven-year-old Marcianus who died around A.D. 126.[49] Parental grief in this context was almost proverbial. But the context was, of course, one of especially heightened feeling, and it is important to reemphasize that the children parents chose to rear embodied their families' hopes for future security and achievement (and not only, as Marcianus's epitaph makes plain, in the upper reaches of society). Those parental aspirations cannot be separated from whatever natural feelings of love and affection they felt. "So many deaths are untimely," Seneca wrote in consolation to Marcia, "yet we make plans for our infants—how they will don the toga, serve in the army, and succeed to their father's property."[50] In similar vein, Cicero maintained that a woman who had aborted herself "cheated the father of his hopes, his name of continuity, his family of support, his house of an heir, and the republic of a citizen-to-be."[51]

More generally, one can detect in certain literary passages a fondness and warmth for children that can hardly have been unique to littérateurs. Images of unsuspecting children who can be induced to take bitter medicine from a honeyed cup, of children and their groundless nighttime fears, of children lovingly welcoming home their father, playing with toys, becoming dizzy after spinning around, being coaxed with cookies to learn their lessons at school—all this suggests a predictable enjoyment of the young in society at large.[52]

Nevertheless, in a society where infant exposure as a form of population control and early childhood death from natural causes were common phenomena, the kind of emotional investment parents made in their children has to be questioned. "Ancient attitudes toward children are singularly paradoxical," it has been said. "Parents in classical antiquity undoubtedly loved their children. . . . And yet the treatment accorded children in ancient society was often severe, even brutal. The exposure of unwanted babies was commonplace. The pedagogy practiced in ancient schools was notoriously harsh."[53] In spite of the admixture of parental hope and affection, therefore, something of an emotional isolation in the life of the child might seem to follow directly from the factors involved in the convention of parental remarriage. "Consider, Marcia," Seneca said, "how rarely it happens that mothers who live in separate households see their children."[54] Seneca may have been referring here to adult children who had established their own households; but the remark is surely not inapposite for younger children, like those of Sulla and Antonius, who had been affected by marital changes in their parents' lives.

Such changes inevitably drew Roman children into wide spheres of familial contact and association, and the result is only to be expected that emotional ties were formed with people in close physical proximity other than parents and siblings. Thus, whatever the importance of the conjugal unit as a vehicle of social reproduction, there can be no doubt that the Roman sense of family extended well beyond the confines of the nuclear grouping. An idea of this Roman sensitivity to familial relationships at large can be gained from an examination of Latin familial vocabulary, which exhibits, by and large, a far greater degree of precision than its English counterpart. The relevant terminology is conveniently set out in a section of the *Digest* entitled "the degrees of relatives and their names," the point of departure of which is the jurisconsult's concern with matters of inheritance and tutelage.[55] It can be summarized as follows.

A. For descendants beyond grandchildren to the seventh degree, Latin used compound forms of the root terms *nepos* (grandson) and *neptis* (granddaughter):

nepos	*pronepos*	*abnepos*	*adnepos*	*trinepos*
neptis	*proneptis*	*abneptis*	*adneptis*	*trineptis*

B. Similarly, for ascendants beyond grandparents to the seventh degree, Latin used compound forms of the root terms *avus* (grandfather) and *avia* (grandmother):

avus	*proavus*	*abavus*	*atavus*	*tritavus*
avia	*proavia*	*abavia*	*atavia*	*tritavia*

C. For uncles, aunts, and cousins, Latin used a set of words that naturally indicated a distinction between paternal and maternal relationship. Words for uncles and aunts also had compound forms to signify further degrees of connection:

patruus (paternal uncle)	*propatruus*	*abatruus*
amita (paternal aunt)	*proamita*	*abamita*
avunculus (maternal uncle)	*proavunculus*	*abavunculus*
matertera (maternal aunt)	*promatertera*	*abmatertera*
consobrini/ae (maternal cousins)		
amitini/ae (paternal cousins)		

D. For in-laws and steprelatives, Latin used a clear set of words that were not based on nuclear family terminology:

socer (father-in-law) cf. also *prosocer*
socrus (mother-in-law) cf. also *prosocrus*
gener (son-in-law) cf. also *progener*
nurus (daughter-in-law) cf. also *pronurus*
levir (brother-in-law)
glos (sister-in-law)
consocer, consocrus (parents-in-law)
vitricus (stepfather) *noverca* (stepmother)
privignus (stepson) *privigna* (stepdaughter)

It should be noted here that although the words for cousins preserve a paternal/maternal distinction, usage may well have been legalistic, since Gaius remarked that *consobrini* was popularly used for all kinds of cousins.[56] Moreover, the paternal/maternal distinction did not exist at all in the vocabulary of descendants and ascendants, and the deficiency had to be accommodated by supplying adjectives, as in English. Further, prepositional compounds were not always used; alternative expressions, using forms of the adjectives *magnus/a, maior, maximus/a* were possible, again as in English. Thus, for example, *proavunculus = avunculus maior,* and *abamita = amita maxima.* Also, the words *levir* and *glos* were very rare. But despite these qualifications, the Latin system of familial vocabulary was far more efficient than the English and avoided such cumbersome usages as "great-great-great-grandson" (= *adnepos*) or "grandfather-in-law" (= *prosocer*).

The terminology was not simply the province of lawyers. In Plautus, for example, the slave Sceledrus can anticipate crucifixion, the fate of his *avos, proavus,* and *abavus,* and the parasite Saturio is proud to follow a profession practiced by his *pater, avos, proavos, abavos, atavos,* and *tritavos.*[57] At a more sober level, the cursus inscription of the relatively undistinguished senator P. Paquius Scaeva draws on a wide range of familial terms, indicating not least how conscious the Roman upper classes were of descent and the importance they attached to preserving the memory of connections that went far beyond the nuclear starting point. Paquius appears as the *filius* of Scaeva and Flavia, the *nepos* of Consus and Didia, and the *pronepos* of Barbus and Diruta; equally, his wife Flavia is described as the *filia* of Consus and Sinnia, the *neptis* of Scapula and Sinnia, and the *pronepos* of Barbus and Dirutia. The married couple were, in fact, cousins, and they are respectively referred to in their inscription as "consobrinus idemque vir" and "consobrina eademque uxor."[58] The greatest potential for emphasizing descent perhaps lay with the family of the emperor. So, with the passage of time and enough acts of adoption, it became possible for Commodus to be celebrated as the *filius* of Marcus (literally true), *nepos* of Antoninus Pius, *pronepos* of Hadrian, *abnepos* of Trajan, and *adnepos* of Nerva. Caracalla could go a step further: he was the *proadnepos* (= *trinepos*) of Nerva.[59]

Aside from the terminology of ascent and descent, a passage in Persius on the topic of inheritance exploits familial vocabulary to humorous effect, adding in the process the collateral dimension:

> age, si mihi nulla
> iam reliqua ex amitis, patruelis nulla, proneptis
> nulla manet patrui, sterilis matertera vixit
> deque avia nihilum superest, accedo Bovillas
> clivumque ad Virbi, praesto est mihi Manius heres.[60]

Further examples from literature and epigraphy are easily accessible, so that all in all the inference is possible from the lexical evidence that in many moments in an individual's life the "family" embraced a much broader constituency than that supplied by the original reproductive unit and that the world of the family was far less circumscribed than the nuclear model implies.[61] For the life of the child especially, the point is made clear by a passage from Cicero's *De Oratore,* in which Cicero speaks autobiographically of the extensive familial contacts of which his boyhood life was composed. Critics of L. Crassus's erudition, Cicero says to his brother Quintus,

> We used at that time to confound, in boyish fashion, by calling witnesses from home, namely our father, our near kinsman [*propinquus*] Gaius Aculeo, and our paternal uncle [*patruus*] Lucius Cicero, inasmuch as our father, and Aculeo, who married our mother's sister [*quocum erat nostra matertera*] . . . and our paternal uncle . . . all severally and often related to us a great deal about Crassus, his application to study, and his intellectual attainments. And since, in the company of our cousins [*consobrini*], the sons of Aculeo, we were not only studying such subjects as attracted Crassus, but were also being instructed by those very teachers whom he made his friends, we, being as we were at his home often perceived—and even we boys could perceive—that . . . nothing seemed strange to him, nothing beyond his range of knowledge.[62]

Cicero's familial frame of reference as a boy was not confined to mother, father, and siblings. Similarly, but much later, Ausonius evokes in the *Parentalia* a world in which a variety of relatives—uncles, aunts, and grandparents—might play important, quasi-parental roles in the social formation of a child.[63]

Beyond kin of various types, the upper-class Roman households among which children moved were also populated by large staffs of dependent slaves and ex-slaves, and it was from the domestic entourage that functionaries such as nurses and pedagogues were drawn to cater to the physical needs of the children of the elite. The upper-class child, in fact, was provided with a succession of child minders from birth to maturity, all of lower-class status, and there is a considerable volume of evidence in literature and inscriptions to show how fixed an element such figures were in the life of the child. When referring to the human newborn, Lucretius, for example, simply assumes the presence of the "alma nutrix," a woman who soothes the infant with her "blanda atque infracta loquela." And Propertius gives his Arethusa a nurse for a companion despite the wife's adult status. Like Giddenis in Plautus's *Poenulus,* the nurse here has taken on the role of *ancilla* now that her special services as a child minder are no longer needed.[64] Identities of individual nurses and pedagogues are given in literature only infrequently. But a little information pertinent to the families of Sulla and Antonius is available. The story was told of Sulla himself that a woman who once encountered him when an infant, before inexplicably disappearing, uttered the words, "The boy will be lucky for you and the republic," addressing herself not to Sulla but to the nurse carrying him.[65] Sulla's son Faustus is said to have been a favorite of his father's freedman Cornelius Epicadus (who became a *grammaticus*), and it is tempting to believe that their closeness continued after Sulla's death, with the freedman in effect serving as Faustus's pedagogue. (However, Epicadus seems to have been nowhere in sight on the day when Faustus was beaten up by his fellow pupil, the future conspirator C. Cassius, for boasting about the great power his father had once wielded.)[66] Antonius's son Antyllus has a pedagogue on record, a certain Theodorus, who is attested with his charge in Egypt when Antyllus was still a boy. But the man was worthless. Theodorus betrayed Antyllus and caused his death, but was soon after crucified, not least for having stolen a precious gem from Antyllus's corpse.[67]

Not all child minders behaved in the abusive manner of Theodorus. Indeed it is noticeable that bonds formed between these servants and the children they cared for endured in some cases over many years, a possible norm implicit in the Propertian example. As an adult, Octavian manumitted his former pedagogue Sphaerus, and Nero was buried by his childhood nurses.[68] In inscriptions, it is not uncommon to find dedications made to servants by adult charges and dedications to adult charges by servants whose technical functions had long been unnecessary. Aware of how firm these ties could be, Cicero actually counseled against maintaining an equality of friendship with nurses and pedagogues once a man achieved maturity.[69] It would be naive to believe that the association between child minder and child was always affectionate, that it always subsisted beyond the charge's childhood; and it should not be forgotten that the nurses and pedagogues themselves were originally forced into associations with elite children by virtue of their inferior social standing, which made them manipulable commodities. However, when contact with a given child or group of children over a period of years was the case, influence on the child was obviously exerted by the child minder, and the connection between the two is not always likely to have been adversely affected or interrupted by compositional alterations in households caused by remarriage. Consequently, the further proposition can be stated that it was as much the child-minding figure as the kin member who at times provided the emotional stability and continuity in the life of the upper-class child, compensating thereby for the distancing between child and parent that social practices could otherwise encourage. Moreover, one of the results of wet-nursing especially was that upper-class children were often brought into contact with the nurses' own children, their *collactanei,* who thus further extended the range of their familial experience.[70]

If that is plausible, it has to be recognized in any characterization of the upper-class Roman family. It is clear that the Latin language had no word for "family" in the customary modern sense of the term.[71] Instead the Romans used the more amorphous words *familia* and *domus,* the vague nature of which was the result of the physical presence in the residential unit of the servile domestic retinue as well as individuals related by blood or marriage ties of one sort or another. Thus, the range of emotional links by which the Roman child could be bound extended well beyond immediate blood connections, that is, family ties in any narrow reproductive sense. From this point of view, drawing on those links as an index of family life, the Roman family has to be regarded as a composite form, a hybrid that encompassed both kin and nonkin members, and one that incorporated a complex set of affective ties in the formation of which proximity was as important an ingredient as immediate nuclear associations.

Notes

1. Quotation from Crook (1967a), 98, but with immediate qualification.

2. Plutarch, *Moralia* 481D–E. For the brothers to whom the work was dedicated, T. Avidius Quietus and Avidius Nigrinus, see C. P. Jones (1971), 51–54.

3. For the *frérèche* (in medieval Europe), observe Herlihy (1985), 137: "in those areas of Europe where partible inheritance prevailed, different forms of household organization took root. The several brothers, all of whom had claim to a share of the inheritance, might keep their common patrimony undivided, even after one or more had married. The result was the joint-family household, also often called by its French name, *frérèche*."

4. The phrase of Stephen Vincenzy, *An Innocent Millionaire* (Toronto, 1983), 21.

5. Plutarch, *Sulla* 35.3–5. On Valeria, see *RE* VIII A, 1 col. 243.

6. See Lyne (1980), 1–4; cf. Hopkins (1983), 84–88. For a clearly defined distinction between romantic love and conjugal love, see Lantz (1981–82), 349.

7. On marriage ages, see Hopkins (1965); Syme (1987a); Shaw (1987b). On consent, see Corbett (1930), 55–57; Treggiari (1982).

8. Corbett (1930), 54.

9. Treggiari (1984) (quotation, 433). Cf. the statement of Stearns and Stearns (1985), 829: "When romance is discouraged in courtship . . . there will probably be less romance (although some) in marriage than when it is encouraged, if only because couples lack appropriate expectations or, in some cases, the vocabulary necessary to express them." See also Corbier (1987).

10. Aulus Gellius, *Attic Nights* 4.3.2; cf. Suetonius, *Caesar* 52.3.

11. Corbett (1930), 107.

12. Quotation from Csillag (1976), 43. The burden of marriage was the theme of a speech once given by the censor of 131–130 B.C., Q. Metellus Macedonicus. Aulus Gellius, *Attic Nights* 1.6, attributes the speech to Macedonicus's nephew, the censor of 102–101 B.C., Q. Metellus Numidicus. But it was Macedonicus, it seems, who impressed Augustus; see Livy, *Periocha* 59; Suetonius, *Augustus* 89.2; *ORF*³ 107–8; cf. Holford-Stevens (1988), 228. McDonnell (1987), however, argues for two speeches and a lack of error on Gellius's part. The important feature is the characterization of marriage as *molestia,* a topos in classical literature but one that Gellius was not obliged to propagate; see McDonnell (1987), 83–84.

13. Valerius Maximus, *Memorable Deeds and Sayings* 4.6; cf. 4.7.

14. Propertius 4.3.

15. Cassius Dio 56.7.2.

16. Cf. Pliny, *Letters* 4.19.

17. Duby (1983), 218. For the lawyers' phrase, see *Digest* 43.10.1.5. Note that it was not to his credit when Sallust described L. Sergius Catilina as "captus amore Aureliae Orestillae" (*Conspiracy of Catiline* 15.2). For the essential qualities of a good Roman marriage, *dignitas* and *concordia,* see Cicero, *Pro Cluentio* 12; cf. J. Griffin (1985), 119 n. 29, referring to a fragment of Seneca that argues "that passionate love of a wife is a form of adultery." The language of passion at Rome is associated above all with the affair, even from the woman's point of view, to judge from the Sulpicia poems in the Tibullan corpus; certainly, "the circumstances of these poems leave much to be guessed," but they have nothing to do with marriage. Lowe (1988), 197. See also, in general, Brown (1988), 12–13, 24, 113, 132, 403.

18. Dixon (1985), 356.

19. Valerius Maximus, *Memorable Deeds and Sayings* 6.7.1; Suetonius, *Augustus* 62.2; 71.1.

20. In 46 B.C., when in his sixties, Cicero married his young ward Publilia, who was little more than a girl, shortly after having divorced Terentia, his wife of thirty years. On medieval Christian marriage, see Duby (1983).

21. Csillag (1976), 71.

22. See Humbert (1972), 76–112; and below, Chapter 7.

23. See Williams (1958); Humbert (1972), 72–74.

24. *ILS* 8393 (27); cf. Lyne (1980), 17: "In this *laudatio* which celebrates and laments an extraordinarily devoted wife and which claims for the marriage an extraordinary felicity,

any actual mention of *love* is conspicuously lacking.'' The following comment on Anglo-Saxon England is not irrelevant to the Roman marriage situation: "Conditions of life such as slavery or captivity made nonsense of an unbreakable marriage bond, and so in cases of necessity the Anglo-Saxons saw no harm in terminating a marriage." Lucas (1983), 68. See also Mitterauer and Sieder (1982), 128–30. Note the use of the word *multivira* at Minucius Felix, *Octavius* 32.8.

25. For a different view, however, see Nörr (1981). On the purpose of the legislation, see Wallace-Hadrill (1981).

26. Cf. Mitterauer and Sieder (1982), 100.

27. Saller and Shaw (1984).

28. Cicero, *De Officiis* 1.54. Quotation from Saller and Shaw (1984), 137.

29. Quotation from Saller and Shaw (1984), 146. For a different picture of familial organization in one particular area of the Roman world, see Hobson (1985).

30. For details of information on the family of Sulla, see Drumann and Groebe (1899–1902), 2:432–33; *RE* IV, 1 cols. 1515–17, 1563, 1596, 1599–1600. On Sulla's marriages, see especially Plutarch, *Sulla* 6.10–12.

31. See B. Rawson (1986a), 35–36.

32. On the date of Cornelia's marriage, see Sumner (1977), 13.

33. Cornelia's children must have been born in close succession, since Q. Pompeius Rufus died in 88 B.C. (Appian, *Civil Wars* 1.56).

34. On the divorce, Plutarch, *Sulla* 34.2.

35. Plutarch, *Lucullus* 4.4.

36. Faustus was too young in 78 B.C. to pronounce his father's funeral oration (Appian, *Civil Wars* 1.106).

37. Plutarch, *Sulla* 33.3 (cf. *Pompeius* 9.2); Pliny, *Natural History* 36.113.

38. Sulla's elder son by Metella should not be forgotten; for his death, Plutarch, *Sulla* 37.2; Seneca, *Consolatio ad Marciam* 12.6.

39. For details of information on the family of Antonius, see Drumann and Groebe (1899–1902), 1:379–84; *PIR*[2] A 800, A 884, A 885; Babcock (1965); Huzar (1986). On Antonius's marriages, see especially Plutarch, *Antonius* 9.1–2, 10.3, 31.1–3. Note that Shaw and Saller (1984) argue that there was little endogamy in Roman society under the Principate; but cf. Corbier (1987), 1275–77.

40. Plutarch, *Antonius* 54.2, 87.1.

41. On Antyllus, Plutarch, *Antonius* 71.3.

42. Plutarch, *Antonius* 87.1–3.

43. See below, Chapter 7.

44. See, typically, for example, Syme (1979), 659–93; Syme (1984), 1364–75.

45. See Wiseman (1985), 15–20.

46. Cicero's speech was the *Pro Cluentio*. For what follows, see *Pro Cluentio* 11–12, 14, 21–23, 25–28, 30–31, 33, 35, 40, 165, 179. It should be emphasized that the very complex history of the family of Auria and Oppianicus (see Figure 6.3) produced a highly extensive network of relationships by marriage. Note the discussion of Moreau (1983).

47. Cicero, *Verrines* 2.1.153.

48. On the topos of the wicked stepmother, see Humbert (1972), 198; Dixon (1988), 155–59; Gray-Fow (1988a). On the more positive side, Gray-Fow (1988b) speculates that the young Octavian was prepared for political life by his stepfather, who taught him

hypocrisy and dissimulation. This, of course, is beyond proof, but it is plain enough that a man could exercise a moral influence over his wife's children.

49. *CIL* 6.7578.

50. Seneca, *Consolatio ad Marciam* 9.2 (cf. 11.5).

51. Cicero, *Pro Cluentio* 32; cf. also *Verrines* 2.3.161, 1.1. Other examples underscore still further how parental grief can scarcely be differentiated from parental expectation when children died prematurely. When Virius Vitalis, a young man from Lugdunum who died aged twenty, was commemorated by his stepfather, the words "in quo spem aetatis conlocaverat" were included on the stone (*ILS* 7723). They can only be taken to mean that the stepfather, who had actually trained Vitalis as a blacksmith and had adopted him as his own son, saw the young man as his means of support in old age. The loss of that support must necessarily have controlled the response to Vitalis's death. The tendency in Roman funerary art to depict children not as they were at the time of death but as they would have been had they lived longer—for which, see Kleiner (1987), 553—is fully consistent with this view. Again, Quintilian leaves no doubt of what he had expected from his older son. Although no more than nine when he died, the boy had already been betrothed to the daughter of his mother's brother (a senator of praetorian rank) and had been given in adoption to a senator of consular rank, the promise of a senatorial career plainly in view (cf. *Institute of Oratory* 6 pr. 13: "ad omnium spes honorum"). Quintilian, not of senatorial background himself, had married into a senatorial family and had taken all the necessary steps to further his own social progress in the next generation. But the son's death terminated those prospects. It is only realistic, therefore, to acknowledge that parental grief for the loss of a child contained a strong element of self-interest and regret. This does not mean that a sense of tragedy at the early ending of life itself was lacking or an absence of "naturalis erga filios caritas" (*Digest* 5.2.15 pr.). But it does mean that a statement such as "It is clear . . . that there was no *general* absence of tender feeling for children as special beings among any premodern European peoples"—Boswell (1988), 37—has to be evaluated carefully. It does not follow that premodern is necessarily identical with modern feeling.

52. Lucretius 1.936–942, 2.55–58, 3.85–90, 3.894–896, 4.11–17, 4.400–403, 6.35–38; Horace, *Satires* 1.1.25–26; cf. also Cicero, *De Finibus* 3.17, 5.42–43; Horace, *Satires* 1.3.133–136, 2.3.246–254; *Epistles* 1.1.62–63, 2.2.141–142; *Ars Poetica* 158–160; and for other references, see Manson (1978) and Manson (1983). In Manson's view, the tender image of the child visible in Roman poetry of the first century B.C. mirrors the growth of a concept that did not exist in earlier eras. Despite the thoroughness of the lexical analysis, however, the argument is vitiated by the fact that no balanced comparison of first-century literature with earlier literature is really possible.

53. Herlihy (1985), 23. Cf. Stearns and Stearns (1985), 818: "That a reduction in infant death rates accompanies (whether as cause or effect) an increase in the emotional investment in children has become a historical commonplace." See also Mitterauer and Sieder (1982), 60–61.

54. Seneca, *Consolatio ad Marciam* 24.2.

55. *Digest* 38.10. See the remarks of Scheid (1975), 350–54.

56. *Digest* 38.10.1.6.

57. Plautus, *Miles* 372–375; *Persa* 57–58.

58. *ILS* 915. On P. Paquius Scaeva and Flavia, see *RE* XVIII, 3 cols. 1119–24; *PIR²* F 248, F 407; Szramkiewicz (1972), 2:424.

59. *ILS* 401, 449.

60. Persius, *Satires* 6.52–56: "Well if none of my father's sisters or his brother's daughters and none of my uncle's great-great-granddaughters are left, and my maternal aunt has died without issue, if my granny's line is extinct, I'll go to the beggars' hill at Bovillae and in no time I'll find some Jack for an heir."

61. Observe the following, randomly assembled: Suetonius, *Augustus* 19.1 (*progener*); *Tiberius* 3.2 (*abnepos*); *Caligula* 10.1 (*proavia*); *Claudius* 26.1 (*proneptis*); *Nero* 35.1 (*abneptis*); Cicero, *De Officiis* 1.54 (*consobrini* and *sobrini*); Ovid, *Heroides* 17.205–206 (*pronurus*); Seneca, *Suasoriae* 1.5 (*amitinus*); Pliny, *Letters* 5.14.8 (*prosocer* and *amita*); Tacitus, *Annals* 1.8 (*nepotes pronepotesque*), 12.64 (*avunculus* and *sobrina*); *ILS* 327 (*neptis* and *matertera*), 1136 (*consocer*), 2947 (*prosocer*), 5484 (*propatruus*). At a late date, Ausonius commemorates in the *Parentalia* an *avunculus* (3), two *materterae* (6, 25), two *patrui* (7), two *amitae* (26, 27), a *consobrina* (28), his *socer* (8), *gener* (14), *consocer* (22), and *consocrus* (30), among others.

62. Cicero, *De Oratore* 2.2.

63. See Ausonius, *Parentalia* 3.7–10 (*avunculus*), 5.9–10 (*avia*), 6.1–2, 11–12 (*matertera*), 25.9–12 (*matertera*), 26.5 (*amita*). Cf. Hopkins (1961); Matthews (1975), 81–84; Guastella (1980); Booth (1982).

64. Lucretius 5.222–231; Propertius 4.3.41; Plautus, *Poenulus* 1124–1126, 1130. See Chapters 2 and 3 above; and cf. Néraudau (1984), 281–87; Mitterauer and Sieder (1982), 66–67 (on the socializing function of servants).

65. *Liber de viris illustribus* 75.1; cf. for the nurse of Cicero and a similar anecdote, Plutarch, *Cicero* 2.1.

66. Suetonius, *Grammarians* 12; Plutarch, *Brutus* 4.4.

67. Plutarch, *Antonius* 81, 87.

68. Cassius Dio 48.33.1; Suetonius, *Nero* 50.

69. Cicero, *De Amicitia* 20.74.

70. For details on *collactanei*, see the chapter appendix.

71. See Saller (1984).

Chapter Appendix

Collactanei were children simultaneously breast-fed by a woman (cf. *Corpus Glossariorum Latinorum* VI s.v. "collactaneus," "qui simul bibit lacte"), who in some cases was a wet nurse (*nutrix*). Little is heard in literary sources of the children of nurses (but cf. Suetonius, *Nero* 35.5), and to some extent a woman's availability as a wet nurse may have depended on the early death of her own child. However, a passage from Augustine (*Confessions* 1.7.11) might be understood to mean that the children of nurses were commonly nursed with their mother's nurslings and that both sets of infants therefore spent considerable time together in early childhood. Plutarch, when speaking of the discord that might arise between brothers dividing their father's estate, refers to the ''nurses and slave-boys who have been brought up'' with them and who are ''their familiar companions,'' as a possible source of contention (*Moralia* 483E). In wet-nursing contracts from Roman Egypt, the stipulation is sometimes met that during the nursing period the nurse is not to breast-feed any child other than the one for whom her services are engaged (e.g., *BGU* 1107), and it might be supposed that the provision customarily applied elsewhere in the Roman world; cf. Néraudau (1984), 286. However, inscriptions identifying *collactanei* and nurses do not support this view.

Table 6.1 summarizes information on *collactanei* available from Latin inscriptions, from both the city of Rome and elsewhere, whether or not nurses are mentioned. (Reference numbers are given for volumes of *CIL*.) All the individuals listed have been assigned a juridical status on the basis of details provided by their respective texts: S = *servus/a:* L = *libertus/a;* I = *ingenuus/a;* F = free. Those designated free may have been *liberti/ae* or *ingenui/ae;* it is impossible to be precise for the most part. But those designated freeborn were usually of upper-class background. It is immediately noticeable that no pair of *collactanei* consisted of two upper-class infants. A few other observations may be made.

The child Atticus (no. 4), who died at the age of four, was the son of the *nutrix* Stacte. Both were almost certainly slaves in the *familia* of the senatorial Statilii Tauri. Stacte's nursling was probably the son of Sisenna Statilius Taurus, cos. A.D. 16, and Atticus his *conlacteus*. L. Volusius Zosimus (no. 5) was also the son of a nurse, Volusia Stratonice, and the *collactius* of his mother's nursling, a child from the family of the senatorial Volusii Saturnini and so again of upper-class status. Stratonice was probably a family freedwoman and her son therefore of servile extraction. Another *conlacteus* of servile background associated with an upper-class nursling was L. Arruntius Dicaeus (no. 3), though the details of this case are less clear than those of the two previous examples. However, it is clear enough from these items that it was possible at Rome for a woman employed as a wet nurse for upper-class children to nurse her own infant at the same time.

The same conclusion might apply in two similar cases, in which, however, in the absence of definite attestation, a nurse's identity can only

Table 6.1. *Collactanei* in Inscriptions*

	Name	Status	Name	Status	Reference
1	M. Vibius Proclus alumnus of Paenia Daphne	F	M. Vibius Felix son of Paenia Daphne	F	6.1903
2	ignotus	—	L. Manlius L.f. Pal. Severus	I	6.2125
3	L. Arruntius L.l. Dicaeus	L	L. Arruntius?	I	6.5939
4	Atticus son of Stacte, nutrix	S?	Sisennae f(ilius)	I	6.6324
5	L. Volusius Zosimus son of Volusia Stratonice, nutrix	F	L. Volusi L.f. ponti f(ilius)	I	6.7393
6	L. Ciartius Scyrus	F	P. Ciartius Helops	F	6.9745
7	M. Vipsanius Agrippinae l. Thales	L	Celer Galli filius	I	6.9901a
8	P. Aelius Pastor	F	Volusia L.f. Salviane	I	6.10760
9	Aphrodisia	S?	Apollaust[. . .	S?	6.12115
10	Ti. Claudius Zeno	F	Ti. Claudius Euaristus	F	6.15323
11	Communio verna Antoniae Augustae	S	Drusus Blandi f(ilius)	I	6.16057
12	Faenia Hygia	F	Faenia L.f. Priscilla	I	6.17682
13	Flavia Fortunata	F	[F]lavius Julianus	F	6.18115
14	Moschis	S?	ignotus/a	—	6.18553
15	Maecilia Cn. l. Eleutheris	L	L. Grattidius Ɔ. l. Eunus	L	6.19112
16	Primitivus	S?	C. Lucilius Festus	F	6.24975
17	Laenas liberta	L	Salvia Tertulla	F	6.25845
18	Hermes	S?	Tatias Adrasti filia	S?	6.27119
19	M. Julius Julianus	F	Vennonius Euelpistus	F	6.28463
20	Ceionius Constantius	F	Tere[n]tia [Pr]ocula	F	6.29690
21	Salvius Victor	F	L. Titius L.f. Pupinia Macer	I	6.29728
22	Januaria	S?	. . .]rinus	S?	6.35492
23	Primigenius	S?	Naevius Clemens	F	6.36193

Table 6.1. Continued

	Name	Status	Name	Status	Reference
24	Annia Aquilina	F	C. Javolenus Severus	F	5.3487
25	Arria Geminia	F	Arrius Germanus p.p. Junior	F	10.1778
26	Helaenus	S?	Klocaerus	S	11.1067
27	Caedius Rufinus	F	C. Tadius Sabinus	F	11.6345
28	Q. Annius Pallas	F	ignotus/a	—	AE 1967.59
29	Cl. Baculus	F	Teltonius Erosion	F	8.3523
30	A. Helice	F?	M. A(ntonius) Maximus	F	2.104
31	Aur. Flavianus	F	Aur. Nemisius	F	3.4218 ˙
32	Ceionia Hilara liber.	L	Ceionia Ferocilla	F	3.8976
33	ignota	—	[Va]l. Therma- tiliana	F	12.337

*See Table Notes at the end of this chapter.

be presumed. M. Vipsanius Thales (no. 7), who died at the age of eighteen, was the *conlactan(eus)* of Sergius Asinius Celer, cos. A.D. 38. Celer's parents were C. Asinius Gallus, cos. 8 B.C., and Vipsania Agrippina, the former wife of Tiberius, and clearly it was she who manumitted Thales. But the identity of Thales's mother is not recorded. However, on the analogy of the cases above, it would seem plausible that Thales's mother was Celer's nurse, a woman in Agrippina's household she would have used as a *nutrix* when Celer was born. Similarly, Communio (no. 11), a slave born into the household of Antonia Minor who died at the age of two, was *collacteus* of Drusus, son of C. Rubellius Blandus, cos. A.D. 18, and Julia, daughter of Drusus Caesar, whom Blandus married in A.D. 33. The reference of Syme (1988), 192 n. 102, to the "brother" of Drusus Blandi f. identified by *CIL* 6.16057 should be regarded as a corruption of "foster brother," and the number of Rubellius Blandus's children by Julia should be consequently amended from four to three. Communio's mother is also unknown. But in all likelihood she would have been a slave belonging to Antonia who served as Drusus's *nutrix*.

Simultaneous nursing of infants of vastly different social rank is evident enough from the examples involving *ingenui* so far noted. But not all *ingenui* were of superior social status. Thus, L. Manlius L.f. Severus (no. 2), although a not inconsequential figure, being described in his inscription as "rex sacrorum, fictor pontificum p(opuli) R(omani), iiii vir Bovillensium," must have been of lesser standing than the members of senatorial families seen earlier. Cf. also L. Titius L.f. Macer (no. 21). Unfortunately his *collactaneus* is unidentifiable. Nor is anything known of the family of Volusia L.f. Salviane (no. 8), who does not appear to be connected with the Volusii Saturnini. However, Faenia Hygia and Faenia L.f. Priscilla (no. 12) were probably of comparable background, despite the free birth of the latter. Both girls died in infancy, before their second birthdays. They were commemorated by Priscilla's brother, L. Faenius Vitalis, as were also the parents of these siblings, L. Faenius Philetus and Faenia Medusa. The parents' shared *nomen* suggests that they had once been slaves in the same household and had been manumitted by their common owner. Being freeborn, Priscilla would have been born after her parents' manumission but remained nonetheless of servile extraction. Faenia Hygia, although free at her death, should therefore be regarded as a child of slave origins, too, deriving from the same *familia* as Priscilla's parents. She and Priscilla were nursed by the same woman. But whether that woman was Medusa or a separate *nutrix* cannot be said. However, the girls' similar background provides a strong contrast with the earlier examples.

Other pairs of *collactanei* with common *nomina* might perhaps be presumed to have both been slaves as children, or children not far removed from slavery (nos. 6, 10, 13), as would pairs whose inscriptions refer to them with only single names (nos. 9, 18, 22, 26; cf. also no. 14). Equally, an undistinguished woman such as Ceionia Ferocilla (no. 32) may have been the patron of her freed foster sibling; or the *alumnus* of a woman such as Paenia Daphne (no. 1) may have become the foster sibling of her own child. Slave origins are certain for the freed pair Maecilia Cn. l. Eleutheris and L. Grattidius Ɔ. l. Eunus (no. 15); although eventually set free by different owners, they must have belonged to the same household as infants.

In most cases it is impossible to determine whether the woman who nursed *collactanei* was formally a *nutrix* or not. Apart from the nurses associated with upper-class families already discussed, the only other certain *nutrix* to appear in the inscriptions is Maria Marcellina, nurse of the praetorian soldier C. Tadius Sabinus and Caedius Rufinus (no. 27). From the inscriptions alone, it is also difficult to judge the extent of the practice of simultaneous breast-feeding, though the rule of the *lex Aelia*

Sentia, that slave *collactanei* could be manumitted by an owner under the age of twenty (Gaius, *Institutes* 1.38–39; *Digest* 40.2.13), could be taken as evidence of a fairly widespread convention. However, inscriptional examples of *collactanei* outside the city of Rome are sparse. (For some literary examples, see *TLL* s.v. *collactaneus, collacteus,* etc.)

The bonds formed between pairs of *collactanei* were sometimes very close, to judge from the terms of endearment found in the inscriptions: "collactaneo dulcissimo et indulgentissimo erga se" (no. 2); "bene merenti et anim[a]e innocenti" (no. 20); "collactaneae pientissimae" (no. 24); "collacticio dulcissimo" (no. 29). This is to be expected given the evidence of the *lex Aelia Sentia.* Cf. also *Digest* 34.4.30.1, a freed *collactanea* benefiting from a will; Juvenal 6.307, with Courtney (1980), 297–98. Yet expressions of intimacy are not found in inscriptions referring to *collactanei* of vastly different social status. So whatever childhood connections may have existed between a pair such as Thales (no. 7) and Sergius Asinius Celer, they were not likely to endure once the aristocratic child reached an age to be educated and prepared for entry into the adult world. A shared infancy was not the prelude to a subsequent common life-style.

Nevertheless, whether composed of children of dissimilar or similar background, pairs of *collactanei* of necessity were associated one with another at the earliest stage of their lives, and that association, under the supervision of a nursing woman, must have assumed a quasi-familial character (recognized by the manumission rules) in a broad sense. That being so, the evidence on *collactanei* illustrates further the difficulty of defining the Roman family.

Table Notes

2. *CIL* 6.2125 = *CIL* 14.2413 = *ILS* 4942. On L. Manlius Severus, see *PIR*[2] M 158; cf. also *RE* I A, 1 cols. 725–26.

3. For discussion of the nursling, see Bradley (1986), 225 n. 8.

4. *CIL* 6.6324 = *ILS* 8539. Cf. Bradley (1986), 226 n. 11.

5. *CIL* 6.7393 = Buonocore (1984), no. 72. Cf. Bradley (1986), 226 n. 15.

6. Cf. above, p. 71, no. 68.

7. *CIL* 6.9901a = *ILS* 8540. On Ser. Asinius Celer, see *PIR*[2] A 1225.

11. On the family of Rubellius Blandus, see Syme (1988), 177–98. On Antonia Minor, see *PIR*[2] A 885.

12. There may possibly be a connection with Nero's praetorian prefect, L. Faenius Rufus (*PIR*² F 102).

14. The inscription is a dedication by an imperial slave and his wife "filiae piissimae . . . et sibi et Moschini conlact." The daughter, who is unnamed, was probably the foster sibling, though this cannot be certain.

19. There may possibly be a connection with Julius Julianus, legate of Arabia in A.D. 125; see *PIR*² I 361a: Syme (1979), 786–87.

28. The inscription does not give the dedicant's identity.

7

Remarriage and the Structure of the Upper-Class Family at Rome

My purpose in this chapter is to work some way further toward clarifying the character of Roman family life, first by calculating the incidence of remarriage among the Roman elite of the late Republic at large and then by confirming the effects of remarriage, or serial marriage, on the structure of the upper-class family. If the extent of remarriage were found to be high, the character of the family would have to be rather different from that produced in circumstances where a low rate of remarriage prevailed. In the former case, a greater number of blended or reconstituted family groupings would be expected than in conditions where married couples remained in stable unions over long periods of time, and in turn a high degree of blending might be expected to lead to a typical family form distinct from that created in situations where reconstitution was of negligible significance. Prominent individuals such as L. Cornelius Sulla and M. Antonius are known to have married several times, and a certain dislocation in their families was the inevitable result. But how typical were case histories such as theirs, and how widespread the consequences?

At once it could be said that because marriage in Rome of the late Republic was intimately bound up with the world of politics, the extraordinary public lives of men like Sulla and Antonius made their matrimonial careers equally extraordinary, so that no generalizations about the family ought to be drawn from their individual histories. On the other hand, the leading historian of the Roman elite has stated, without ambiguity, that ''the more that is discovered about persons of note at

Rome, the more marriages come to light or have to be postulated,'' and it becomes very difficult therefore to resist the impression that repeated marriage was common.[1] Indeed, random remarks drawn from the correspondence of Cicero suggest, from a contemporary perspective, the apparent ordinariness of the event, and make clear the assumption that step relationships were viewed as a fully predictable and accepted aspect of Roman family life. Thus:

> In this letter I am recommending Q. Fufidius. . . . He is the stepson [*privignus*] of my particular friend and connection M. Caesius. . . .
>
> [Nicias] said that to his knowledge Talna had recently proposed to Cornificia, Quintus' daughter, a much-married lady by no means in her first youth [*vetulam sane et multarum nuptiarum*]. . . .
>
> I can't at this stage add anything about Tubero's wife and stepdaughter [*privigna*] to my speech for Ligarius. . . .
>
> But how much faith to put in one of [Octavian's] years and name and heredity and education—that's a great question. His step-father thinks none at all [*vitricus quidem nihil censebat*]—I saw him at Astura.
>
> Paula Valeria, Triarius' sister, has divorced her husband for no reason the day he was due to get back from his province. She is to marry D. Brutus. [Caelius Rufus to Cicero][2]

One could point, too, to the volume of law dealing with the ramifications of repeated marriage, even though it has to be kept in mind that bulk alone is not in itself an index of common social behavior. The Roman jurists simply take it for granted that remarriage was normative.[3]

To test the impression, however, it is obviously desirable to try to measure, if only approximately, the actual rate of remarriage in a specific population, and that is what I wish to do here for the consular families of the period from 80 B.C to 50 B.C.—that is, to see how many of the consuls and their wives in the ''last generation of the Roman Republic'' were involved in repeated marriage. The group chosen for study is, of course, exceptional in that it includes the most politically successful figures of a whole era. But most of these men did not gain success (or notoriety) comparable to that of the dynasts, and the tactic of working with a finite sample may create a relatively objective basis from which to explore the upper-class family in wider compass. As the implications of repeated marriage are pursued, the main contention will be that if the Roman family is to be properly understood, a core reproductive unit of coresident parents and children cannot be studied in isolation, but a much broader framework of reference has to be adopted.

II

The topics on which information is ideally required are straightforward enough: how many of the consuls in the period stated were married; how many were married more than once; how many of their wives were married more than once; and how many children were born to each marriage. Immediately, however, the point has to be made that a precise calculation of the rate of remarriage is beyond reach, for despite the high social and political profile of the fifty-nine consuls concerned, full records of their matrimonial histories, and so of their wives' histories, just do not exist (see Table 7.1).[4] Some consuls are known to have married once but may have remarried or have been previously married without any trace of the fact having survived in the extant evidence, while others are not known to have married at all, even though it is highly unlikely under the prevailing social conditions of the age that they never did so.[5] To illustrate: L. Afranius, consul in 60, is known to have had a son and so to have married; but the identity of his wife is not recorded.[6] Further, since Afranius's son was *adulescens* in 49, it is possible that Afranius was married more than once, though nothing more than the possibility can be registered. More awkward still is Q. Caecilius Metellus Pius, consul in 80. Metellus belonged to a family that had dominated Rome's political life at the turn of the first century and whose members continued to rise to the consulship throughout the generation under scrutiny. It would stretch all limits of belief to imagine that he never married, but no wife can be securely identified for him.[7] Under these circumstances, accordingly, it is probable that the incidence of both marriage and remarriage is underrepresented in the sample as a whole, so that any figure proposed for the rate of remarriage must be judged minimal.

What, then, emerges from the marriage histories of the consuls themselves? First, information is utterly lacking for eight men, who thus have to be excluded from consideration. But evidence of a single marriage, actual or presumable from the attestation of legitimate offspring, exists for the remaining fifty-one, and a record of remarriage appears in eight instances.[8] At first blush the incidence of remarriage in the group as a whole does not seem especially noteworthy, about

Table 7.1. Consuls, 80–50 B.C.

B.C.			
80	1. L. Cornelius Sulla	2.	Q. Caecilius Metellus Pius
79	3. P. Servilius Vatia	4.	Ap. Claudius Pulcher
78	5. M. Aemilius Lepidus	6.	Q. Lutatius Catulus
77	7. D. Junius Brutus	8.	Mam. Aemilius Lepidus Livianus
76	9. Cn. Octavius	10.	C. Scribonius Curio
75	11. L. Octavius	12.	C. Aurelius Cotta
74	13. L Licinius Lucullus	14.	M. Aurelius Cotta
73	15. M. Terentius Varro Lucullus	16.	C. Cassius Longinus
72	17. L. Gellius Poplicola	18.	Cn. Cornelius Lentulus Clodianus
71	19. P. Cornelius Lentulus Sura	20.	Cn. Aufidius Orestes
70	21. Cn. Pompeius Magnus	22.	M. Licinius Crassus
69	23. Q. Hortensius	24.	Q. Caecilius Metellus Creticus
68	25. L. Caecilius Metellus	26.	Q. Marcius Rex
67	27. C. Calpurnius Piso	28.	M'. Acilius Glabrio
66	29. M'. Aemilius Lepidus	30.	L. Volcacius Tullus
65	31. L. Aurelius Cotta	32.	L. Manlius Torquatus
64	33. L. Julius Caesar	34.	C. Marcius Figulus
63	35. M. Tullius Cicero	36.	C. Antonius
62	37. D. Junius Silanus	38.	L. Licinius Murena
61	39. M. Pupius Piso	40.	M. Valerius Messalla
60	41. Q. Caecilius Metellus Celer	42.	L. Afranius
59	43. C. Julius Caesar	44.	M. Calpurnius Bibulus
58	45. L. Calpurnius Piso Caesoninus	46.	A. Gabinius
57	47. P. Cornelius Lentulus Spinther	48.	Q. Caecilius Metellus Nepos
56	49. Cn. Cornelius Lentulus Marcellinus	50.	L. Marcius Philippus
55	21. Cn. Pompeius Magnus	22.	M. Licinius Crassus
54	51. L. Domitius Ahenobarbus	52.	Ap. Claudius Pulcher
53	53. Cn. Domitius Calvinus	54.	M. Valerius Messalla
52	21. Cn. Pompeius Magnus	55.	Q. Caecilius Metellus Pius Scipio
51	56. Ser. Sulpicius Rufus	57.	M. Claudius Marcellus
50	58. L. Aemilius Paullus	59.	C. Claudius Marcellus

16 percent. But in all likelihood the rate should be raised considerably to take account of twelve likely instances of remarriage that can be deduced from prosopographical and chronological studies.[9] For example, D. Junius Brutus, consul in 77, is known to have married a Sempronia, on record in 63, and to have had a son, D. Brutus Albinus, who was born (it is thought) about 81; but because the son's *cognomen* belongs to the family of the Postumii, it can be argued that the mother of Albinus was a Postumia and that Sempronia was his stepmother. Two marriages have to be allowed, therefore, to the consul of 77, even though the first is not

directly attested.[10] Again, it is known that M. Pupius Piso, consul in 61, divorced his wife about 82 when he was aged approximately thirty-three.[11] Between that time and the year of his consulship, there was every opportunity for Piso to remarry, and it is more than reasonable to assume that he did so in view of the general importance of marriage in Roman upper-class society. Admittedly, an element of doubt must remain in these cases, but all things considered, the doubt is slight. So if the twelve cases of likely remarriage are added to the certain cases, the rate of remarriage rises to about 39 percent, which can be taken to indicate, potentially at least, a significant degree of familial reconstitution in the lives of those affected by the remarrying consuls.

The degree becomes more significant still if account is taken of the remarrying consular wives and the focus set on the conjugal units brought into existence by any consul's marriage. There are sixteen instances of certain remarriage and three cases of likely remarriage among the consular wives, so that remarriage on the part of at least one spouse becomes visible in about 47 percent of the families created by the consuls' marriages.[12] This implies that almost one of every two families in which the husband became consul felt the impact of reconstitution in one way or another, and for reasons already stated the result might well be conservative.[13] It is true that there are four cases of consular marriages that show no sign of children issuing from them[14]—caused, no doubt, by an absence of evidence rather than failure of the couples to reproduce at all—and this means that the degree of familial blending consequent upon remarriage cannot quite be regarded as equal to the rate of remarriage among the principals. I suspect, however, that it can have been little different in reality, and such a profusion of intermingling must be assumed in some way to have affected the essential character of the Roman family.

The familial blending remarriage caused is easily demonstrable. Among stepparents one can note Servilia, the second wife of L. Licinius Lucullus, consul in 74, and stepmother to his children by his first wife, Clodia; P. Cornelius Lentulus Sura, consul in 71, stepfather to his wife Julia's three sons from her previous marriage to M. Antonius Creticus; D. Junius Silanus, consul in 62, stepfather to his wife Servilia's son by M. Junius Brutus; Porcia, the second wife of M. Calpurnius Bibulus, consul in 59, and stepmother to his son (or sons) from an earlier marriage; and L. Marcius Philippus, consul in 56, stepfather to his wife Atia's children by C. Octavius.[15] Likewise, among stepsiblings and half-siblings one can observe that the three daughters of D. Junius Silanus, consul in 62, had an older half-brother from Servilia's first marriage to M. Brutus; and the daughter and son of L. Calpurnius Piso Caesoninus, consul in 58, were half-siblings widely separated in age, twenty-five years.[16] The son of L. Marcius Philippus, consul in 56, had as stepsiblings the son and daughter of Marcius's wife, Atia, from her marriage to C. Octavius; and the son and two daughters of C. Claudius Marcellus, consul in 50, were the elder half-siblings of their mother's two daughters by M. Antonius.[17] It could happen that a child was exposed to the influence of a stepparent at a very tender age, as in the case of Marcella, the younger daughter of C. Claudius Marcellus, who was born in 40 or 39, soon after her father's death, and whose mother, Octavia, quickly married M. Antonius.[18] And it could happen, too, that a stepmother who was much younger than her remarrying husband was in fact much the same age as, or even younger than, his children from earlier marriages. Thus, when M. Tullius Cicero, consul in 63, married his ward Publilia in December 46—he was sixty, she about fifteen—his daughter Tullia was aged about thirty and had already been married herself more than once.[19] Complex, if more distant, associations could also arise, for the marriages of Marcia to M. Porcius Cato and Q. Hortensius, consul in 69, made her a stepmother twice over and indirectly united Cato's children by Atilia and Hortensius's by Lutatia. Atia, the successive wife of C. Octavius and L. Marcius Philippus, brought together Octavius's daughter by Ancharia and Marcius's son from an earlier union—with the sequel that the son took as his own wife his stepmother's younger sister.[20]

The factors that governed remarriage and the reconstitution of families hardly need to be spelled out. Men died prematurely from the accidents of warfare, women from the hazards of childbirth, both from the ravages of uncontrollable disease.[21] In addition, the fluctuations of Roman politics affected not only first marriages but the high rate of divorce and subsequent formation of new alliances as well. And in a society where sentiment was at best no more than incidental to the arrangement of a marriage, there could be little opposition to serial marriage if the wider demands of society were to be met.

The main points of interest to emerge from the material considered so far are:

1. that upper-class families at Rome were not composed predominantly of married couples who as individuals expected only one-spousal partner in their lives and of children who expected their parents' union to be severed only by death in old age;

2. that, on the contrary, many, perhaps most, men and women would anticipate at least two marriages in the course of their adulthood, the birth of children in each marriage, and stepparental association with other children;

3. that the offspring of upper-class parents would anticipate, whether in their early or more mature years, the appearance in their familial worlds of stepparents, half-siblings, and stepsiblings.

It is difficult, naturally, to say what emotional effects these social norms produced among family members, though a certain lack of permanence in family life might be postulated; and, as in later periods of history, the stereotype of the wicked stepmother should be allowed to derive from the widely experienced tensions between child and stepparent that frequent remarriage created.[22] However that may be, it is clear that the Roman family, if captured at a precise moment in time, was in many instances rather more than a simple reproductive unit of father, mother, and offspring. How, then, as a type, is it to be characterized?

III

To speak of the Roman family is to speak of an entity that can be defined in various ways, according to context. If, for example, one speaks of the family of the Metelli dominating Roman political life at the turn of the first century, the meaning—all kin, or at least all male kin—is vastly different from speaking of, say, the flight in 40 of Ti. Claudius Nero from Naples to Sicily with his family—that is, his wife, Livia, and his infant son, Tiberius.[23] Since the Roman upper class of the late Republic was a relatively circumscribed body, it would be difficult to dispute the observation that "the harder one looks, the clearer it becomes that *all* the great politicians were linked by family ties of one sort or another."[24] But to investigate the Roman family in the sense of all kin would for present purposes bring little advantage, because the concept is too amorphous to be really useful. At the same time, the value of concentrating on the core reproductive unit alone should already have been brought into question by the evidence of familial blending. It may be preferable, therefore, to consider the general categories of household formation used by modern historians and sociologists—in which coresidence is the prime criterion of concern—as a set of alternatives from which the most appropriate classification for Roman conditions might be selected. The following broad types can be noted:[25]

1. *Simple family household:* a term used to indicate a coresident domestic group comprising "a married couple, or a married couple with offspring, or a widowed person with offsping," but most often used simply to mean the "nuclear family," that is, a household consisting "in its entirety of man, wife and children.

2. *Extended family household:* a term used to indicate "a conjugal family unit with the addition of one or more relatives other than offspring, the whole group living together.

3. *Multiple family household:* a term used to indicate "all forms of domestic group which include two or more conjugal family units connected by kinship or marriage."

What correlations can be made between these concepts and the Roman household?

It was customary for a Roman senator to maintain a residence within the city, no matter what properties he possessed elsewhere, not least as a basis from which to pursue his public career. Evidence on senators' town houses is plentiful and has been conveniently catalogued.[26] However, to understand typical living arrangements, it is vital to know when in a senator's, or aspirant senator's life he established a household independent of that of his parents, a point that had not been reached, for example, by the two brothers of M. Licinius Crassus, consul in 70, when they married. According to Plutarch, Crassus's "two brothers were married while their parents were still alive and the whole family had their meals together."[27] The Crassi, that is, formed a multigenerational or multiple-family household. (And, it should be noted, Plutarch continues that "when one of his brothers died Crassus married the widow and had children by her.") Moreover, in an earlier age the elder Cato's son had continued to live in his father's house after marrying, while sixteen relatives of the second-century senator Q. Aelius Tubero, all Aelii, are said to have lived together in one house with a multitude of wives and children.[28]

Yet circumstances such as these were probably exceptional.[29] Cicero, when defending M. Caelius Rufus in 56, argued that a single young man close to thirty who was embarking on a public career could be expected to have his own residence in Rome, even though the criticism Caelius had incurred for not living in his father's house could be taken to imply that not everyone would have agreed.[30] Still, it was a possibility that Cicero's own son, Marcus, should have had his own residence in Rome before the age of twenty when he was as yet unmarried. Sulla, as a young man and probably before his first marriage, too, rented accommodation in a house shared by independent freedman. And the younger Cato, who had been orphaned in early life, also acquired his own house once he inherited his patrimony, almost certainly before his first marriage at the age of twenty-two.[31] Obviously enough, much must have depended on individuals' financial circumstances, and the story of the coresidential Aelii was clearly told to point up their poverty.[32] But most senatorial families were not impoverished, and by and large it can be accepted that young men of the senatorial class often set up their own households at the time of first marriage—if indeed they had not already done so—and that multigenerational households, though not true aberrations, were not the norm. In modern jargon, Roman upper-class marriage was neo-local, though *patria potestas* might for a time continue to exert a restraining influence on the independence of the young married man.[33] The establishment of a separate household comprising a newly married couple—that is, a simple family household—created the potential for the swift appearance of a complete nuclear family, and it becomes tempting, as a result, to assert the primacy in Roman society of that entity.

But the Roman household did not consist of the married couple and their children alone; it included also their domestic staff, and "in attempting to construct types of family grouping," it has been said, "the historian must take into account all those who play a part in the house or household community in its entirety, whether they are related to each other or not."[34] The involvement in the lives and affairs of their masters of the slaves and former slaves who made up the domestic retinue could at times reach a very intimate level; the close relationship between Cicero and Tiro is proof enough of that.[35] To be sure, no one would wish to maintain that a tie of this sort existed between the master and every member of the household staff, and the distinction between servant and blood relative was not forgotten. However, when the privileged servant took his former owner's name upon manumission, a blurring of that distinction could certainly occur; and it remains true that the practical tasks of child care, typically handled by servants, brought certain domestics into the emotional orbit of the infant children of the household and kept them there until adulthood and beyond. The luxurious mansions owned by upper-class Romans, housing both the core unit of owner, wife, and unmarried children and other core units made up from the members of the domestic retinue, were from a certain point of view multiple-family residences. Therefore, given this physical, practical, and emotional interaction between kin and nonkin household members, the concept of the simple family household or nuclear household seems inadequate as a realistic point of central reference for understanding Roman familial behavior and mentality. (When the infant Tiberius was in flight with his mother and father, Livia even then had his nurse with the child.) Admittedly, modern typologies may allow for the inclusion in the simple family household of servants, but usually servants whose stay in the household was brief and whose role was dissimilar from that of the Roman servants closely associated with the socialization of children over time.[36]

Of greater importance, none of the types of household formation itemized above will successfully accommodate the complexities of Roman family life consequent upon remarriage. True, the term *nuclear household* is sometimes used to refer to a coresident domestic group made up of remarried parents, their common children, and their other children from previous marriages, and this may have a certain validity for the Roman family in cases where remarriage followed spousal death. (The problem of the servants, however, would still be left.) But the situation is rather different in cases where remarriage followed divorce. At Rome it was the legal rule that the children of a divorced couple were to remain in the household of their father.[37] After the departure of their mother from the household, they would thus be physically separated from her, though still, of course, related to her. In turn, if the mother remarried and had children by a new husband, the half-siblings would belong to different households but would nonetheless still be bound by a familial tie. To illustrate: Livia, the mother of the younger Cato, was married twice. To her first husband, Q. Servilius Caepio, she bore three children (two daughters and a son), the last of whom was born in 98; the following year or a little later, Caepio divorced Livia, who at once married a M. Porcius Cato, to whom she had borne two further children by 91, when both she and her second husband were dead. The older of these children, the young Cato himself, was born in 95, the other (his sister) somewhat later.[38] The point of interest here is that for about five years or so before her death, Livia, residing in the new husband's household and bearing his children, was presumably distanced from her older children, all of whom were still quite young but living in their father's household. So, too, the half-siblings, though sharing a common parent, were situated in two distinct physical settings. It cannot be said that the two households formed two totally separate families, because continuing family ties between close relatives not coresident created a link between them. And to emphasize the fact of the link—of a kind that must have been common indeed in view of the frequency of divorce and remarriage at Rome—is not to wander back in the direction of defining the family as all kin. A line of common sense can be drawn.

Consequently, it does not seem to be a useful strategy to try to locate the Roman family within a typology that, in stressing the factor of coresidence, encourages household and family to be regarded as synonymous and the family as essentially static; but as the fact of serial marriage naturally suggests, it is better to pursue the dynamic element in family history and to allow for the possibility that different configurations within the same family, of complex character, might arise at different stages of the family's development or life course.[39] The matrimonial career of Cn. Pompeius Magnus illustrates the point.

Pompeius's first wife, Antistia, was the daughter of the Antistius who presided in 86 at Pompeius's trial for embezzlement. During the trial Antistius is said to have been so impressed by the defendant that he offered Pompeius his daughter in marriage. A betrothal was arranged, and a few days after Pompeius's acquittal the marriage was celebrated.[40] Antistia, it can be supposed, was several years younger than her husband, who was just about nineteen and marrying for the first time. But as far as is known there was no issue from the marriage, which after only four years came to an end. The reason was that in 82 Sulla, in a deliberate act of political calculation, pressured Pompeius into an alliance with him by encouraging the young man to divorce Antistia and marry instead Sulla's stepdaughter, Aemilia. Pompeius obliged. But the situation was hampered by the fact that Aemilia already had a husband, M'. Acilius Glabrio, consul in 67, and indeed was in the late stages of a pregnancy. Yet her divorce, too, was quickly arranged, the marriage to Pompeius effected, and Aemilia's presence in a new household established. It happened that the new marriage was very brief, for Aemilia died giving birth to her child (M'. Acilius Glabrio), so again Pompeius was still without a child of his own.[41] Technically, however, he did become a stepfather in 82, though contact between Pompeius and the infant Glabrio was probably negligible. Although born in Pompeius's house, the child was presumably transferred to his father's house to be reared.

From about 80 until the end of 62, Pompeius was married to Mucia, the daughter of a Metella and half-sister of the Metelli who were consuls in 69 and 68.[42] There is no explicit testimony to prove that the match was politically contrived, but in view of Mucia's Metellan connections, it can hardly have been otherwise. The marriage produced three children—Cn. Pompeius, Pompeia, and Sex. Pompeius—all of whom were probably born in the early years of the union.[43] In 77, Pompeius was away on campaign and wintered with his army in the Cisalpina before moving in 76 to Spain, where he remained occupied with the war against Q. Sertorius until 71. The amount of time he spent with his young children cannot therefore have been great. Whether the children had any association with their stepbrother Glabrio is unknown, but the point of their indirect familial relationship is to be noted.

Returning to Rome in 62 from his great eastern expeditions, Pompeius promptly divorced Mucia for her alleged infidelities during his absence.[44] The marriage had lasted for eighteen years or so and in Roman terms had been successful: children had been produced. But for most of the time the principals had been separated by the demands of Pompeius's career. In due course Mucia became the wife of M. Aemilius Scaurus (once briefly Pompeius's brother-in-law) and bore him a son.[45] Pompeius thus acquired a second stepson, his children a half-brother considerably younger than themselves and one who belonged, though related to them, to a different household.

In yet another politically motivated move, Pompeius in 59 next married Julia, Caesar's daughter, the marriage at once requiring cancellation of Julia's impending union with Q. Servilius Caepio and making her the stepmother of Pompeius's children.[46] Yet it happened that she was of their generation, being practically coeval with Sex. Pompeius and so about sixteen when she married a husband thirty years her senior.[47] Despite the difference in age, the marriage is said to have been passionate on both sides, and in the five years it lasted Julia became pregnant twice. The first pregnancy terminated in a miscarriage caused by Julia's belief that Pompeius had been killed in a bout of urban violence; and the second concluded with Julia dying in childbirth, her daughter surviving only a few days.[48] Had she lived, the child would have been much of an age with Pompeius's grandchildren; Pompeia, married soon after 59, had had two children by 46 when her first husband died.[49]

Like Julia, Pompeius's last wife, Cornelia, daughter of Pompeius's colleague in the consulship of 52, was much younger than her husband, and the criticism was made when they married in 52 that she would have been a more suitable bride for one of Pompeius's sons. As it was, she became a second coeval stepmother to Pompeius's children.[50] The marriage lasted until 48, when Cornelia became a widow for the second time (her first husband had been P. Licinius Crassus, son of the triumvir), but as far as is known it did not produce any new children for Pompeius, who at the time of his death was almost fifty-nine.[51]

From this summary of one man's marriages, it should be clear that the life course of families comprising remarrying individuals and their offspring was rather different from that of the modern affective nuclear family as usually understood— not least, perhaps, because of the Roman woman's continuing ties to her family of origin after marriage *sine manu*.[52] Typically the contemporary nuclear family proceeds through a number of well-differentiated and predictable stages: the marriage of a coeval couple who set up a new household; a period of child rearing, in which a small number of children tend to be closely clustered in age; the disappearance from the household of the adult children as they pursue their own livelihoods, marry, and establish their own households; and, finally, a long period extending from middle to old age—sometimes called the "empty nest phase"—in which the conjugal pair are free to follow their own interests, their responsibilities for providing and nurturing discharged.[53] A model of this kind, however, is not at all appropriate for Roman families such as that of Pompeius when considered over time. In 70, for example, the year of Pompeius's first consulship, his family consisted of himself, his wife Mucia, and their young children—but with the young Glabrio already a curious appendage. In 55, the year of Pompeius's second consulship, it consisted of himself, now middle-aged, a young wife capable of childbearing (or so it could be thought), her coeval adult stepchildren, whose mother had remarried, grandchildren in all probability, and another stepson, the young Scaurus, lurking in the background. If Mucia's point of view is adopted, her family in, say, 65, was composed of herself, her husband Pompeius (absent in the East), and her children (who had a stepbrother elsewhere); while in, say, 55, it had altered radically to consist of herself, her new husband M. Aemilius Scaurus, the young son she had borne him, this boy's much older half-siblings, not living in Scaurus's palatial house naturally, and probably grandchildren. Pompeius was not an especially prolific husband, but the permutations of "family" arising from his marriages become endless without in any way destroying the validity of the term. What emerges, in fact, is a sequence of nuclear formations (in a reproductive sense) that gradually lead to familial links beyond the immediate household in an irregular and disjointed manner. But there is nothing predictable in all of this, particularly from the chronological angle.

IV

Now the objection could still be brought forward that many individuals did not have marriage histories comparable to that of Pompeius, and that for their families the nuclear model might remain suitable no matter what the variations elsewhere. At a more detailed level, it could be urged that the deep concern displayed for his wife and children by Cicero in the crises first of his exile and secondly of the civil war between Caesar and Pompeius reflects a characteristic Roman preoccupation with the nuclear family.[54] The point is important and worth dwelling on, for the affliction Cicero felt at his forced separations from Terentia, Tullia, and Marcus is beyond all doubt, as are his anxieties about their well-being and the tenderness of the letters he sent to them.[55]

Yet in the letters to Atticus written in exile (far greater in number than those to the immediate family in the extant collections), it is Cicero's brother Quintus who, among Cicero's family members as a whole, claims the most attention, with his children receiving relatively scant mention and Terentia hardly any at all: "Give a helping hand to Quintus, best and kindest of brothers"; "Be good to my brother Quintus"; "I beg and adjure you to care for my poor brother Quintus, whom I have ruined, unlucky wretch that I am," Cicero wrote at various points through 58; and when appropriate he spoke warmly to Atticus of his nephew and son-in-law as well.[56] The pattern is the same in the correspondence from the civil war years. Thus, expressions of concern for family members depended to some degree on the identity of the addressees to whom the letters were sent (not to mention a notion such as "fraternus amor"),[57] and once all the relevant items are examined, it cannot be said that Cicero's concern was limited to wife and children alone. Cicero's sense of familial obligations was not narrowly circumscribed but spanned a wide range of familial connections. Indeed, it is striking to observe how the domestic framework of reference used by Cicero and his contemporaries in their letters may embrace the "whole house" (with the stress falling on children and fortune) yet exclude any mention of wives.[58]

Again, from the basis of the common difference in age between husband and wife at the time of first marriage, with the man typically being up to a decade older than the woman, it could be argued that the Roman family conformed to what modern historians have called a "Mediterranean" type of family in reference to traditional Europe.[59] The Roman correspondence is indeed undeniable, and the demographic implications for the exercise of *patria potestas* are noteworthy. But once the tendencies of the Mediterranean family are examined in full, many are found to be incompatible with the evidence on Roman upper-class families.[60] The Mediterranean domestic group was "seldom" formed by the marriage of the head of the household, whereas his takeover of an already existing household was "frequent"; and the proportion of widows who married was "very low," while the proportion of multi-generational households was "high." The lack of overlap with Roman practices seems conclusive. Possibly, then, the Roman family should simply be described as a "conjugal family," a term perhaps capable of accommodating the effects of repeated marriage without extending into the dubious territory of the family as all kin. But even this is difficult to reconcile with the following description of the historical conjugal family from a modern sociologist:

> Compared with other family systems, there was [in the conjugal family] a freer choice of mate. Courtship and marriage were based on mutual attraction, and parental controls operated only to determine who was allowed to meet whom. The age of marriage, therefore, was not very young; marriage took place when the couple were in a position to exercise choice, both in the sense of knowing what they were doing, and in that of being self-supporting economically. Further, a married couple looked to each other for an "emotional input-output balance" based on affection. . . . Another guiding principle was egalitarianism.[61]

Beyond this, there was a "relative exclusion of a wider range of kin and affines from the everyday affairs of the couple and their children."[62] The contrast with the Roman situation—even to judge from the history of Pompeius alone—is self-evident.

In the end, therefore, it may be the contemporary Western family, under the impact of the modern "divorce revolution," that provides the best analogue for the upper-class Roman family (if a comparison is to be found at all). It has been reported of the United States for 1977 that 43 percent of all marriages were second marriages for a least one partner, and for 1980 that one of every five married couples included at least one partner who was previously divorced. Similarly, in Britain in 1981, every third marriage was a remarriage for at least one spouse. The effect of the divorce revolution has been to make repeated marriage a genuine expectation for large numbers of the population and for blended families to become a staple feature of the social landscape.[63] At Rome divorce was only one of the driving forces that produced among the elite a high rate of remarriage. But in the widespread creation of extensive relationships—through stepparents, stepsiblings, and half-siblings—the result was the same. For many Romans, consequently, the family—even the "immediate" family—was an intricate formation that cannot be successfully reduced to one modular construct. Recognizing this, it seems better to place the emphasis not on typology but only on those features visible in the personal history of Pompeius which commonly, and perhaps typically, shaped the complicated familial worlds of the Roman upper class:

1. the arranged nature of most marriages, especially those controlled by the world of politics, and the relative unimportance of sentiment in compacting marital unions;
2. the impermanence of the marriage bond and the ease of its dissolution;
3. the frequency of premature death and consequent availability of a surviving spouse to enter a new union;
4. the likelihood that an individual's children would be broadly spaced in age;
5. the likelihood that some of an individual's children would belong to the same generation as his or her grandchildren;
6. the likelihood that husband and wife would either be significantly distanced in age or belong to different generations;
7. the immanence of the belief that marriage and procreation were culturally induced social obligations, not the result of individualistic choices;
8. the creation through serial marriage of networks of familial relationships which extended beyond the immediate household.

Because of these factors, the upper-class Roman family certainly has to be regarded as a dynamic entity, but one that in its life course had little regularity of shape. It was, rather, an extremely fluid organism, subject to constant interruption, disruption, and reconstitution. It embraced both kin and nonkin members within a single household and beyond, and combined elements of nuclearity with more extensive associations of vital importance. Perhaps it is not altogether surprising, therefore, that the most common term of reference used by Romans to designate their families was not an abstract noun but simply, as Cicero so often wrote, the open-ended adjectival form, *mei*.

V

The suggestion I have wanted to make is that in upper-class society at Rome in the late Republic the rate of remarriage was so high that familial blending of the sort that can be seen clearly in the individual histories of certain politically prominent figures was very common, and that the extensive familial associations that remarriage created, both over time and within and without the household, have to be fully taken into account in defining the Roman family. Those associations, in fact, encourage assessment of the Roman family within its own terms rather than according to typologies derived from later historical studies. (I would not, however, want at all to deny the value of the comparative evidence.) Two questions follow: is a high rate of remarriage perceptible in the Roman upper class in generations later than that singled out here, and is there any indication of frequent remarriage, and its consequences, in other sectors of the social hierarchy? Each question deserves full-scale study in its own right. But two brief comments may be made by way of coda.

First, among the consuls of the generation beginning in 49, some men are immediately recognizable as figures who married more than once, and the same is true of many of their wives. The issue is clouded to some degree by the increasing dominance in the sources of what was to become the imperial family, but it cannot be denied that men such as P. Vatinius, consul in 47, P. Cornelius Dolabella, consul in 44, M. Vipsanius Agrippa, consul in 37, Paullus Aemilius Lepidus, consul in 34, and so on, were continuing, when remarrying, a social convention long in evidence before the emergence of an imperial dynasty.[64] Moreover, at a much later date an abundance of remarriages is implied by Pliny in his account of a court case in which he took part as an advocate.[65] His client was Attia Viriola, a woman who had been disinherited by her aged father, "ten days after he had fallen in love and brought home a stepmother for his daughter." Attia Viriola had thus been compelled to go to court to recover her inheritance. "Fathers, daughters and stepmothers," Pliny says, "all anxiously awaited the verdict," a remark that is meaningless without the presumption of frequent changes of marriage partners in Roman society of the high empire. Divorce and remarriage were not topics that Pliny considered suitable for his "decorous pages."[66] But Pliny knew the real world: he was married three times himself.

Second, a few passages from the *Metamorphoses* of Apuleius can be noted. On accidentally meeting his friend Socrates in Hypata, the itinerant food merchant Aristomenes informs Socrates that in his home city of Aegina he is believed dead and that his wife's parents are encouraging their daughter to find a new husband. After his encounter with the witch Meroe, Aristomenes himself (he tells Lucius) had abandoned his city and family and created a new life in Thessaly, complete with a new wife. The ghost of the young nobleman Tlepolemus visits Charite to ask her not to marry his murderer, accepting however the obvious expectation that a young widow should remarry. The baker to whom Lucius the ass is sold is married to his daughter's stepmother, and the decurion to whose slave Lucius is later entrusted has two sons by successive wives, the one half-brother being considerably older than the other and perhaps about the same age as his stepmother.[67] If the *Metamorphoses* is taken to be evidence broadly reflecting genuine social conditions, remarriage seems to have been prevalent, under the high empire, at many levels of provincial society.[68] And, like Pliny, there were few who knew the familial complications of remarriage better than Apuleius himself.

Notes

1. Syme (1986), 302; cf. 20, "The more that is known about any senator, the more consorts accrue."

2. Cicero, *Letters to Friends* 279.1; *Letters to Atticus* 299.4, 328.2, 390.2; *Letters to Friends* 92.2.

3. On the law, see Humbert (1972), 181–299.

4. A numbered list of consuls is provided in the table, and I use the relevant numbers in the notes that follow as appropriate. I have drawn information on the consuls' marriages and on their wives from standard prosopographical sources—and especially from the works of Syme—but in view of the abundance of the secondary literature, I cannot be certain that I have collected every pertinent detail. However, I do not think that the approximate calculation given below is seriously out of order. Some examples of upper-class remarriage in the late Republic were given by Humbert (1972), 85–87, who concluded of consular

marriages in the period 80–30 that "plus du tiers de ces unions ne fut pas unique, soit du fait du mari, soit du fait de la femme." See also Brunt (1988), 453.

5. Cf. Syme (1986), 172: "At Rome it was not easy to discover an aristocrat still a bachelor in his late twenties."

6. Caesar, *Civil Wars* 1.74, 1.84.

7. No wife is given by Syme (1986), Table I. Metellus, however, is known to have adopted the future consul of 52, Q. Caecilius Metellus Pius Scipio (Cassius Dio 40.51.3), which implies that, if married, Metellus had no surviving son at the time of the adoption, around 64–63. Syme (1986), 244.

8. Absence of information: nos. 2, 11, 12, 25, 27, 31, 48, 57. Note that although no marriage for C. Calpurnius Piso, cos. 67, is known, Syme (1979), 502, assigns him a putative grandson. Record of remarriage: nos. 1, 13, 21, 23, 35, 43, 44, 50.

9. Nos. 4, 7, 10, 15, 17, 19, 37, 39, 40, 45, 49, 59.

10. Syme (1979), 516–17; Syme (1984), 1243–44; Syme (1986), 18.

11. Syme (1979), 501; Syme (1986), 36.

12. Certain remarriage: the wives of nos. 1, 4, 19, 21, 22, 23, 28, 35, 37, 38, 39, 40, 44, 49, 50, 59. Likely remarriage: the wives of nos. 17, 43, 55.

13. Obviously, I have counted only once cases where both husband and wife remarried. Discounting the likely instances of remarriage, the figure for certain remarriage is about 32 percent.

14. The marriages of nos. 15, 19, 41, 46.

15. Servilia, L. Licinius Lucullus, Clodia: see Wiseman (1974), 113–14. P. Cornelius Lentulus Sura, Julia, M. Antonius Creticus: see Sumner (1973), 138. D. Junius Silanus, Servilia, M. Junius Brutus: see Syme (1986), 19, 25–26. Porcia, M. Calpurnius Bibulus: see Syme (1986), 206, with Table II; Syme (1987a), 322; Syme (1987b). L. Marcius Philippus, Atia, C. Octavius: see Syme (1979), 134; Syme (1986), 403; cf. Wiseman (1985), 16–17 (Figure I).

16. Syme (1986), 19, 25–26, with Table II, 330; cf. Syme (1987a), 329.

17. Syme (1986), Table III (note that C. Octavius also had another daughter from his first marriage to Ancharia).

18. Syme (1986), 140, 143; Syme (1987a), 328.

19. Shackleton Bailey (1966), 325; Shackleton Bailey (1965), 280.

20. *RE* VIII, 2 cols. 2472–73, 2478; cf. Syme (1986), Table II; Syme (1979), 134; Syme (1986), 403, with Table III.

21. See Syme (1986), 15–31.

22. Observe Stone (1979), 66: "It is impossible to stress too heavily the impermanence of the Early Modern Family, whether from the point of view of husbands and wives, or parents and children. None could reasonably expect to remain together for very long, a fact which fundamentally affected all human relationships." The generalization follows remarks on remarriage, among other things. See also Sieder and Mitterauer (1983), 342, on the lack of privacy and intimacy in families characterized by instability.

23. Suetonius, *Tiberius* 6.1.

24. Wiseman (1987), 84; cf. Brunt (1988), 39.

25. The definitions and quotations are taken from Laslett (1972), 28–32. They are deliberately kept broad and minimal and are intended simply to serve as a rough guide for discussion. The refinements of household formations to be found in the secondary literature

on the modern family are numerous and often, it seems, constructed on an ad hoc basis. The results are thus confusing. For a review, see Mitterauer and Sieder (1982), 1–21; Goldthorpe (1987), 56–87.

26. See Shatzman (1975), 238–463.

27. Plutarch, *Crassus* 1.1.

28. Plutarch, *Cato the Elder* 24; Valerius Maximus, *Memorable Deeds and Sayings* 4.4.8; Plutarch, *Aemilius* 5.6, 28.9. See Crook (1967b), 111–18, in reference to joint families.

29. B. Rawson (1986a), 14. But remember *Digest* 7.8.4–6 and Plutarch, *Moralia* 481D–E.

30. Cicero, *Pro Caelio* 17–18. See Shatzman (1975), 311; Wiseman (1985), 62, 64–65.

31. Cicero, *Letters to Atticus* 271.2; Plutarch, *Sulla* 1.2, 1.4; *Cato the Younger* 1.1, 4.1. See Shatzman (1975), 393; Syme (1986), 20.

32. Crook (1967b), 117.

33. B. Rawson (1986a), 16–17. However, Saller (1987b) stresses on demographic reasoning that the number of adult sons affected by *patria potestas* cannot have been great.

34. Mitterauer and Sieder (1982), 15. Shatzman (1975), 482, maintains that "senators had at least 25–30 domestics at their residence in Rome" in the later Republic. I would regard this as a very low estimate.

35. On Tiro, see Treggiari (1969), 259–63.

36. See Laslett (1972), 29.

37. Rawson (1986a), 35–36.

38. Syme (1986), 25.

39. See Berkner (1972), 405, 410, and note the remarks Åkerman (1981), 172: "The effects of remarriage on family and household structure have so far only been analysed for Möklinta parish [Sweden] for the seventeenth century. . . . The pronounced dominance of ordinary nuclear families which usually appears in such studies, is not found here. In 1690 particularly, various kinds of extended families constituted the majority. This tendency is clearer when remarriages are considered. In extended three-generation families (the most complex form), remarriages were found in 17 cases out of 40. In ordinary three-generation families remarriages were as frequent as 10 out of 30. . . . It is not surprising that families thus formed became very complex."

40. Plutarch, *Pompeius* 4. On the date, see Gruen (1968), 244–46; Sumner (1973), 111 (just possibly 85).

41. Plutarch, *Pompeius* 9; *Sulla* 33.

42. The date of the marriage to Mucia can only be approximated; for its end, Cicero, *Letters to Atticus* 12.3. See Syme (1979), 66–67; Syme (1986), 255.

43. Sex. Pompeius, the younger son, must have been born by 76 or, alternatively, in the 60s; Syme (1986), 255 n. 4.

44. Cicero, *Letters to Atticus* 12.3; Suetonius, *Caesar* 50.1; Cassius Dio 37.49.3.

45. Asconius p. 28C. See Syme (1979), 122 n. 1; Syme (1986), 261, 264.

46. Plutarch, *Pompeius* 47.6; Suetonius, *Caesar* 21.

47. On Julia's date of birth, see Syme (1984), 1237.

48. Plutarch, *Pompeius* 53.3–4.

49. Syme (1986), 255, 257.

50. Plutarch, *Pompeius* 55.1–2. Cornelia was born around 70; Syme (1986), 246.

51. Pompeius was born September 29, 106; Sumner (1973), 129. P. Crassus: Plutarch, *Pompeius* 55.1. It was not beyond expectation that Pompeius and Cornelia should have children; see *Digest* 1.17.15.2 for the general assumption of men's ability to reproduce until the age of sixty; contrast *Digest* 19.1.21 pr.: an *ancilla* aged fifty or more is not considered capable of conception.

52. See. B. Rawson (1986a), 19: "This meant that in some sense she did not belong to her husband's *familia*." See further Pomeroy (1976).

53. See Mitterauer and Sieder (1982), 48–69; Sieder and Mitterauer (1983), 340.

54. See Saller (1987a), 67: "This fundamental concern stood out unmistakably in the letters Cicero sent off during periods of crisis in the late Republic. During his exile and the civil war he repeatedly wrote about the need to protect his wife, daughter and son."

55. See, for example, Cicero, *Letters to Friends* 6.3, quoted in Chapter 8 below.

56. Cicero, *Letters to Atticus* 56.2, 59.2, 68.5. See also *Letters to Atticus* 53.4, 54, 55.2, 60.4, 64.2-3; *Letters to Friends* 9.3; *Letters to Quintus* 3.3.

57. Cicero, *Letters to Friends* 2.10; cf. *Digest* 28.5.59.1.

58. See, for example, Cicero, *Letters to Friends* 25.2, 73.9, 153.2, 259.2; and below, Chapter 8.

59. Saller (1987b); Shaw (1987b).

60. Cf. Saller (1987b), 30 n. 22. The characteristics of the Mediterranean family are set out in Laslett (1983), 526–27, from which the following quoted words and phrases are taken.

61. Goldthorpe (1987), 63.

62. Goldthorpe (1987), 62.

63. Goldthorpe (1987), 231–33.

64. On the consuls mentioned, see Wiseman (1971), 56–57; Syme (1986), 36, 56–57, 73, 109–11, 143–47. Rousselle (1988), 91–92, argues that senators did not remarry frequently under the Principate, and Raepsaet-Charlier (1981–82) argues for a low rate of divorce among aristocratic Romans. But I remain unconvinced by either case. Note on the frequency of divorce, and on divorce as the natural sequel to marriage, Tertullian, *Apology* 6.6 (admittedly polemical).

65. Pliny, *Letters* 6.33, corroborated by *Digest* 5.2.4.

66. Syme (1988), 468.

67. Apuleius, *Metamorphoses* 1.6, 1.9, 8.8, 9.31, 10.2.

68. On the *Metamorphoses* as a historical source, see Millar (1981).

8

A Roman Family

One of the more daunting obstacles confronting the historian of the Roman family is the rarity of private documents such as diaries, correspondence, or journals that allow individual families to be studied over time from the perspective of one or more of their members. Most sources provide only external and isolated views of Roman family life, random snapshots, as it were, taken by a passing tourist from the window of a bus or train. But private records are not altogether lacking. In the surviving letters of Cicero, a great amount of precious information about the life of one particular family is available, both across time and from within the family itself, and it allows, for example, Cicero's relationships with his wife Terentia, his daughter Tullia, and his son Marcus to be understood at a level of intimacy that is beyond reach for other Roman families. The following quotation, taken from a letter Cicero wrote in April of 58 B.C. when he was leaving Italy for exile, is a powerful statement of the strength of his feelings for Terentia, Tullia, and Marcus, and it vividly illustrates the importance of nuclear family attachments in Roman society. It is just one of many unequivocal expressions of family sentiment from Cicero that can still be read and appreciated:

> Ah, what a desperate, pitiful case is mine! What now? Shall I ask you to come—a sick woman, physically and spiritually exhausted? Shall I *not* ask then? Am I to live without you? . . . Be sure of one thing: if I have you, I shall not feel that I am utterly lost. But what is to become of my Tulliola? You at home must take care of that—I have nothing to suggest. But assuredly, however matters turn out, the poor little girl's marriage and good name must be a primary consideration. Then there is my son. What

will he do? I hope that *he* will always be with me, my darling child. I cannot write any more now. Grief clogs my pen.[1]

My purpose in this chapter is to use Cicero's letters as a guide to illustrating how the Roman family functioned and operated—that is, to laying bare something of the essence of the Roman family. Starting from the premise that the correspondence can reveal clues to the nature of Roman family life, I shall pursue a theme and dwell on certain episodes that seem suggestive of how the Roman family ought to be understood; and I intend throughout to emphasize Cicero's assumptions about life within his family.

First, however, the limitations of the evidence have to be acknowledged. Cicero's letters present expressions of opinion and sentiment generally free of the constraints that writing for a public audience imposed. But they do not span the whole of Cicero's adulthood. A few items belong to the early and middle 60s of the first century B.C., but most date to an interval of rather less than twenty years, coming to a close a few months before Cicero's death on December 7, 43. This is unfortunate on many counts. But from the viewpoint of family history, it means that when the correspondence picks up in earnest—take 60 as a fixed point of convenience when Cicero was forty-six—the configuration of Cicero's immediate family was already well defined, and his perspective was already that of a middle-aged, consular *paterfamilias*. There is almost nothing to be learned from the correspondence about Cicero's parents, his decision to marry, his reasons for choosing Terentia as his wife, the birth and early life of Tullia, and so on. (The birth of Marcus, in 65, is announced in one of the earliest extant letters.) Still worse, the letters are not evenly distributed over the period they cover, and many (and many of those germane to this study) belong to periods of crisis of one sort or another: the period of Cicero's exile, from early 58 to the late summer of 57; the period of his governorship of the province of Cilicia in 51–50 (a crisis in the sense that Cicero was then apart from Terentia and Tullia); and the period from 49 on, when Rome was wracked by civil war and political turmoil. The evidence is thus imperfect. Its value, however, remains very high.[2]

II

Attention can be directed first to a sequence of passages which suggest, in a general way, how Cicero and his contemporaries thought of "the family.'' They are passages in which Cicero evokes, for himself or his addressee, what can be called a domestic framework of reference. The first two are from an anguished letter Cicero wrote in 58, in exile, to his brother Quintus. The third belongs to a letter of early 54 addressed to M. Licinius Crassus, the consul of 70 and 55, to whom Cicero pledged support while Crassus was in Syria. The fourth is from a letter of consolation written in 52 to the man who had been Cicero's quaestor during his consulship (in 63) but who had just been convicted in the courts, T. Fadius. The fifth is from a letter of 50, when Cicero was en route to Cilicia, written to his predecessor in the province, Appius Claudius Pulcher (consul in 54), then under indictment for treason. The sixth, of more or less the same date, also concerns Pulcher but is from a letter to M. Caelius Rufus (praetor in 48), a long-standing associate. And the final extract is from another letter of consolation, sent in 46 (it seems) to Cn. Domitius Ahenobarbus (consul in 32), at a time, after Pharsalus, of personal political uncertainty for the addressee. They are as follows:

> That much-lauded Consulship of mine has robbed me of you, and my children, and my country, and my possessions; I only hope it has robbed you of nothing but myself.

> Once I was happy indeed, in my brother, children, wife, means, even in the very nature of my wealth, the equal of any man that ever lived in prestige, moral standing, reputation, influence.

> Yes, I have succeeded in making plain, not only to your entire domestic circle but to the community at large, that I am your very good friend. Your wife, the paragon of her sex, and your two sons, whose filial affection, high character, and popularity do them honour, rely on my counsels and promptings and my active support.

> *You* have your property and your children. You also have me and others closely attached to you in friendship and good-will.

> If it is especially characteristic of a crafty fellow to measure all things by the yardstick of his own interest, what, may I ask, could be more in mine, more advantageous and convenient to me than connection with a personage of the highest birth and rank, whose riches, talents, children, and relations by blood and marriage would be a source of pride and strength to me?

> Why on earth should I *not* be gratified to welcome the friendship of such a man—in the prime of life, wealthy, successful, able, surrounded by children, by connections of blood and marriage, and by friends . . .

> Therefore I implore and conjure you in the name of our old association and
> friendship, and of the abundant good-will I bear you and you equally bear
> me; preserve yourself for me, for your mother, your wife, and all your
> family, to whom you are and have ever been most dear.[3]

Cicero's concern in these passages is to list the elements that define
what it is that is most precious in a man's life. Four rubrics are visible—
country, resources, friends, and family—of which the last receives by far
the most attention. Variously, the family can include wives and children,
parents and siblings, and a wider circle of relatives by blood or by
marriage that is in fact limitless.[4] In other words, "family" can embrace
both immediate and more distant relatives, who can be summoned from a
pool of general availability as specific circumstances dictate. In the third
extract, the terms of reference are confined to the nuclear, M. Crassus's
wife and sons (Tertulla, M. Crassus, and P. Crassus). But in all the other
passages except the fourth, the terms are more diverse, and since
Crassus's sons were men in their early thirties in 54, it is unlikely that
Cicero was thinking of a narrow nuclear household when the third
passage was written. Sometimes, in examples one, four, five, and six,
one nuclear element—children—is mentioned, but its complement—the
children's mother—is not. This could be explained by assuming that the
relevant mothers were not living when Cicero spoke of their children, and
it is certainly the case that the mothers of the children of T. Fadius and of
Appius Claudius Pulcher are unidentifiable. But with the first item there
is no doubt: Cicero refers to his own brother and children but fails to
mention his wife, who, however, is included with the others in the second
passage.

What emerges, therefore, is that when Cicero wishes to conjure up a
sense for his contemporaries of the family, he by no means restricts
himself to husband, wife, and children but appeals to a much broader
range of kin members. Moreover, it is very difficult for him to segregate
family from resources (wealth, means, possessions), so that in expressions of what a man holds most dear the human and the material are very
closely conjoined.[5] It is these two categories together, indeed, that make
up Cicero's domestic framework of reference.

The formulation was by no means peculiar to Cicero. In letters written
to him by *others,* the following statements are found, fully in accord with
those already quoted from Cicero. First, from 49, Caelius Rufus strongly
admonishing Cicero not to offend C. Julius Caesar:

I beg and implore you, Cicero, in the name of your fortunes and your children, to take no steps which will jeopardize your well-being and safety.

Accordingly, if you care for yourself, for your only son, for your household, for your remaining hopes, if I and your excellent son-in-law have any influence with you . . .

Then, in the winter of 45–44, P. Vatinius (consul in 47), writing of a captive terrorist:

But what am I to say to those who demand redress by process of law for the plunder of their property, the seizure of their ships, the slaughter of brothers, children, and parents?

And in 43, L. Munatius Plancus (consul in 42), writing from Transalpine Gaul of M. Aemilius Lepidus (consul in 46), the future triumvir:

I urged Lepidus to . . . collaborate in aiding the commonwealth. I exhorted him to think more of himself, his children, and his country than of one ruined, desperate bandit.[6]

It is of interest here that in the first two passages Caelius Rufus makes no mention of Terentia, and that in the second Marcus and Tullia's husband, P. Cornelius Dolabella, are referred to but not Marcus's sister and Dolabella's wife. Similarly, in the extract from Plancus's letter, Lepidus's wife, Junia (sister to M. Brutus), is not mentioned with her children, though she was certainly alive in 43.[7] Relatives from the reproductive triad are everywhere in these passages, as they must be. But they are selectively mentioned on the one hand and juxtaposed with more wide-ranging terms on the other—fortunes, household, brothers, parents—which connote a very open-ended understanding of "family."

That observation does not mean that the importance of the bonds that could exist in Cicero's world between husbands and wives or between parents and children has to be minimized; it suggests only that those bonds did not necessarily have, at all times and in all cases, an absolute and exclusive primacy in the Roman familial mentality. To take evidence again from Cicero's exile, there is no question at that time of Cicero's devotion to wife and children. Here is a forty-eight-year-old man, married for almost twenty years (and with a daughter who herself has been married for several years), writing in the most affecting manner:

And then at the same time I miss my daughter, the most loving, modest, and clever daughter a man ever had, the image of my face and speech and mind. Likewise my charming, darling little boy, whom I, cruel brute that I am, put away from my arms. Too wise for his years, the poor child already understood what was going on.

As for my loyalest of wives, poor, unhappy soul, I did not let her come with me so that there should be someone to protect the remnants of our common disaster, our children.

My brother, I need not commend my daughter (and yours) and our Marcus to your care . . . while you are safe, they will not be orphans. . . . Please look after Terentia too.[8]

These remarks, obviously, are from a letter to Cicero's brother Quintus (written at Thessalonica on June 13, 58). But it is not for that reason alone, nor because Cicero and Quintus had failed to rendezvous as Quintus returned to Rome from his governorship of Asia, that Cicero gives in the letter equally strong expression to his feelings for his brother and his nephew (Quintus's son, also named Quintus). The first passage above is preceded by these words:

You can imagine how I weep as I write these lines, as I am sure you do as you read them. Can I help thinking of you sometimes, or ever think of you without tears? When I miss you, I do not miss you as a brother only, but as a delightful brother almost of my own age, a son in obedience, a father in wisdom. What pleasure did I ever take apart from you or you apart from me?

The second is preceded by these:

Likewise your son, my image, whom my boy loved like a brother and had begun to respect like an elder brother.[9]

The elder Quintus, it can be noted, was two years or so younger than Cicero, the younger Cicero a little more than a year older than Marcus.

The conclusion this letter encourages, then, as does the other evidence so far considered, is that to a large extent the Roman family was an amorphous, undifferentiated entity that cannot be reduced to an easily defined basic type or model. But to the degree that definition is possible, it is clear that Romans did not conceive of their families as discrete, insular cells or conjugal units but as networks of kin members far more communal in aspect and orientation. Corroboration comes from the evidence in the letters on Cicero's own familial network.

III

The following are a number of illustrations from specific moments in the history of Cicero's family.

On January 20, 60, Cicero, in Rome, wrote to T. Pomponius Atticus, his friend but also the brother of his brother's wife, in Greece. "I am so utterly forsaken," he said, "that my only moments of relaxation are those I spend with my wife, my little daughter, and my darling Marcus."[10] The language is warm and affectionate, and the intimate scene Cicero sketches suggests almost a modern notion of the core family functioning as a place of refuge from the cares of the world.[11] But without dwelling unduly on the fact that, in physical terms, the Roman house lacked the private character of the modern single-family residence and could not accommodate anything like the modern concept, the context of Cicero's remark has to be fully appreciated. Cicero's need, he told Atticus at the beginning of his letter, was for a special friend in whom he could confide openly and honestly. The two individuals who came immediately to mind for the purpose were Atticus and Quintus. But both men were absent from Rome, and among Cicero's public acquaintances there was no one he considered suitable or trustworthy enough to fulfill the role of confidant. Thus, "I am so utterly forsaken. . . ."

One should not, of course, expect that a fifteen-year-old daughter or a five-year-old son could really have met Cicero's needs at this time. But for understanding the nature of marriage and the limitations of the core family in Roman society, it is revealing that as he articulated his desire for a confidant, Cicero thought first and foremost not of his wife but of a male companion (or male collaterals, in fact). Terentia was not her husband's peer and could not be the companion he craved. So again, in a letter from 54, when Cicero was lamenting the condition of the state, it was the company of Atticus and Quintus that occurred to him as the most natural source of personal consolation, not the company of his wife.[12] When the need for solace arose, a man's thoughts were not always dominated by images of his wife and children.

In December 45, Cicero reported to Atticus a conversation he had recently had with their nephew, the young Quintus, the principal theme of which had been the cause of Quintus's dejection.[13] The issue of Quintus marrying was under discussion, but he had been unable to decide whom to take as a wife. (The understanding is that there were several candidates to choose from.) So, he informed Cicero, he had incurred the displeasure of both his mother, Pomponia, and his uncle Atticus. Now, however, he had decided to follow the wishes of mother and uncle in order to dispel their annoyance. Cicero accordingly congratulated him on his resolve and urged him to go through with the marriage quickly, not least because that would make his father happy, too. "I shall take your advice," were Quintus's last words.

What is of interest here is the involvement of Pomponia and Atticus in Quintus's choice of a bride (implicit in the displeasure Quintus communicated to Cicero). Pomponia's involvement is predictable. Marriage in upper-class Roman society was a matter for arrangement, principally by parents, and since Pomponia was at this point in her life divorced (and not remarried), she may have felt especially assertive about her son's immediate future. Atticus's involvement, however, is less explicable, unless one assumes that the marriage of a young man of senatorial origin was of concern to all the members of the family community to which he belonged and who might, indeed, be affected in one way or another by it. Cicero himself clearly felt that he had every right to contribute to the process of giving advice to his nephew, as he thought appropriate, and, as will shortly be seen, that was only the logical continuation of a long-standing part Cicero had played in the young Quintus's upbringing.[14]

In 44, the prospect surfaced that the older Quintus should remarry (not surprisingly), and the name of a potential new wife, Aquilia, appears in a letter Cicero wrote to Atticus about the matter.[15] As it happened, Cicero denied that Quintus wanted to marry again, and certainly there never was a match with this woman. It is difficult to tell, therefore, how serious the candidacy of Aquilia to become Quintus's wife actually was. But it is noteworthy, for present purposes, that the possibility of the marriage was taken seriously enough by the young Quintus for him to send letters to both Atticus and his father to state his opposition to the prospect. "The main point was," Cicero told Atticus, "that he would not stand Aquilia as a stepmother." If parental control of children's marriages was the norm in Roman society, adult children's participation in the arranging of parental remarriages is a not altogether unexpected corollary.[16] Here, however, the young Quintus's behavior, as it affected and drew in both his uncles, shows once more that Roman marriage was not at all the private concern of the marrying principals but the concern of all those in the family community likely to be affected by it. The marriage of one member of a kin network had implications and repercussions that none could afford to ignore, and it is the kin network at work that is visible in this episode.

IV

One feature of the history of Cicero's family is not confined to a fixed moment in time but extends over many years: the attitude Cicero and Quintus adopted of "sharing" each other's children.

A passage was quoted above in which Cicero spoke of Tullia and Marcus as Quintus's children as well as his own—"my daughter (and yours) and our Marcus"—a mode of reference signifying the brothers' closeness, to be sure, but something, it could perhaps be argued, that was no more than a social affectation. After all, the polite convention of speaking of "our children" occurs in a number of letters Cicero wrote to men with whom he had no familial connection at all.[17] But there is more in view than mere convention in letters composed at times of intense concern and anxiety, such as the letter from Cicero's period of exile just referred to or one to Quintus from May of 54, when Quintus was far away from his son in Gaul and Britain (with Caesar), which contains these words:

> I shall carefully attend to your charges, both in conciliating people and in not estranging certain persons. But my greatest concern will be to see your boy (our boy) every day, which goes without saying, and to look into what he is learning as often as possible. If he is willing to accept it, I shall even offer my services as his teacher, having gained some practice in this employment, in bringing our younger boy forward during this holiday season.[18]

In the late spring of 53, Quintus wrote to Cicero from Transalpine Gaul:

> My dear Marcus, as I hope to see you again and my boy and my Tulliola and your son, I am truly grateful at what you have done about Tiro. . . .[19]

On other occasions, Cicero wrote to his brother of his nephew as "your and my boy Quintus" and "our little boy."[20] It is as though Tullia, Marcus, and the young Quintus were the common property of the brothers, to be shared and enjoyed without any need for a rigid line of parental demarcation.

V

At this stage I move to a more discursive examination of the way in which Cicero and Atticus, as relatives by marriage, exercised a supervisory function in the lives of their married siblings, Quintus and Pomponia, and of their siblings' son Quintus.

The marriage of Quintus and Pomponia took place about 70, at a time when Quintus was beginning to enter Roman public life. Both politically and socially, a respectable marriage was desirable for this purpose, and it should not be coincidental that Quintus married more or less at the time he held the quaestorship, the first major step in the senatorial career of honors. He was a little past thirty years of age. Rather unusually, however, his wife was a woman several years older than Quintus. Upper-class women at Rome typically married for the first time in their middle to late teens, and for a woman to be marrying for the first time in her late thirties was irregular. Thus, it is a legitimate speculation that Pomponia has been married at least once before her marriage to Quintus, that she had lost a husband (or husbands) to death or divorce, that she had experienced pregnancy, and that she had long been used to managing her own household. She cannot be assumed, therefore, to have been compliant and submissive in the manner of a young woman leaving her parental home when her marriage to Quintus began. The marriage lasted for about twenty-five years, ending in divorce in 45–44. The young Quintus was its only issue.[21]

The marriage began, as did most upper-class Roman marriages, by arrangement. And it was Cicero, the older brother, who negotiated on Quintus's behalf, with Atticus, his friend since childhood, negotiating for Pomponia.[22] The Roman marital ideal was that husband and wife should live together in growing concord, and although most marriages at the upper levels of society were unions of convenience, it did not always follow that they were discordant or even loveless. With Quintus and Pomponia, however, there is no sign that harmony ever grew between them, and one can only conclude that they were totally incompatible (to put it in modern terms). The letters do not allow a day-to-day or even year-by-year case history of the marriage to be compiled. But they give a series of glimpses of the life Quintus and Pomponia lived together. The main observable feature is a sequence of disruptions that seem attributable most of all to their conflicting temperaments or, perhaps, to the manner in which they had been brought together in the first place. The first glimpse belongs to November of 68 and comes from a letter Cicero wrote to Atticus responding to some earlier remarks Atticus had made about Pomponia's distressed condition of the moment.[23] Quintus was currently away from Rome, Pomponia presumably living in the house Quintus would have provided when they married. Pomponia, however, had taken some complaint about her husband to her brother, who in turn consulted Cicero, who in turn gave advice to Quintus. The cause of the friction is not revealed, though Cicero implies that the fault lay with Quintus. It would be pointless to try to guess what it was. But the custodial role played by Cicero and Atticus in the episode is very noticeable: each dealt with his respective sibling, and their collective efforts brought success (it seems). Cicero was able to assure Atticus that his advice to Quintus could be expected to smooth out the situation, and later in the same month Quintus and Pomponia were reunited and more comfortable together.[24] Some months later, in May of 67, Cicero informed Atticus that Pomponia was pregnant, a sign, he said, that the marriage was "as I have always wished and worked for."[25]

Between 67 and 61, nothing is heard of the marriage. But Quintus's career progressed well enough. In 65 he held the aedileship, in 62 the praetorship, and in the spring of 61 he left Rome to take up what was to become a three-year term as governor of the province of Asia.[26] Quintus and Pomponia were now the parents of a six-year-old boy, and they had a new house in the Carinae.[27]

In 61, however, there was another problem. In December, having received from Atticus copies of letters to Atticus from Quintus, Cicero wrote to his friend about a rift that had developed between Pomponia's husband and her brother before Quintus left for Asia.[28] There had been some hope that the rift could be closed, if Quintus had been able to meet Atticus in Greece en route to his province. But no meeting, and no reconciliation, had taken place. Again, the elliptical quality of much of the correspondence prevents a clear view of the problem. But Pomponia was almost certainly involved in the antagonism between Atticus and Quintus:

> Where the blame for this unhappy rift may lie is easier for me to judge than to put into writing. I am afraid that in defending my own relations I might

have hard things to say of yours. For it is plain to me that even if his domestic circle did nothing to cause the damage, they could at least have counteracted it when they found it.[29]

Cicero was by no means ignorant of his brother's shortcomings. But he evidently saw fault on Pomponia's side, and without doubt there was again a lack of harmony between husband and wife. Yet, while Quintus was in Asia, the life of the family community as a whole was kept on a relatively even keel. Pomponia delivered news from Atticus to Cicero, received holiday invitations from Terentia, was addressed by Quintus on financial matters, and moved with her son into another house Quintus acquired, this time on the Palatine close to that of Cicero and Terentia.[30] The communal nature of the family's life that Cicero's letters illuminate was thus physically intensified. As correspondents, Cicero and Atticus continued to keep watch over their siblings' marital life, tactfully but uninterruptedly.

For the next ten years details on the marriage are sparse. In April of 56, Cicero one day went next door, as it were, to visit the young Quintus, who earlier had been too sick to attend a party Cicero had given to celebrate the betrothal of Tullia to Furius Crassipes. He reported the visit to his brother, who was in Sardinia at the time, engaged in Cn. Pompeius's efforts to improve Rome's grain supply; and he mentioned how amused he had been by the young Quintus's comments on feelings between Pomponia and Terentia (not especially warm, it seems).[31] More significantly, he added that although Quintus was away, Pomponia had been complaining about him. Enduring marital concord was thus still an unrealized ideal in the marriage of Quintus and Pomponia.

There was nothing amusing in an episode Cicero reported to Atticus in May of 51, in which the boorish behavior of Pomponia was plain for all to see. The circumstances were as follows.[32] Cicero himself was about to take up the governorship of Cilicia, and Quintus was to accompany him as a member of his staff. As they departed, the brothers' wives and children traveled with them on the Italian leg of their journey, and at one point Quintus decided to provide a holiday entertainment for the dependents of his estate at Arcanum, one of the stepping-stones on the way. From their ancestral home of Arpinum, the previous point of sojourn, Quintus sent ahead his freedman Statius to make arrangements for a dinner. When the main party arrived, he asked Pomponia to summon the women of the estate while he did the same for the men. Pomponia, however, took umbrage at the fact that Statius, rather than she herself, had been invited to prepare the dinner. So she refused to carry out her charge and never attended the celebration at all. She secluded herself from her relatives and would not accept the food Quintus sent her, prompting the observation from him (to Cicero) that this was precisely the sort of peevishness he had to put up with all the time. The following day Cicero discovered that Pomponia had refused to spend the night with her husband, and by the time the two sets of spouses separated (wives did not accompany their husbands to their provinces), Pomponia's distemper still had not abated. In writing to Atticus of all this, Cicero said that Quintus's behavior throughout the episode had been irreproachable and that Pomponia ought to be reprimanded for her misconduct. The implication was that it was Atticus's familial obligation to respond to the initiative Cicero had taken, by writing, and to help regulate Pomponia's marriage further by a timely and diplomatic intervention.

Whatever Atticus did, the discord was not dispelled, and a year or so later, while Quintus was still in the East, the first rumblings of divorce were heard.[33] Quintus had had enough and was ready to end the marriage, he confided to Statius. But Cicero told Atticus that he opposed the idea and that his brother had erred in confiding his intentions to the freedman. They should therefore recruit the young Quintus to help them head off the prospect of convulsion in the family. The prospect did materialize, but it took five years to do so. In 49, family solidarity prevailed over personal factors. As civil war began, Cicero included Pomponia in his deliberations about the safety of the women of the family (should Terentia, Tullia, and Pomponia stay in Rome or leave?), and for a time Pomponia appears to have lived in Cicero's villa near Formiae.[34] But letters to Atticus from May of 49 indicate that Quintus and Pomponia remained estranged, so the end was assuredly in sight.[35] It is not until early 44, however, that evidence of the divorce becomes available, by which time Pomponia's dowry was being repaid.[36] Quintus then was fifty-eight, Pomponia about sixty-four, their son about twenty-three.

To judge from Cicero's evidence, Quintus and Pomponia's marriage was punctuated by periodic upsets whose cumulative effect was far more serious than any of its constituent parts. Because the evidence is discontinuous, the disagreements may seem exaggerated. (Had more evidence survived, further episodes of friction might well have emerged.) As it is, tensions in the marriage are evident enough; and yet, almost paradoxically, the union lasted for a substantial period of time. How is that to be explained, when divorce at Rome was a comparatively easy recourse?

Part of the answer may lie in the fact that for much of the period from 61 to 48, Quintus's career kept the couple physically distanced from each other. From March of 61 until the autumn of 58, Quintus was in Asia; in 57–56, he was in Sardinia; from 54 to 52, he was in Gaul and Britain; and after an interval of just six months in Italy, he was in Cilicia in 51–50. When civil war broke out in 49, Quintus was back in Italy but quickly left for Greece, not returning until the autumn of 47.[37] Pomponia was with him for none of these excursions. One can only guess, of course, at the effects they had. On one hand, they may have fostered alienation and may have made the occasions of reuniting very difficult; on the other, they may have acted as safety valves, preventing tensions from complete eruption and encouraging optimism for the future. It is impossible to say.

But one certain sustaining element was the interest of Cicero and Atticus, over the years, in preserving their siblings' marriage. Their interest depended on the continuing assumption that the union brought dividends to the family community as a whole (for example, social and political benefits) and that the sensibilities of the principals were of less import than the well-being of the family group. It is perceptible in a sequence of remarks exchanged between Cicero and Atticus that take for granted the notion that the Roman family was an extensive institution composed of many members, and that any member might intervene, naturally and predictably, in the affairs of any of the core units to be found in the overall community:

> You write to me of your sister. She will tell you herself how anxious I have been that my brother Quintus should feel towards her as a husband ought. Thinking that he was rather out of temper I sent him a letter designed to mollify him as a brother, advise him as my junior, and scold him as a man on the wrong track; and from what he has since written to me on a number of occasions I feel confident that *all is as it ought to be and as we should wish.*

> My brother Quintus seems to me to feel towards Pomponia *as we wish* and is now with her on his estates at Arpinum.

> As to my brother, I feel sure that things are *as I have always wished and worked for.*

I have told you about this, perhaps at greater length than was called for, to show you that *lessons and advice are called for from your side as well as from mine.*

Whatever step he [Quintus] proposed to take in such a matter he ought not to have written to a freedman. I shall do my utmost to prevent any action contrary *to our wishes and to what is right.*

In fact I was greatly impressed by the dutiful, affectionate way he [young Quintus] spoke. It makes me the more hopeful that nothing untoward will happen. *So I wanted you to know.*

Young Quintus has certainly acted like a good son in reconciling his father's mind towards your sister, not it is true without a good deal of encouragement from me, but I was spurring a willing horse. Your letter too has greatly stimulated him. Altogether I am satisfied that the matters stands *as we wish.* [38]

The theme of "all is as it ought to be and as we should wish" (seen in the emphasized phrases) connotes intervention, management, and manipulation, the natural corollaries, in fact, of marriage by arrangement. In a milieu where marriage was negotiated on the basis of variables such as family pedigree, financial resources, social respectability, and political prominence, every compact affected many more people than the marriage partners themselves; and once a match had been contrived, nothing was more reasonable, or proper, than that those who had arranged should work to keep productive and intact what they had brought into being. Indeed, there was something of an obligation to do so. [39] To Cicero and Atticus, the social, political, and economic yield from their siblings' marriage was enormous. The influence and esteem of each, in the public world, was enhanced by familial association with the other. The correspondence on family matters that constantly passed between them (collaterals, remember, not principals) is proof of their efforts to keep Quintus and Pomponia in peaceful union. In turn, those efforts are proof of how the life of the Roman family has to be judged not simply in the confining terms of the model of the conjugal unit but in terms that place that unit in its full, extensive familial context. In this case, it is the vigilant care Cicero and Atticus afforded the union of Quintus and Pomponia that forces recognition of the wider scene.

VI

Despite the divorce, there was to be a final installment in the history of
Quintus and Pomponia. But I want first to turn to the young Quintus and
his relationship with his two uncles.

In the spring of 49, with Rome in deep political crisis, Cicero sent
several letters to Atticus that included criticism of their nephew. From the
middle of April through the middle of May, anger and irritation poured
from Cicero's pen when he thought of young Quintus, and he insisted
more than once that neither his own strictness nor his brother's overindulgence could be blamed for the way the nephew's natural untowardness
had manifested itself. Quite unexpectedly, Quintus had taken off from
Cicero's villa near Formiae, where most of the family had gathered for
safety's sake, and had gone to Rome to join the cause of Caesar, having
sent ahead a letter announcing his imminent arrival. Cicero feared that his
treachery would bring disaster to uncle and father, pointlessly as it turned
out. But Quintus's lack of commitment and faithfulness to the family was
distressing:

> My compliance towards him has always been seasoned with plenty of
> strictness and I have nipped many serious offences of his in the bud—not
> just the odd peccadillo. As for his father's mildness, it should have earned
> his affection rather than such callous disregard. We took so grave a view of
> his letter to Caesar that, while saying nothing to you, I think we made the
> boy's life pretty uncomfortable. But this journey of his and his pretence of
> filial duty is something I don't care to characterize. So much I know, that
> after an interview with Hirtius he was summoned by Caesar, and spoke to
> him about my thorough hostility to his interests and my design of leaving
> Italy. Even this I write with hesitation. But it is no fault of ours, nature is
> the enemy.
>
> There is much in him that is extraordinary, but an utter lack of straightfor-
> wardness and sincerity. I wish you had taken the young man in hand. His
> too indulgent father undoes all my disciplinary measures. Without him, if
> that were possible, I could govern the lad. For *you* it is possible. But I don't
> insist. As I say, it is a great task.
>
> As for our young man, I cannot help feeling affection for him, but I plainly
> see that he has none for us. I have never met with such a lack of moral
> constitution, such estrangement towards his family, such secretiveness.
> What an incurable spate of annoyances! But I shall take care that he gets

some direction, and am already doing so. His abilities are extraordinary, it is his character that needs attention.

. . . he has always been indulged by his father, but indulgence does not make a boy untruthful or grasping or wanting in natural affection, though it may make him headstrong, overbearing, and aggressive. Accordingly he has these faults too, the products of over-indulgence, but they are tolerable, at least I suppose I may call them so, young people being what they are nowadays. But the qualities that cause me, fond of him as I am, more pain even than the miseries of our present condition, do not arise from any compliance on our part. They have their own roots. No doubt I should tear them up if I had the opportunity. But the times are such that I must put up with all.[40]

Quintus was now about eighteen, of an age to be forming his own political judgments and making his own decisions. Yet one of the most arresting features of Cicero's correspondence in the spring of 49 is the underlying assumption that Cicero and Atticus, his uncles, had not just the capacity but the absolute right to influence, direct, and mold Quintus's behavior. The assumption is explicit in such pronouncements as "I shall handle young Quintus pretty strictly" and "I shall give the young man what he needs, as you ask."[41] It has been seen, too, in the episode of Quintus's marriage deliberations. But to understand it fully, the details of Cicero's involvement in Quintus's childhood have to be brought into play.

Of Quintus's earliest years nothing is known.[42] The first appearance he makes in the historical record, at the age of seven or so, is in a letter Cicero wrote to Atticus in 60.[43] Since Quintus's father was then in Asia, one would imagine that it was Pomponia who had chief responsibility for the boy. But from Cicero's remarks now and in the following year, something of a share in Quintus's upbringing, on his and Atticus's part, is already noticeable. Cicero was concerned that Atticus should take care of Quintus during an apparent illness, and that Quintus and Pomponia should not be disturbed, in their new house on the Palatine, by the renovations Cicero was making to his own. In 59, moreover, Quintus was studying with a tutor named Aristodemus, who was also the tutor of Cicero's son; the cousins must have been taught together.[44]

Cicero's interest in his nephew continued through the next several years. In 58, Quintus's name was included in expressions of guilt Cicero made, in exile, for the problems he had inflicted on the family community. In 56, Cicero was writing of him warm-heartedly to Atticus. Atticus was again instructed to look after the boy, and in 55 Quintus actually stayed with the maternal uncle for a while.[45] Also in 56, Cicero wrote to his brother, in Sardinia, to say that Quintus was studying (and doing well) with a new tutor, Tyrannio, the lessons being given in Cicero's house under his personal supervision.[46] As seen earlier, when Tullia's betrothal to Crassipes was celebrated, Quintus was unable to attend, but Cicero visited him soon after and found him not only recovered but full of entertaining conversation.

By 54, Quintus was a teenager. With his father away in Gaul, Pomponia must again have had chief responsibility for her son, and a hint of the authority she commanded appears in a passing comment Cicero made to his brother, in September of that year, that Quintus had not been allowed to join Cicero on a visit he made to Arpinum.[47] But Quintus could hardly have been a source of antagonism between Cicero and Pomponia. Cicero continued to supervise closely Quintus's education, supplying yet another tutor in the personage of the rhetor Paeonius; he had Quintus to dinner when Pomponia dined out; and, to judge from a letter of December of 54, Quintus occasionally stayed at Cicero's house.[48] So the guiding and protective role of Cicero—that of a quasi-parent, as it were—complemented that of the mother, to the full approval of Quintus's absent father. Cicero's affection for Quintus is very plain in the letters of this year:

> I pardon your continual enquiries about young Quintus, but I hope you on your side will pardon me if I refuse to admit that you love him any more than I do myself.

> I love your son as you ask and as he deserves and as I ought, but I am letting him go because I don't want to take him away from his teachers and because his mother * is leaving. Without her I am terrified of the young fellow's appetite![49]

From 54 to 51, Quintus disappears from view. He reemerges in 51, a sixteen-year-old, accompanying Cicero to Cilicia with his father and his cousin. But, despite the father's presence, the quasi-parental function long since discharged by Cicero continued. The expedition to Cilicia was doubtless intended as an educational exercise for Quintus and Marcus, both to experience travel in the eastern Mediterranean and to be given an exploratory insight into the workings of Roman provincial government. But the province's hostile climate brought certain risks to safety, and for the winter of 51–50 the boys were sent, as a precautionary measure, to the court of Deiotarus of Galatia. There they studied with the infamous Dionysius.[50] It was Cicero's intention—not his brother's—he told Atticus (always keeping the other uncle in touch), to dispatch Quintus and Marcus to Rhodes in the event of a real military crisis.[51] A little later, Cicero announced to Atticus his intention to give Quintus his toga of manhood—at Laodicaea, as he left his province, at the Liberalia in the spring (March 17).[52] Quintus's father was fully occupied with military affairs during the winter and had thus instructed Cicero to arrange for the celebration of Quintus's coming of age. Clearly there was nothing inappropriate about an uncle supervising this important family occasion.

It was during the Cilician interlude, however, that Cicero appears to have first become aware of shortcomings in Quintus's character. He told Atticus that Quintus needed to be kept on a tight rein and that "the boy's nature, though gifted, is complex, and I have plenty to do guiding it!"[53] It was now that the issue of his parents' divorce began to arise, so perhaps the two developments were related. Certainly when Quintus learned that his father and mother might divorce—which he did by accident—he did not take the news calmly:

> I think, indeed I am sure, that young Quintus has read a letter addressed to his father. He is in the habit of opening them and does so at my suggestion, in case there might be something we ought to know about. This particular letter contained the same item [i.e., the possibility of the divorce] about your sister which you wrote to me. I could see that the boy was dreadfully upset. He cried as he lamented over it to me. In fact I was greatly impressed by the dutiful, affectionate, thoughtful way he spoke. It makes me the more hopeful that nothing untoward will happen.[54]

The evidence is too thin to allow for intense penetration of Quintus's emotional state. But Cicero's remarks are enough to show that Quintus found the thought of his parents' divorce disturbing even though he had been separated from one or the other for long intervals during his childhood. But this small insight into how a child in upper-class Roman society could be affected by parental divorce offsets the cavalier attitude to marital disruption frequently apparent in the sources, and it suggests a complexity in Roman family life often concealed from sight. At Cicero's instigation, however (and it is difficult, again, to avoid notions of the manipulative here), Quintus's passive, emotional reaction was converted into something more active and constructive. Cicero urged Quintus to try to reconcile his parents, and a few weeks later he could write to Atticus:

"Young Quintus has certainly acted like a good son in reconciling his father's mind towards your sister."[55]

Cicero thus had no difficulty in appreciating Quintus's finer points. But it was the opposite side of Quintus's character that began to predominate. Had Cicero left his brother in charge of Cilicia when his term as governor expired, he said to Atticus, there would have been trouble with their nephew.[56] The boy had "a fine conceit of himself," which Atticus understood as well as Cicero: Atticus and Quintus's father had recently had an unpleasant exchange of letters over him.[57] But as yet there was no serious problem. In 50, before returning to Italy, Quintus spent a little time with his father at Atticus's home in Buthrotum.[58] Since the older Quintus remained in the East, however, it was Cicero the uncle who was left to oversee the young Quintus's well-being, and his pity for his nephew (as much as for his son) provided him, in early 49, with an excuse for political prevarication.[59] Subsequently Cicero contemplated sending both boys to Greece for safety's sake but then chose to seclude them in his villa near Formiae; his concern never faltered, and decisions were made on Quintus's behalf.[60] Until April, indeed, the solidarity of the family network remained intact. Lamenting his lack of decisiveness in not having retreated from Italy with Cn. Pompeius, Cicero alleged wife, daughter, son, and nephew as the cause; but the boys, he thought, could still go on receiving lessons from Dionysius.[61] The cohesiveness of the domestic group was destroyed only by Quintus's inexplicable bolt to Caesar.

From 60 to 49, then, Cicero played a prominent role in his nephew's upbringing. He was genuinely fond of Quintus, spent considerable time with him, in various places, and had a particular interest in his formal education. In turn, Quintus was able to treat Cicero's household as his own and, as far as can be told, had a sympathetic relationship with his uncle. Cicero's quasi-parental activities, furthermore, did not cause tension among the adult members of the family circle. True, Quintus was separated from his father for much of his early life; so it could be argued, conveniently but simply, that the uncle filled an unfortunate void. But there was nothing unusual about the older Quintus's career in and of itself, and the absences it caused were of a type that must have been common in upper-class Roman society. The collaborative parental function of Cicero cannot therefore have been extraordinary.

The notion, indeed, that a child like Quintus "belonged" not to his parents alone but to a wider range of kin is strongly evident in the constant flow of correspondence about the boy between the uncles, in the assumption that Cicero and Atticus should cooperate, or work individually with his parents, to regulate Quintus's behavior, and in the understanding that Cicero and Atticus each had a stake in their nephew's future. The attitudes and actions of the men were a logical extension of the custodial position they occupied with regard to their siblings' marriage.[62] The evidence, it has to be recognized, assumes that the uncles' concerns and initiatives were the result of conventional expectations. Cicero's brother, after all, once told young Quintus to regard Cicero as his teacher.[63] Of course, since there are no extant letters from Atticus to Cicero, Atticus's participation in shaping the early life of Quintus is less perceptible than that of Cicero. But there is no question that it is perceptible. Children were a collective responsibility, as Cicero and Quintus themselves had once been in their childhood. In the *De Oratore* Cicero speaks briefly (and tantalizingly) of the contribution made to his and Quintus's joint education by their father, their paternal uncle, L. Cicero, their maternal uncle (by marriage), C. Aculeo, and their cousins, the sons of Aculeo.[64] The history of the young Quintus thus replicates, in much greater detail, the same pattern of extensive family participation and cooperation in the socialization of children. The life of the Roman family lived as the life of a family community cannot be clearer.

The durability of the network, too, is worth emphasis. The efforts Cicero and Atticus made to keep Quintus and Pomponia in peaceful concord ultimately failed, as has been seen, and in the late stages of the marriage young Quintus was just playing off one parent against the other.[65] Even so—and there is now a curious final twist—the last appearance Quintus and Pomponia make in the historical record indicates that a marriage of a quarter of a century, with all the familial ramifications involved, could not easily be set aside and forgotten. In the proscriptions of 43, when M. Antonius and Caesar's heir were wreaking havoc against the optimate rump, Cicero, Quintus, and the young Quintus were violently put to death. They had tried to escape the assassins sent to murder them but were betrayed by servants. Cicero's brother and nephew were killed first at Rome, Cicero himself a short while after at the villa near Formiae. After he was slain, Cicero's head and hands were severed, to gratify the vengeful appetite of the victim of the *Philippics*.[66] The man who had betrayed him was a certain Philologus, a former slave who had once belonged to Quintus and whom Cicero himself had instructed in literature and philosophy. This is the way Plutarch describes his fate, once he had fallen into the custody of Antonius:

> However, in all this Antonius did show one sign of decent feeling. He handed over Philologus to Pomponia, the wife of Quintus. And she, once she had got the man in her power, inflicted all sorts of terrible punishments on him and finally made him cut off his own flesh bit by bit, roast the pieces, and then eat them.[67]

The gruesomeness of the incident cannot be gainsaid. But this grim episode was perhaps Pomponia's finest familial and marital moment. In spite of the divorce, the sad conclusion to an arranged marriage that brought little satisfaction to either spouse, the bonds of sentiment and loyalty that the union created, that Cicero and Atticus had labored so long to maintain, and that were now cruelly brought back to life by the horror of brutal death, could not be utterly destroyed.

VII

Through the almost two decades covered by the correspondence, Cicero's family configuration underwent a vast transformation. If, again simply for the sake of convenience, the two fixed points of 60 and 44 are taken, the contrast stands out sharply.

In 60, Cicero himself was forty-six and had been married to Terentia for approximately seventeen years; their daughter Tullia was fifteen, their son Marcus five.[68] This family unit, however, cannot properly be thought of as nuclear (strictly speaking). Since Tullia was in 60 married to C. Calpurnius Piso Frugi (quaestor in 58), it was already spread over two households. Beyond this, Cicero had a brother aged forty-three, who was married to the older Pomponia, and a nephew aged six. Through them Cicero was related by marriage to his friend since childhood, Atticus, who himself in 60 was as yet unmarried.

By 44, when Cicero was sixty-two, the changes are dramatic. Cicero and Terentia have divorced, and so have Quintus and Pomponia. Cicero, as it happens, has divorced twice. After separating from Terentia, he quickly married and as quickly divorced his second wife, his ward Publilia, a woman young enough to be his granddaughter. Meanwhile,

Tullia's husband had died in 57, and since then she had had one and possibly two other husbands, by the second of whom, P. Cornelius Dolabella (consul in 44), she had two sons, neither of whom survived infancy. Shortly after the birth of the second child, Tullia herself died. Atticus had married, in 56, a woman named Pilia, and in 44 their daughter, Attica, was seven years old. Pilia, however, may also have been dead by this time. That left Cicero's son Marcus and nephew Quintus, who were, as yet, unmarried.[69]

By definition, no family can ever be a static entity. So the metamorphosis visible in Cicero's familial world between 60 and 44 is in one sense the simple result of a normal evolutionary process. Under the impact of marriage and divorce, birth and death, the shape of the family constantly altered, while within the family as a whole any number of conjugal units can be seen: Cicero and Terentia, Atticus and Pilia, Tullia and Dolabella, and so on (plus offspring, as appropriate). But what Cicero's letters show at any point along the evolutionary scale is that the familial ideology dominant among the individuals who comprise the family is not that of the conjugal cell but that of the family group as a whole. It is the well-being of the kin network as a network that governs familial attention in the world represented by Cicero's correspondence, a fact that is consistent, of course, with the amorphous character of the Roman domestic framework of reference seen earlier and a fact that is illustrated most clearly of all by the history of the involvement of Cicero and Atticus in the lives of their siblings and their siblings' child.

It could be said, in counterpoint, that despite its relative richness, the evidence of the letters is nonetheless distorted. On family matters, it is only the voice of Cicero that is being heard, not the voice of Terentia or Tullia or anyone else, so that the communal character of family life Cicero reveals is an aberration, attributable to one individual's preoccupation with the people to whom he was related. But this is not compelling. The very nature of the letter—a form of *communication* between individuals—presupposes a community of interest between author and recipient. Cicero's letters make obvious the fact that all the members of the family network were constantly communicating with one another, as circumstance and occasion required, to provide news, seek help, and give advice. It was not, that is to say, merely a question of correspondence being exchanged between Cicero and Atticus, or between Cicero and Quintus, but between Atticus and Quintus, between Terentia and Atticus, between the young Quintus and Atticus, between Marcus and young Quintus, even between Pilia and Quintus. The flow of correspondence was multidirectional and ceaseless.[70]

But if the communal family mentality is best seen in the way Cicero worked to preserve his brother's marriage and in the way he contributed to the upbringing of his nephew, it is manifest, too, in a host of other details randomly tossed up by the correspondence: how Cicero refers to his cousin L. Tullius Cicero (a member of Cicero's family network in boyhood) as Atticus's "family connection"; how Cicero welcomes Pilia's views on Tullia's marriage to Dolabella; how Cicero is seen involved in the negotiations surrounding the proposed marriage of Attica; how Atticus is instructed to "make inquiries" about the family of a woman young Quintus was interested in marrying; how Dolabella is naturally expected to fall under the benign influence of Cicero once he entered the network; how Cicero, Terentia, and Atticus were involved in the divorce of Tullia and Dolabella; how Cicero describes his affection for Atticus as that of love for a second brother.[71] It is evident further still in a final string of quotable passages that to some extent can be categorized as social niceties or family pleasantries. But underlying them all is the assumption that the recipient (Atticus in this case) cares to hear them:

> We are expecting Quintus back any day. Terentia has a bad attack of rheumatism. She is very fond of you and of your sister and mother, and sends her best love, as does my darling little Tullia. Take care of yourself and your affection for me, and be sure of my brotherly affection in return.

> But let us keep all this for our strolls together at the Compitalia. Remember the day before. I shall have the bath heated. Terentia invites Pomponia as well, and we shall have your mother over too. Please bring me Theophrastus on Ambition from Quintus' library.

> As for yourself, do come without fail, if you can bear to stick down here for a while, and bring Pilia, as is right and proper and as Tullia much wishes.

> I am much beholden to your little daughter for so carefully instructing you to give me her love, and to Pilia also; but the former's attention is more remarkable in that she is so affectionate all this time to someone she has never seen. So on your side please give my love to both.[72]

This mentality, ubiquitous and all-encompassing in the letters, did not necessarily cause any weakness in the bond between husband and wife or in that between parent and child. After all, in the personal history of

Cicero, the one safely controversial element is his passion for his daughter Tullia. It did mean, however, that the individual bonds between husband and wife and parent and child failed to combine and to reinforce each other, and so the conjugal unit could not emerge in the Roman domestic framework of reference as a dominant all-exclusive entity. Rather, the bonds remained discrete, separate threads in a densely and extensively woven fabric; and it was the fabric as a totality that dominated the Roman familial mind.

Notes

1. *Letters to Friends* 6.3.
2. On Cicero's background, see variously Shackleton Bailey (1971), 1–5; Stockton (1971), 1–5; E. Rawson (1975), 1–11; Mitchell (1979), 2–9; cf. also Gratwick (1984), 32.
3. *Letters to Quintus* 3.1, 3.6; *Letters to Friends* 25.2, 51.2 (cf. Gruen [1974], 349), 73.9 (cf. Gruen [1974], 353–54), 93.2, 221.2.
4. The Latin terms include *frater, liberi, coniunx, uxor, propinqui, adfines, parens, tui omnes*.
5. The Latin terms include *fortunae, copiae, pecunia, opes*.
6. *Letters to Friends* 153.1, 153.2, 259.2, 390.1.
7. See Syme (1986), 35.
8. *Letters to Quintus* 3.3, 3.10.
9. *Letters to Quintus* 3.3.
10. *Letters to Atticus* 18.1.
11. See Dixon (1988), 25. Cf. *Letters to Friends* 249.2, on Tullia alone.
12. *Letters to Atticus* 92.2.
13. *Letters to Atticus* 354.
14. Note the remark of Plutarch (*Moralia* 491D): "But while care for brothers themselves is an excellent thing, yet even more excellent is it to show oneself always well disposed and obliging in all matters to brothers' fathers-in-law and brothers-in-law."
15. *Letters to Atticus* 367.
16. Compare the involvement of Sicinius Pontianus in the marriage of his mother to Apuleius; Apuleius, *Apologia* 70–73, 83. See Corbier (1982), 694, 727–28, for the background.
17. For example, *Letters to Friends* 20.24, 203.5, 218.4.
18. *Letters to Quintus* 17.2.
19. *Letters to Friends* 44.1.
20. *Letters to Quintus* 10.2, 12.1. Cicero appears to have been genuinely fond of children. Note, for instance, his interest in Atticus's daughter; *Letters to Atticus* 112.2, 125.4.
21. For the chronological details on Quintus and Pomponia, see Shackleton Bailey (1980), 3–4; cf. *MRR* II 139 on Quintus's quaestorship. According to Cornelius Nepos, *Life of Atticus* 17.1, Pomponia was close in age to her brother Atticus (as Cicero and Quintus),

who was born late in 110; Summer (1973), 129. Whether she was younger or older than Atticus is unknown. But since she gave birth to her son in 67, her age at marriage should be put at approximately forty. On marriage ages generally, see Syme (1987a); Shaw (1987b).

22. Cornelius Nepos, *Life of Atticus* 5.3. There was nothing odd in Cicero's behavior; cf. Plutarch, *Moralia* 491E: "But above all we should be troubled at a brother's unmarried and childless state, and by exhortation and raillery take part in pressing him on every side into marriage and in getting him well fastened in the bonds of lawful matrimony." On the social eminence of Atticus, see Millar (1988).

23. *Letters to Atticus* 1.2.

24. *Letters to Atticus* 2.2.

25. *Letters to Atticus* 6.5.

26. See Shackleton Bailey (1980), 3–4; *MRR* II 158, 173, III 209 (cf. *Letters to Atticus* 15.1); McDermott (1971).

27. See Shatzman (1975), 425.

28. *Letters to Atticus* 17.1–5, 7.

29. *Letters to Atticus* 17.3.

30. *Letters to Atticus* 21.11, 23.4, 27.5, 24.7.

31. *Letters to Quintus* 10.1.

32. *Letters to Atticus* 94.3–4.

33. *Letters to Atticus* 116.1, 117.8.

34. *Letters to Atticus* 138.3, 142.1.

35. *Letters to Atticus* 202.1–3, 207.3.

36. *Letters to Atticus* 367.5, 407.2.

37. For the details, see Shackleton Bailey (1980), 3–4; McDermott (1971).

38. *Letters to Atticus* 1.2, 2.2, 6.5, 94.4, 116.2, 117.8, 120.1.

39. Cf. Plutarch, *Moralia* 491D: "But a brother's wife should be esteemed and reverenced as the most holy of sacred things; if her husband honours her, we should applaud him; if he neglects her, we should sympathize with her annoyance; when she grows angry, soothe her; if she commits some trifling fault, take part in urging her husband to a reconciliation; and if some private difference arise between yourself and your brother, bring complaints to her and so do away with the reasons for complaint."

40. *Letters to Atticus* 195.6, 197.2, 201.6, 202.3–4. See also 196.1, 198.3, 200.2.

41. *Letters to Atticus* 203.3, 204.4.

42. A biography of the young Quintus is provided by Garrido Božić (1951). Presumably Quintus was provided from birth onward with the servants who customarily carried out the tasks of child care in elite Roman households, in the way that Cicero later provided slaves for his short-lived grandson, the child of Tullia and P. Cornelius Dolabella; *Letters to Atticus* 267.3.

43. *Letters to Atticus* 22.1.

44. *Letters to Atticus* 22.1, 24.7, 27.5.

45. *Letters to Atticus* 60.4, 68.5; *Letters to Quintus* 3.3; *Letters to Atticus* 77.1, 77.3, 85.2.

46. *Letters to Quintus* 8.2.

47. *Letters to Quintus* 21.7.

48. *Letters to Quintus* 21.7, 21.14, 21.19, 23.4 (cf. 23.1), 27.9. For a nephew temporarily living with his uncle, cf. Apuleius, *Apologia* 86.

49. *Letters to Quintus* 21.7, 27.9. The elder Quintus may genuinely have missed his son while in Gaul: see *Letters to Friends* 44.1.

50. *Letters to Atticus* 110.3, 113.9, 115.12.

51. *Letters to Atticus* 111.4.

52. *Letters to Atticus* 113.9, 115.12.

53. *Letters to Atticus* 113.9, 115.12, 116.2.

54. *Letters to Atticus* 117.8.

55. *Letters to Atticus* 120.1. For the cavalier attitude, note *Letters to Friends* 92.2 (April of 50, to Caelius Rufus): ''Paula Valeria, Triarius' sister, has divorced her husband for no reason the day he was due to get back from his province. She is to marry D. Brutus. There have been a good many extraordinary incidents of this sort during your absence which I have not yet reported.'' For ideal devotion of child to parent, from Coriolanus in early Roman history to Q. Sertorius in the epoch of Cicero, see Plutarch, *Coriolanus* 4.3, *Sertorius* 2, 22.6.

56. *Letters to Atticus* 121.4.

57. *Letters to Atticus* 121.4; cf. 123.3.

58. *Letters to Friends* 126.

59. *Letters to Atticus* 135.3.

60. *Letters to Atticus* 136.3, 141.4, 142.1, 144.2; cf. 143.

61. *Letters to Atticus* 172.4, 156.1, 159.

62. Plutarch again has a relevant commentary: ''And indeed it is an uncle's duty to rejoice and take pride in the fair deeds and honours of a brother's sons and to help give them an incentive to honourable achievement, and, when they succeed, to praise them without stint; for it is, perhaps, offensive to praise one's own son, yet to praise a brother's is a noble thing, not inspired by selfishness but honourable and truly divine; for it seems to me that the very name of uncle admirably points the way to goodwill and affection for nephews'' (*Moralia* 492C). For divine uncles, note *Letters to Atticus* 22.1.

63. *Letters to Quintus* 21.19.

64. Cicero, *De Oratore* 2.2. Cicero gives in the correspondence some expression of children's obligations to their parents (e.g., *Letters to Atticus* 176.2, *Letters to Friends* 277.1), but his own parents are scarcely mentioned. His father's death is chronicled, as briefly as possible, in *Letters to Atticus* 2.2 (and similarly, with no sign of grief on either side, the death of Atticus's grandmother is reported at 8.1). The only mention of his mother is made by Quintus, in a letter to Tiro, *Letters to Friends* 351.2.

65. *Letters to Atticus* 341.2, 342.1, 344.1, 354.1, 364.4.

66. For the accounts of Cicero's death, see Livy, *Fragment* 120; Appian, *Civil Wars* 4.19–20; Plutarch, *Cicero* 47–49; cf. Shackleton Bailey (1971), 276–77.

67. Plutarch, *Cicero* 49.2–3.

68. See Shackleton Bailey (1971), 22–23.

69. See Shackleton Bailey (1971), 201–15; Gratwick (1984), 32, 36–37.

70. Observe, for instance, *Letters to Atticus* 104.7 (Pilia to Quintus), 150.3 (Terentia to Atticus), 199.1 (Tullia to Cicero), 341.2 (young Quintus to Cicero), 371.3 (young Quintus

to his father), 391 (Marcus to Cicero), 425.4 (exchange of letters between Marcus and young Quintus), *Letters to Friends* 157 (Dolabella to Cicero).

71. *Letters to Atticus* 1.1, 122.1, 327.4, 408.2; *Letters to Friends* 94.1, 168, 169, 63.5.

72. *Letters to Atticus* 1.8, 23.4, 78.2, 115.22.

Bibliographical References

Africa, Thomas W. 1977–78. "The Mask of an Assassin: A Psychohistorical Study of M. Junius Brutus." *Journal of Interdisciplinary History* 8: 599–626.

Åkerman, Sune. 1981. "The Importance of Remarriage in the Seventeenth and Eighteenth Centuries." In J. Dupâquier, E. Hélin, P. Laslett, M. Livi-Bacci and S. Sogner, eds., *Marriage and Remarriage in Populations of the Past.* New York. Pp. 163–75.

Astin, Alan E. 1978. *Cato the Censor.* Oxford.

Babcock, Charles L. 1965. "The Early Career of Fulvia." *American Journal of Philology* 86: 1–32.

Bagnall, Roger S. 1968. "Three Papyri from Oxyrhynchus." *Bulletin of the American Society of Papyrologists* 5: 135–50.

Baldwin, Barry. 1973. *Studies in Lucian.* Toronto.

Barnes, T. D. 1967. "Hadrian and Lucius Verus." *Journal of Roman Studies* 57: 65–79.

———. 1981. *Constantine and Eusebius.* Cambridge, Mass., and London.

Beard, Mary. 1986. "New Lines on Ancient Life." *Times Literary Supplement,* June 20, 1986. P. 672.

Berkner, Lutz K. 1972. "The Stem Family and the Developmental Cycle of the Peasant Household: An Eighteenth-Century Austrian Example." *American Historical Review* 77: 398–418.

Biezunska-Malowist, I. M. 1977. *L'esclavage dans l'Egypte gréco-romaine, Seconde partie: Période romaine.* Wroclaw.

Binkowski, Edyth, and Beryl Rawson. 1986. "Bibliography 1: Sources for the Study of the Roman Family." In Beryl Rawson, ed., *The Family in Ancient Rome: New Perspectives.* London and Sydney. Pp. 243–57.

Birks, Peter. 1981. "Other Men's Meat: Aquilian Liability for Proper User." *Irish Jurist* 16: 141–85.

Birley, Anthony R. 1981. *The Fasti of Roman Britain.* Oxford.

———. 1987. *Marcus Aurelius: A Biography,* revised ed. London.

————. 1988. *The African Emperor: Septimius Severus*. London.

Biscottini, Maria Valentina. 1966. "L'archivio di Tryphon, tessitore di Oxyrhynchos." *Aegyptus* 46: 60–90.

Bonner, Stanley F. 1977. *Education in Ancient Rome*. Berkeley and Los Angeles.

Booth, Alan D. 1982. "The Academic Career of Ausonius." *Phoenix* 36: 329–43.

Boswell, John. 1988. *The Kindness of Strangers: The Abandonment of Children in Western Europe from Late Antiquity to the Renaissance*. New York.

Boulogne, Reinier. 1951. *De Plaats van de Paedagogus in de romeinse Cultuur*. Groningen.

Boulvert, Gérard. 1970. *Esclaves et affranchis impériaux sous le haut-empire romain: Rôle politique et administratif*. Naples.

————. 1974. *Domestique et fonctionnaire sous le haut-empire romain: La condition de l'affranchi du prince*. Paris.

Bowersock, G. W. 1969. *Greek Sophists in the Roman Empire*. Oxford.

Bradley, K. R. 1978. *Suetonius' Life of Nero: An Historical Commentary*. Brussels.

————. 1984. "The Social History of the Roman Elite: A Perspective." *Echos du monde classique/Classical Views* 3: 481–99.

————. 1985. "Ideals of Marriage in Suetonius' *Caesares*." *Rivista Storica dell'Antichità* 15: 77–95.

————. 1986. "Wet-nursing at Rome: A Study in Social Relations." In Beryl Rawson, ed., *The Family in Ancient Rome: New Perspectives*. London and Sydney. Pp. 201–29.

————. 1987. *Slaves and Masters in the Roman Empire: A Study in Social Control*. New York and Oxford.

————. 1989a. "History Old and New: A Perspective." *Echos du monde classique/Classical Views* 8: 333–40.

————. 1989b. *Slavery and Rebellion in the Roman World, 140 B.C.–70 B.C.* Bloomington, Indianapolis, London.

Brown, Judith C. 1986. *Immodest Acts: The Life of a Lesbian Nun in Renaissance Italy*. New York and Oxford.

Brown, Peter. 1988. *The Body and Society: Men, Women and Sexual Renunciation in Early Christianity*. New York.

Brunt, P. A. 1958. Review of W. L. Westermann, *The Slave Systems of Greek and Roman Antiquity* (and others). *Journal of Roman Studies* 48: 164–70.

———— 1974. "The Roman Mob." In M. I. Finley, ed., *Studies in Ancient Society*. London. Pp. 74–107.

————. 1975. "The Administrators of Roman Egypt." *Journal of Roman Studies* 65: 124–47.

————. 1988. *The Fall of the Roman Republic and Related Essays*. Oxford.

Buonocore, Marco. 1984. *Schiavi e liberti dei Volusi Saturnini*. Rome.

Burford, Alison. 1972. *Craftsmen in Greek and Roman Society*. Ithaca, N.Y.

Burn, A. R. 1959. "Two Inscriptions Found in Dunbartonshire." *Journal of Hellenic Studies* 79: 159.

Calder, William M. III. 1983. "Longus 1.2: The She-Goat Nurse." *Classical Philology* 78: 50–51.

Campbell, J. B. 1984. *The Emperor and the Roman Army*. Oxford.

Carter, John M. 1982. *Suetonius, Divus Augustus*. Bristol.

Champlin, Edward. 1974. "The Chronology of Fronto." *Journal of Roman Studies* 64: 136–59.

Christes, Johannes. 1979. *Sklaven und Freigelassene als Grammatiker und Philologen im antiken Rom*. Wiesbaden.

Clarke, G. W. 1974. *The Octavius of Marcus Minucius Felix*. New York.

Clarke, M. L. 1967. "Quintilian: A Biographical Sketch." *Greece and Rome* 14: 24–37.

———. 1981. *The Noblest Roman: Marcus Brutus and His Reputation*. London.

Cohn Haft, L. 1957. "A Note on the Διδασκαλικαι and a Correction in the Reading of P. Vars, ser nov, 7." *Aegyptus* 37: 266–70.

Conrad, Robert Edgar. 1983. *Children of God's Fire: A Documentary History of Black Slavery in Brazil*. Princeton.

Corbett, Percy Ellwood. 1930. *The Roman Law of Marriage*. Oxford.

Corbier, Mireille. 1982. "Les familles clarissimes d'Afrique proconsulaire (Ier–IIIe siècle)." *Tituli* 5: 685–754.

———. 1987. "Les comportements familiaux de l'aristocratie romaine (IIe siècle avant J.-C.–IIIe siècle après J.-C.)." *Annales ESC:* 1267–85.

Courtney, E. 1980. *A Commentary on the Satires of Juvenal*. London.

Crook, J. A. 1967a. *Law and Life of Rome*. London.

———. 1967b. "*Patria Potestas*." *Classical Quarterly* 17: 113–22.

Csillag, Pál. 1976. *The Augustan Laws on Family Relations*. Budapest.

Curchin, Leonard A. 1982. "Jobs in Roman Spain." *Florilegium* 4: 32–62.

———. 1983. "Familial Epithets in the Epigraphy of Roman Britain." *Britannia* 14: 255–56.

———. 1984. "Familial Epithets in the Epigraphy of Roman Spain." In *Mélanges offerts en hommage au révérend père Etienne Gareau*. Ottawa. Pp. 179–82.

DeMause, Lloyd. 1974. "The Evolution of Childhood," In Lloyd De Mause, ed., *The History of Childhood*. New York. Pp. 1–73.

Demos, John Putnam. 1982. *Entertaining Satan: Witchcraft and the Culture of Early New England*. New York and Oxford.

———. 1986. *Past, Present and Personal: The Family and the Life Course in American History*. New York and Oxford.

Dixon, Suzanne. 1984. "Roman Nurses and Foster-mothers: Some Problems of Terminology." *Australasian Universities Language and Literature Association Proceedings* 22: 9–24.

———. 1985. "The Marriage Alliance in the Roman Elite." *Journal of Family History* 10: 353–78.

———. 1988. *The Roman Mother*. London and Sydney.

Drumann, W., and P. Groebe. 1899–1902. *Geschichte Roms*[2]. Leipzig.

Duby, Georges. 1983. *The Knight, the Lady and the Priest: The Making of Modern Marriage in Medieval France*. New York.

Fildes, Valerie. 1986. *Breasts, Bottles and Babies: A History of Infant Feeding*. Edinburgh.

———. 1988. *Wet Nursing: A History from Antiquity to the Present*. Oxford and New York.

Finley, M. I. 1969. "The Silent Women of Rome." In M. I. Finley, *Aspects of Antiquity*. New York. Pp. 129–42.

————. 1980. *Ancient Slavery and Modern Ideology*. New York.

————. 1981. "The Elderly in Classical Antiquity." *Greece and Rome* 28: 156–71.

Forbes, Clarence A. 1955. "The Education and Training of Slaves." *Transactions of the American Philological Association* 86: 321–60.

Frank, Tenney. 1940. *Rome and Italy of the Empire*. Volume V in Tenney Frank, ed., *An Economic Survey of Ancient Rome*. Baltimore.

Frier, Bruce Woodward. 1977. "The Rental Market in Early Imperial Rome." *Journal of Roman Studies* 67: 27–37.

Gardner, Jane F. 1986. *Women in Roman Law and Society*. London and Sydney.

Garnsey, Peter, and Richard Saller. 1987. *The Roman Empire: Economy, Society and Culture*. Berkeley and Los Angeles.

Garrido Božić, I. M. 1951. "Quintus Filius." *Greece and Rome* 20: 11–25.

Garrido-Hory, M. 1981. *Martial et l'esclavage*. Paris.

Geer, R. M. 1931. "Notes on the Early Life of Nero." *Transactions of the American Philological Association* 62: 57–67.

Gilliam, J. F. 1971. "A Legionary Veteran and His Family." *Bulletin of the American Society of Papyrologists* 8: 39–44.

Golden, Mark. 1988a. Review of Beryl Rawson, ed., *The Family in Ancient Rome: New Perspectives*. *Echos du monde classique/Classical Views* 7: 78–83.

————. 1988b. "Did the Ancients Care When Their Children Died?" *Greece and Rome* 35: 152–63.

Goldthorpe, J. E. 1987. *Family Life in Western Societies: A Historical Sociology of Family Relationships in Britain and North America*. Cambridge.

Gordon, A. E. 1958. *Album of Dated Latin Inscriptions* I. Berkeley and Los Angeles.

Gourevitch, Danielle. 1984. *Le mal d'être femme: La femme et la médecine dans la Rome antique*. Paris.

Gratwick, A. S. 1984. "Free or Not so Free? Wives and Daughters in the Late Roman Republic." In Elizabeth M. Craik, ed., *Marriage and Property*. Aberdeen. Pp. 30–53.

Gray-Fow, Michael J. G. 1988a. "The Wicked Stepmother in Roman Literature and History: An Evaluation." *Latomus* 47: 741–57.

————. 1988b. "A Stepfather's Gift: L. Marcius Philippus and Octavian." *Greece and Rome* 35: 184–99.

Griffin, Jasper. 1985. *Latin Poets and Roman Life*. London.

Griffin, Miriam T. 1976. *Seneca: A Philosopher in Politics*. Oxford.

————. 1985. *Nero: The End of a Dynasty*. New Haven and London.

Grodzynski, Denise. 1984. "Ravies et coupables: Un essai d'interprétation de la loi IX, 24, 1 du Code théodosien." *Mélanges de l'Ecole Française de Rome: Antiquité* 96: 697–726.

Gruen, Erich S. 1968. *Roman Politics and the Criminal Courts, 149–78 B.C.* Cambridge, Mass.

————. 1974. *The Last Generation of the Roman Republic*. Berkeley and Los Angeles.

Guastella, Gianni. 1980. "I Parentalia come testo antropologico: l'Avunculato nel mondo celtico e nella familia di Ausonio." *Materiali e Discussione per l'Analisi dei Teste Classici* 4: 97–124.

Guida, Augusto. 1985. "More on She-Goat Nurses." *Classical Philology* 80: 142.

Heichelheim, F. M. 1938. *Roman Syria*. Volume IV in Tenney Frank, ed., *An Economic Survey of Ancient Rome*. Baltimore.

Herlihy, David. 1985. *Medieval Households*. Cambridge, Mass., and London.

Herrmann, Johannes. 1958. "Vertragsinhalt und Rechtsnatur der ΔΙΔΑΣΚΑΛΙΚΑΙ." *Journal of Juristic Papyrology* 11–12: 119–39.

Himmelfarb, Gertrude. 1987. *The New History and the Old: Critical Essays and Reappraisals*. Cambridge, Mass., and London.

Hobson, Deborah W. 1985. "House and Household in Roman Egypt." *Yale Classical Studies* 28: 211–29.

Holford-Stevens, Leofranc. 1988. *Aulus Gellius*. London.

Hopkins, M. K. 1961. "Social Mobility in the Later Roman Empire: The Evidence of Ausonius." *Classical Quarterly* 11: 239–49.

———. 1965. "The Age of Roman Girls at Marriage." *Population Studies* 18: 309–27.

Hopkins, Keith. 1983. *Death and Renewal: Sociological Studies in Roman History 2*. Cambridge.

Howell, Peter. 1980. *A Commentary on Book One of the Epigrams of Martial*. London.

Humbert, M. 1972. *Le remariage à Rome*. Milan.

Hunt, A. S., and C. C. Edgar. 1932. *Select Papyri I*. Cambridge, Mass.

Huzar, Eleanor G. 1986. "Mark Antony: Marriages vs. Careers." *Classical Journal* 81: 97–111.

Jones, A. H. M. 1964. *The Later Roman Empire 284–602: A Social, Economic and Administrative Survey*. Oxford.

———. 1974. "The Cloth Industry under the Roman Empire." In A. H. M. Jones, *The Roman Economy: Studies in Ancient Economic and Administrative History*, ed. P. A. Brunt. Oxford. Pp. 350–64.

Jones, C. P. 1971. *Plutarch and Rome*. Oxford.

———. 1986. *Culture and Society in Lucian*. Cambridge, Mass., and London.

Jongmann, Willem. 1988. *The Economy and Society of Pompeii*. Amsterdam.

Joshel, Sandra R. 1986. "Nurturing the Master's Child: Slavery and the Roman Child-Nurse." *Signs* 12: 3–22.

Kampen, Natalie. 1981. *Image and Status: Roman Working Women in Ostia*. Berlin.

Kinsey, T. E. 1979. "Melior the Calculator." *Hermes* 107: 501.

Klapisch-Zuber, Christine. 1985. *Women, Family, and Ritual in Renaissance Italy*. Chicago and London.

Kleiner, Diana E. E. 1987. "Women and Family Life on Roman Funerary Altars." *Latomus* 46: 545–54.

Lambert, Garth R. 1982. *Rhetoric Rampant: The Family Under Siege in the Early Western Tradition*. London, Ontario.

Lantz, Herman R. 1981–82. "Romantic Love in the Pre-Modern Period." *Journal of Social History* 15: 349–70.

Laslett, Peter. 1972. "Introduction: The History of the Family." In Peter Laslett, ed., *Household and Family in Past Time*. Cambridge. Pp. 1–89.

———. 1983. "Family and Household as Work Group and Kin Group: Areas of Traditional Europe Compared." In Richard Wall, ed., *Family Forms in Historic Europe*. Cambridge. Pp. 513–63.

Lattimore, Richmond. 1962. *Themes in Greek and Latin Epitaphs*. Urbana, Ill.

Levick, Barbara. 1978. "Concordia at Rome." In R. A. G. Carson and Colin M. Kraay, eds., *Scripta Nummaria Romana: Essays Presented to Humphrey Sutherland.* London. Pp. 217–33.

Lewis, Naphtali. 1983. *Life in Egypt under Roman Rule.* Oxford.

Lowe, N. J. 1988. "Sulpicia's Syntax." *Classical Quarterly* 38: 193–205.

Lucas, Angela M. 1983. *Women in the Middle Ages: Religion, Marriage and Letters.* Brighton.

Lutz, Cora C. 1947. "Musonius Rufus, The Roman Socrates." *Yale Classical Studies* 10: 3–147.

Lyne, R. O. A. M. 1980. *The Latin Love Poets: From Catullus to Horace.* Oxford.

McDermott, William C. 1971. "Q. Cicero." *Historia* 20: 702–17.

McDonnell, Myles. 1987. "The Speech of Numidicus at Gellius, *N.A.* 1.6." *American Journal of Philology* 108: 81–94.

MacMullen, Ramsay. 1980. "Women in Public in the Roman Empire." *Historia* 29: 208–18.

Manca Masciardi, Mariadele, and Orsolina Montevecchi. 1984. *I contratti de baliatico.* Milan.

Manson, Michel. 1978. "*Puer Bimulus* (Catulle, 17, 12–13) et l'image du petit enfant chez Catulle et ses prédécesseurs." *Mélanges d'Archéologie et d'Histoire de l'Ecole Française de Rome* 90: 247–91.

———. 1983. "The Emergence of the Small Child at Rome (Third Century B.C.–First Century A.D.)." *History of Education* 12: 149–59.

Matthews, John. 1975. *Western Aristocracies and Imperial Court, A.D. 364–425.* Oxford.

Maxey, Mima. 1938. *Occupations of the Lower Classes in Roman Society.* Chicago.

Meeks, Wayne A. 1983. *The First Urban Christians: The Social World of the Apostle Paul.* New Haven and London.

Meiggs, Russell. 1973. *Roman Ostia*². Oxford.

Millar, Fergus. 1977. *The Emperor in the Roman World.* London.

———. 1981. "The World of the *Golden Ass.*" *Journal of Roman Studies* 71: 63–75.

———. 1984. "The Mediterranean and the Roman Revolution: Politics, War and the Economy." *Past and Present* 102: 3–24.

———. 1988. "Cornelius Nepos, 'Atticus' and the Roman Revolution." *Greece and Rome* 35: 40–55.

Mitchell, Thomas N. 1979. *Cicero: The Ascending Years.* New Haven and London.

Mitterauer, Michael, and Reinhard Sieder. 1982. *The European Family: Patriarchy to Partnership from the Middle Ages to the Present.* Oxford.

Moeller, Walter O. 1976. *The Wool Trade of Ancient Pompeii.* Leiden.

Mohler, S. L. 1940. "Slave Education in the Roman Empire." *Transactions of the American Philological Association* 71: 262–80.

Montevecchi, O., and M. Manca Masciardi. 1982. "Contratti di baliatico e vendite fiduciare a Tebtynis." *Aegyptus* 62: 148–61.

Moreau, Philippe. 1983. "Structures de parenté et d'alliance à Larinum d'après le *pro Cluentio.*" In M. Cébeillac-Gervasoni, ed., *Les "Bourgeoisies" municipales italiennes aux IIe et Ier siècles av. J.-C.* Paris and Naples. Pp. 99–123.

Musurillo, Herbert. 1972. *The Acts of the Christian Martyrs.* Oxford.

Néraudau, Jean-Pierre. 1984. *Etre enfant à Rome.* Paris.

Nielsen, Hanne Sigismund. 1987. *"Alumnus:* A Term of Relation Denoting Quasi-Adoption." *Classica et Mediaevalia* 38: 141–88.

Nörr, D. 1981. "The Matrimonial Legislation of Augustus." *Irish Jurist* 16: 350–64.

Oglivie, R. M. 1965. *A Commentary on Livy, Books 1–5.* Oxford.

Pearl, Orsamus. 1985. "Apprentice Contract." *Bulletin of the American Society of Papyrologists* 22: 255–59.

Pflaum, H.-G. 1960–61. *Les carrières procuratoriennes équestres sous le haut-empire romain.* Paris.

Pollock, Linda A. 1983. *Forgotten Children: Parent-Child Relations from 1500 to 1900.* Cambridge.

———. 1987. *A Lasting Relationship: Parents and Children over Three Centuries.* London.

Pomeroy, Sarah B. 1975. *Goddesses, Whores, Wives, and Slaves: Women in Classical Antiquity.* New York.

———. 1976. "The Relationship of the Married Woman to Her Blood Relatives in Rome." *Ancient Society* 7: 215–27.

Prosperi Valenti, Giuseppina. 1985. "Attori-bambini del mondo romano attraverso le testimonianze epigrafiche." *Epigraphica* 47: 71–82.

Raepsaet-Charlier, Marie-Thérèse. 1981–82. "Ordre sénatorial et divorce sous le haut-empire: Un chapitre de l'histoire des mentalités." *Acta Classica Universitatis Scientiarum Debreceniensis* 17–19: 161–73.

Rawson, Beryl. 1986a. "The Roman Family." In Beryl Rawson, ed., *The Family in Ancient Rome: New Perspectives.* London and Sydney. Pp. 1–57.

———. 1986b. "Children in the Roman *Familia.*" In Beryl Rawson, ed., *The Family in Ancient Rome: New Perspectives.* London and Sydney. Pp. 170–200.

Rawson, Elizabeth. 1975. *Cicero: A Portrait.* London.

Richardson, L. Jr. 1988. *Pompeii: An Architectural History.* Baltimore and London.

Robertis, Francesco M. de. 1963. *Lavoro e lavoratori nel mondo romano.* Bari.

Rousselle, Aline. 1988. *Porneia: On Desire and the Body in Antiquity.* Oxford.

Ste. Croix, G. E. M. de. 1981. *The Class Struggle in the Ancient Greek World.* London.

Saller, Richard P. 1984. *"Familia, Domus,* and the Roman Conception of Family." *Phoenix* 38: 336–55.

———. 1986. *"Patria Potestas* and the Stereotype of the Roman Family." *Continuity and Change* 1: 7–22.

———. 1987a. "Slavery and the Roman Family." In M. I. Finley, ed., *Classical Slavery.* London. Pp. 65–87.

———. 1987b. "Men's Age at Marriage and Its Consequences in the Roman Family." *Classical Philology* 82: 21–34.

———. 1988. *"Pietas,* Obligation and Authority in the Roman Family." In *Festschrift für Karl Christ zum 65. Geburtstag.* Darmstadt. Pp. 393–410.

Saller, Richard P., and Brent D. Shaw. 1984. "Tombstones and Roman Family Relations in the Principate: Civilians, Soldiers and Slaves." *Journal of Roman Studies* 74: 124–56.

Scheid, John. 1975. "Scribonia Caesaris et les Julio-Claudiens." *Mélanges de l'Ecole Française de Rome: Antiquité* 87: 349–75.

Scobie, Alex. 1983. *Apuleius and Folklore.* London.

Scullard, H. H. 1981. *Festivals and Ceremonies of the Roman Republic*. London.

Segalen, Martine. 1986. *Historical Anthropology of the Family*. Cambridge.

Shackleton Bailey, D. R., ed. 1965. *Cicero's Letters to Atticus, Volume I*. Cambridge.

———. 1966. *Cicero's Letters to Atticus, Volume V*. Cambridge.

———. 1971. *Cicero*. London.

——— 1980. *Cicero: Epistulae ad Quintum Fratrem et M. Brutum*. Cambridge.

Shatzman, Israel. 1975. *Senatorial Wealth and Roman Politics*. Brussels.

Shaw, Brent D. 1987a. "The Family in Late Antiquity: The Experience of Augustine." *Past and Present* 115: 3–51.

———. 1987b. "The Age of Roman Girls at Marriage: Some Reconsiderations." *Journal of Roman Studies* 77: 30–46.

Shaw, Brent D., and Richard P. Saller. 1984. "Close-kin Marriage in Roman Society." *Man* 19: 432–44.

Shelton, J. C. and J. G. Keenan. 1971. "Four Papyri from Second-Century Tebtunis." *Zeitschrift für Papyrologie und Epigraphik* 7: 173–83.

Sherwin-White, A. N. 1966. *The Letters of Pliny: A Historical and Social Commentary*. Oxford.

Sieder, Reinhard, and Michael Mitterauer. 1983. "The Reconstruction of the Family Life Course." In Richard Wall, ed., *Family Forms in Historic Europe*. Cambridge. 309–45.

Slater, W. J. 1974. "Pueri, turba minuta." *Bulletin of the Institute of Classical Studies* 21: 133–40.

Stambaugh, John E. 1988. *The Ancient Roman City*. Baltimore and London.

Stearns, Peter N., and Carol Z. Stearns. 1985. "Emotionology: Clarifying the History of Emotions and Emotional Standards." *American Historical Review* 90: 813–36.

Stockton, David. 1971. *Cicero: A Political Biography*. Oxford.

Stone, Lawrence. 1979. *The Family, Sex and Marriage in England, 1500–1800*. Harmondsworth.

———. 1987. *The Past and the Present Revisited*. London and New York.

Straus, J. A. 1977. "Quelques activités exercées par les esclaves d'après les papyrus de l'Egypte romaine." *Historia* 26: 74–88.

Sumner, G. V. 1973. *The Orators in Cicero's Brutus: Prosopography and Chronology*. Toronto and Buffalo.

———. 1977. "The Pompeii in Their Families." *American Journal of Ancient History* 2: 8–25.

Sussman, George D. 1982. *Selling Mothers' Milk: The Wet-Nursing Business in France*. Urbana, Ill.

Syme, Ronald. 1971. *Emperors and Biography: Studies in the Historia Augusta*. Oxford.

———. 1979. *Roman Papers, Volumes I and II*. Oxford.

———. 1984. *Roman Papers, Volume III*. Oxford.

———. 1986. *The Augustan Aristocracy*. Oxford.

———. 1987a. "Marriage Ages for Roman Senators." *Historia* 36: 318–32.

———. 1987b. "M. Bibulus and Four Sons." *Harvard Studies in Classical Philology* 91: 185–98.

———. 1988. *Roman Papers, Volumes IV and V*. Oxford.

Szramkiewicz, Romuald. 1972. *Les gouverneurs de province à l'époque augustéenne*. Paris.

Taubenschlag, R. 1955. *The Law of Egypt in the Light of the Papyri*. Warsaw.

Thompson, E. P. 1968. *The Making of the English Working Class*. Harmondsworth.

Treggiari, Susan. 1969. *Roman Freedmen during the Late Republic*. Oxford.

―――. 1975a. "Jobs in the Household of Livia." *Papers of the British School at Rome*. 43: 48–77.

―――. 1975b. "Family Life among the Staff of the Volusii." *Transactions of the American Philological Association* 105: 393–401.

―――. 1976. "Jobs for Women." *American Journal of Ancient History* 1: 76–104.

―――. 1979a. "Lower-Class Women in the Roman Economy." *Florilegium* 1: 65–86.

―――. 1979b. "Questions on Women Domestics in the Roman West." In *Schiavitù, manomissione e classi dipendenti nel mondo antico*. Rome. Pp. 185–201.

―――. 1981. "*Contubernales* in *CIL* 6." *Phoenix* 35: 42–69.

―――. 1982. "Consent to Roman Marriage: Some Aspects of Law and Reality." *Echos du monde classique/Classical Views* 1: 34–44.

―――. 1984. "*Digna Condicio:* Betrothals in the Roman Upper Class." *Echos du monde classique/Classical Views* 3: 419–51.

Turner, E. G. 1968. *Greek Papyri: An Introduction*. Princeton.

Wallace-Hadrill, Andrew. 1981. "Family and Inheritance in the Augustan Marriage Laws." *Proceedings of the Cambridge Philological Society* 27: 58–80.

―――. 1988. "The Social Structure of the Roman House." *Papers of the British School at Rome* 56: 43–97.

Watson, Alan. 1967. *The Law of Persons in the Later Roman Republic*. Oxford.

Weaver, P. R. C. 1972. *Familia Caesaris: A Social Study of the Emperor's Freedmen and Slaves*. Cambridge.

Weinstock, Stefan. 1971. *Divus Julius*. Oxford.

Westermann, W. L. 1914. "Apprentice Contracts and the Apprentice System in Roman Egypt." *Classical Philology* 9: 295–315.

Whitehorne, John E. G. 1984. "Tryphon's Second Marriage (POXY. II 267)." In *Atti del XVII congresso internazionale di papirologia*. Naples. Pp. 1267–74.

Wiedemann, Thomas. 1989. *Adults and Children in the Roman Empire*. New Haven and London.

Wilkes, J. J. 1969. *Dalmatia*. London.

Williams, Gordon. 1958. "Some Aspects of Roman Marriage Ceremonies and Ideals." *Journal of Roman Studies* 48: 16–29.

Wilson, Harry Lanford. 1910. "Latin Inscriptions at the Johns Hopkins University. IV." *American Journal of Philology* 31: 25–42.

―――. 1912. "Latin Inscriptions at the Johns Hopkins University. VII." *American Journal of Philology* 33: 168–85.

Wipszycka, Ewa. 1965. *L'industrie textile dans l'Egypte romain*. Wroclaw.

Wiseman, T. P. 1971. *New Men in the Roman Senate, 139 B.C.–A.D. 14*. Oxford.

―――. 1974. *Cinna the Poet and Other Roman Essays*. Leicester.

―――. 1985. *Catullus and His World: A Reappraisal*. Cambridge.

―――. 1987. *Roman Studies: Literary and Historical*. Liverpool.

Zambon, Angela. 1935. "ΔΙΔΑΣΚΑΛΙΚΑΙ." *Aegyptus* 15: 3–66.

―――. 1939. "Ancora sulle ΔΙΔΑΣΚΑΛΙΚΑΙ." *Aegyptus* 19: 100–102.

Zimmer, Gerhard. 1982. *Römische Berufsdarstellungen*. Berlin.

Index of Principal Names and Subjects

Names are listed in the familiar forms generally used in the text; e.g., Cicero, not M. Tullius Cicero.